Secrets for Parenting Healthy,
Happy Daughters

Raising
Girls
With
ADHD

Secrets for Parenting Healthy,
Happy Daughters

Raising
Girls
With
ADHD

James W. Forgan, Ph.D., and Mary Anne Richey

PRUFROCK PRESS INC.
WACO, TEXAS

Dedication

Jim dedicates this book to his amazing and beautiful daughter, Emily, remembering the times they've spent together reading, camping, and laughing.

Mary Anne dedicates this book to her wonderful grandchildren and all of the devoted teachers she has known who have gone "above and beyond" to make a difference in the lives of girls with ADHD.

Acknowledgements

Projects like this require the work of many individuals, and we'd like to thank Jodi MacNeal for her editing expertise, Dr. Marshall Teitelbaum and Dr. Tommy Schechtman for sharing their expertise on diagnosis and medical management of ADHD, Dr. Judith Aaronson-Ramos for her suggestions for reviewing alternative dietary treatments, the families who contributed their experiences, and our spouses for their loving support.

Library of Congress Cataloging-in-Publication Data

Forgan, James W.
 Raising girls with ADHD : secrets for parenting healthy, happy daughters / by James W. Forgan,
Ph.D., and Mary Anne Richey.
    ages cm
 Includes bibliographical references.
 ISBN 978-1-61821-146-0 (pbk.)
 1. Attention-deficit hyperactivity disorder. 2. Attention-deficit-disordered children. 3. Girls--
Mental health. 4. Child rearing. 5. Parent and child. I. Richey, Mary Anne, 1947- II. Title.
 RJ506.H9F668 2014
 618.92'85890082--dc23
                            2013045618

Edited by Lacy Compton

Cover and layout design by Raquel Trevino

ISBN-13: 978-1-61821-146-0

Printed in the United States of America.

At the time of this book's publication, all facts and figures cited are the most current available.
All telephone numbers, addresses, and website URLs are accurate and active. All publications,
organizations, websites, and other resources exist as described in the book, and all have been
verified. The authors and Prufrock Press Inc. make no warranty or guarantee concerning the
information and materials given out by organizations or content found at websites, and we are
not responsible for any changes that occur after this book's publication. If you find an error, please
contact Prufrock Press Inc.

Prufrock Press Inc.
P.O. Box 8813
Waco, TX 76714-8813
Phone: (800) 998-2208
Fax: (800) 240-0333
http://www.prufrock.com

Table of Contents

Chapter 1

Girls and ADHD

Each self-assessment helps you reflect on your daughter and your parenting practices and is a preview of the chapter's content.

1. When I think about myself and where I am emotionally right now, I . . .

    a. am still deciding if she really has ADHD or not.

    b. am overwhelmed with all of the things she needs and that I need to do to help.

    c. know she has ADHD, and I'm ready to take action to help.

    d. am hoping this is a phase and that she will quickly outgrow this.

2. My daughter's type of ADHD is . . .

    a.   Hyperactive-Impulsive.

    b.   Inattentive.

    c.   Combined Type.

    d.   I don't know.

3. My daughter's ADHD occurs with . . .

    a.   anxiety.

    b.   depression.

    c.   low self-esteem.

    d.   learning problems.

    e.   other.

    f.   none of the above.

4. When I think about discussing my daughter's ADHD with our extended family, I . . .

    a.   wouldn't touch it with a 10-foot pole.

    b.   have already had that conversation.

    c.   have it on my to-do list.

    d.   believe they will be warm and supportive.

5. When I think about my daughter and her ADHD, I believe . . .

    a.   she has more strengths than weaknesses.

    b.   she has more weaknesses than strengths.

    c.   she has an equal number of strengths and weaknesses.

    d.   I'm unsure about exactly what she needs.

There is no doubt that raising a girl is difficult, but raising a girl with Attention Deficit/Hyperactivity Disorder (ADHD), whether Inattentive Type (what once was called ADD) or the Hyperactive-Impulsive Type, is even tougher. When you have a girl with ADHD, you may face issues that generally aren't on other parents' radar screens, such as:

◇ impulsivity in acting before considering the consequences,
◇ organizational problems,
◇ intense emotional displays,
◇ excessive talking,
◇ forgetfulness,
◇ fragile self-esteem,
◇ self-doubt,
◇ constant procrastination,
◇ difficulty with time management,
◇ daydreaming and missing information,
◇ underachievement,
◇ co-occurring disorders,
◇ relationship issues, and
◇ social difficulties.

Fortunately, there are professionals and resources to help you work through many of the parenting challenges of raising girls with ADHD. *You don't have to conquer everything on your own.* With some effort, you can find support groups with other parents of girls with ADHD (see http://ADHDaware.com or http://Chadd.org), valuable books, and professionals such as counselors, psychologists, or medical doctors. Locating the right people to help you takes some energy, time on the phone and Internet, and research, but it *is* worth the effort. Not only will you feel supported, but you'll also be making an investment in your daughter. In our own parenting and private practices, we know it is much better to be proactive and provide assistance to ward off problems than to be reactive and face even larger problems.

If you do not have a professional to help guide you, don't worry. We are sharing some of our most valuable tips and strategies with you. At the end of each chapter, you will find points to consider and action steps you can take right away to help your child. Share these with your spouse or a family member so you'll have an ally in choosing the best strategies for supporting your daughter in school and at home. And in most chapters we link you to specific steps for creating a personalized Dynamic Action Plan (see Chapter 7). The beauty of your Dynamic Action Plan is that it will allow you and your daughter to build upon today's successes while following a plan for her promising future.

What Makes Parenting Girls With ADHD Different From Parenting Boys With ADHD?

Many people are familiar with how ADHD presents in boys but are less clear about its presentation in girls. In addition to the obvious boy-versus-girl gender differences, there are distinct differences in the presentation and effects of ADHD in boys versus girls. This is an area of emerging research, so always be on the lookout for new information. In our review of the literature of the differences in ADHD in girls and boys, we found that girls with ADHD:

◊ are diagnosed with ADHD at an older age;
◊ are more frequently diagnosed with inattention and have less hyperactivity and impulsivity;
◊ have more emotional comorbidities during the teenage years;
◊ have a greater likelihood of internalizing problems and difficulty regulating emotions, which can lead to self-esteem issues;
◊ have increased feelings of guilt and self-doubt;
◊ have more hormonal issues, specifically estrogen and its effects on medication;

◇ can have greater risk of early sexual activity;

◇ experience more friendship difficulties;

◇ have greater turmoil in the mother-child relationship;

◇ struggle more with societal expectations, which traditionally have expected girls to be more nurturing and accommodating;

◇ may be held more accountable for poor organization and sloppy papers in school, which may be excused as typical "boy" behavior in males;

◇ may work harder to compensate for or hide their symptoms in an effort to meet parent/teacher expectations;

◇ may be misdiagnosed with other forms of psychopathology—for example, inattention and poor peer interaction may be misdiagnosed as depression;

◇ have differences in brain structure and development;

◇ have lower levels and different manifestation of Oppositional Defiant Disorder and Conduct Disorder than males—girls may be more likely to have covert behaviors like lying whereas boys may have more overt, aggressive symptoms like physical aggression;

◇ are more disliked than boys by ratings of same-sex peers or have higher peer rejection rates;

◇ are more likely to self-harm, cut, and self-mutilate; and

◇ exhibit more excessive talking.

Girls With ADHD Can Be Successful

"Behind each successful girl with ADHD is a proud but tired parent." Actually, we hope you are not alone and that there are a lot of people who have contributed to your girl's success. Our goal in writing this book is to provide you with hope, inspiration, and anticipation that your girl will grow into a successful young woman with ADHD. We believe in the expression, "knowledge is power," but more importantly, *applied* knowledge is power, and that is why you'll find many self-reflection activities throughout this book. We start with the one below to set the positive tone of this book. Throughout the pages, you'll find words of inspiration, hope, and anticipation of great things to come for your girl.

Read through the list of positive words that follow in Figure 1 and place a check mark next to each word that you believe describes your daughter. Your daughter has many positive qualities, and we hope you remember this and (perhaps when you feel discouraged or are butting heads) look back upon this list to reaffirm that she is full of natural talent.

Remember, although the research literature on girls with ADHD may appear pessimistic and girls with ADHD do face challenges, they also have the ability to become highly successful women. We see this from women with ADHD who have been successful, including Mary Kate Olsen, Erin Brockovich, Michelle Rodriguez (actress), and Emily Dickinson.

Yes, it's challenging to raise a successful girl with ADHD, but here's the good news, it's not impossible. You can raise a successful girl with ADHD by surrounding yourself with the right people, maintaining a positive attitude, accepting her strengths and weaknesses, instilling confidence, and nurturing her natural abilities.

Your daughter with ADHD is unique, special, and talented, and has her own set of strengths and skills. She has characteristics and abilities that you understand. Despite her ADHD, you can nurture your daughter's qualities to help her grow into a successful woman. Like other people, she has four fundamental needs that must be met: sense of worth, belonging, purpose, and competency. Your daughter can probably accomplish anything she sets her mind to if you nurture these four areas.

❒ adorable	❒ animated	❒ artistic	❒ assertive
❒ astounding	❒ attractive	❒ authentic	❒ beautiful
❒ big-hearted	❒ blessed	❒ brave	❒ brilliant
❒ bubbly	❒ caring	❒ charitable	❒ charming
❒ cheerful	❒ clean	❒ clever	❒ courageous
❒ creative	❒ dazzling	❒ delightful	❒ distinguished
❒ eager	❒ efficient	❒ elegant	❒ encouraging
❒ energized	❒ enthusiastic	❒ excited	❒ faithful
❒ fun	❒ generous	❒ good	❒ gorgeous
❒ graceful	❒ happy	❒ healthy	❒ helpful
❒ honest	❒ imaginative	❒ independent	❒ instinctive
❒ intelligent	❒ intuitive	❒ joyful	❒ kind
❒ knowledgeable	❒ leader	❒ lively	❒ marvelous
❒ natural	❒ neat	❒ optimistic	❒ popular
❒ positive	❒ prepared	❒ pretty	❒ proud
❒ quick	❒ quiet	❒ ready	❒ reliable
❒ remarkable	❒ respectful	❒ safe	❒ serious
❒ sincere	❒ smart	❒ sparkling	❒ spirited
❒ strong	❒ stylish	❒ supportive	❒ thankful
❒ thorough	❒ trustworthy	❒ upbeat	❒ vocal
❒ vibrant	❒ vigorous	❒ visual	❒ welcoming
❒ willing	❒ wonderful	❒ youthful	❒ zestful
Other: _____	Other: _____	Other: _____	Other: _____

Figure 1. List of positive attributes.

What Does Success for Girls With ADHD Look Like?

We don't define success as accumulating things. The expression, "The person with the most toys wins" is a fallacy. Our definition of being successful doesn't mean owning the best car or a huge house, having tons of money or an extraordinary career. Although these things can be nice and often project the image of success, they don't reflect internal success—the type of success you need to feel satisfied and fulfilled.

We've worked with too many families to know that what you see portrayed on the outside does not always mirror what's happening on the inside. One client told us, "My life is a mess, my kids are a mess, and my relationships are a mess. Sometimes I'm just going through the motions." She was what most people would consider successful: beautiful physical features, an amazing smile, plenty of money, and her own business. To the casual observer, she appeared to have it all together, but true peace was absent and chaos and confusion brewed inside.

As we stated in our previous book, *Raising Boys With ADHD*, we believe success is about being comfortable with your natural abilities and believing that you make a difference in this world. This might come from enjoying the company of others, investing your time in the well-being of your child or spouse, excelling in your job, or being active at your church or synagogue. Ultimate success for girls with ADHD is more about accepting strengths and weaknesses, living independently and earning a living as an adult, and helping make our world a better place. As a mom with ADHD told Jim,

> I grew up with a lot of money, millions of dollars and I mingled with some of the A-list people that would blow your mind. I was given everything and bounced from here to there, but I truly was not

satisfied until I actually earned my first $150 by selling some of the clothes I made. I was 19 years old and felt so fulfilled because I knew that I could make it on my own even if the millions went away.

It's your job as a parent to help your daughter identify her purpose, develop her talents, and learn how to get along with people. It's not a high-paying or cushy job, but it is *extremely* rewarding and, in our opinion, one of the most important jobs you'll ever do.

Girls With ADHD Are Everywhere

It's harder to recognize girls with ADHD than boys, but believe us, girls with ADHD are *everywhere* and are found in every country. ADHD is not a disorder exclusive to the United States. The American Psychiatric Association (2013) stated in the fifth edition of the *Diagnostic and Statistical Manual of Mental Disorders* (DSM 5) that, "Population surveys suggest that ADHD occurs in most cultures in about 5% of children" (p. 61). Furthermore, ADHD is diagnosed more frequently in boys than girls, with a ratio of 2:1 in children. However, as the DSM 5 states, "Females are more likely than males to present with primarily inattentive features" (p. 63).

The prevalence of ADHD in the United States varies from 5%–12% depending on the source of the data and how it was collected. According to the National Institutes of Mental Health (2010) website, the average age of ADHD diagnosis for both boys and girls is 7 years old. The Centers for Disease Control and Prevention (2010) website indicated that parents reported that approximately 9% of children 3–17 years of age (5 million) have been diagnosed with ADHD as of 2010. Boys (12%) were more likely than girls (5%) to have ever been diagnosed with ADHD as children. Ultimately, the ratio evens out to 1:1 as more females are diagnosed during adolescence and adulthood. Many girls may miss the opportunity to benefit from interventions that could have occurred in childhood had they been diagnosed earlier. As Dr. Ellen Littman (2012), a licensed clinical psychologist who has written extensively on girls with ADHD, noted, "there remains a referral bias, in that girls are less frequently referred, and a diagnostic bias, in that the diagnostic criteria still exclude many girls" (p. 18).

There are very few studies following girls with ADHD. Two of the most comprehensive recently released, the Berkeley Girls ADHD Longitudinal Study (BGALS) and the Milwaukee Study, showed that girls with childhood ADHD continue to exhibit impairment into adulthood and may need ongoing treatment (Hinshaw, Barkley, & Hechtman, 2012). Even though it's harder to identify girls because, as a group, they are not as hyperactive/impulsive and don't stand out as much as boys with ADHD, it is critical for girls to receive a correct diagnosis so they can begin the journey of learning how to manage their symptoms and receive support. Many girls with undiagnosed ADHD have hidden struggles, but they struggle just the same with maintaining attention, completing homework, staying organized, keeping up with family chores, and relating to peers—especially to other girls.

Did I Cause It?

Not intentionally, but in many cases a parent's genetics probably contribute to a child having ADHD. When a child is diagnosed with ADHD, parents often comment to us that their daughter is a lot like they were as a child. It doesn't help one bit to cast blame on yourself or your spouse and wonder who your daughter "got it" from. If you do suspect a genetic link, try instead to find some sympathy and compassion for what your daughter is facing.

It is important for you to remember that your parenting style and the decisions you've made usually are not your girl's main issues. Being a more skilled parent will not make ADHD go away. Poor parenting does not *cause* ADHD (but as we'll see later in the book, it certainly can aggravate the situation). Can we, as parents, improve the way we deal with our daughters with ADHD? Absolutely, and we'll spend a good bit of this book sharing ways to help you do just that.

Overcoming ADHD

We often advise parents not to worry so much about the label but to focus on proactive steps they can take to help their daughter. To raise a successful daughter with ADHD, you must start doing things differently as soon as possible after you first learn she has ADHD.

Recognize That ADHD Is a Disorder

ADHD is in the *Diagnostic and Statistical Manual of Mental Disorders* (DSM-5), and brain imaging studies document that structural brain differences exist in people with ADHD, so there is no denying it's a true neurobiological disorder. Even though your daughter looks fine on the outside, her mind is wired very differently. Taking a "disorder perspective" provides understanding. When talking to others about her ADHD, we recommend that you recognize her as an individual first and then consider how ADHD impacts her. In the educational world, this is known as using the "person-first" type of language. In other words, the ADHD does not define her but rather, she defines how ADHD affects her. Part of your parenting job is helping her understand how she can manage her ADHD, and you are taking a great step by reading this book and teaching yourself more about ADHD. Increasing your knowledge about ADHD is key to raising a successful girl. Surprisingly, many myths about ADHD exist (see Table 1). Are there any you still believe?

Table 1
Myths About ADHD

Myth	Fact
Poor parenting causes ADHD.	ADHD is neurological and often genetic.
If you have one child with ADHD, all of your children will have it.	Not all children in the same family have ADHD.
ADHD is not a disability.	ADHD is a recognized disability in the Americans with Disabilities Act (ADA) and the Individuals with Disabilities Education Act (IDEA).
Medication is the only treatment for ADHD.	Medication is only one treatment option.
Teachers want inattentive girls on medication.	Teachers want their students to give their best effort.
If a girl is not hyperactive, then she doesn't have ADHD.	Girls who are inattentive but not hyperactive can have ADHD.
A girl who can focus for long periods of time on an interest cannot have ADHD.	Girls with ADHD can focus on highly interesting and engaging topics.
A girl with good grades can't have ADHD.	A girl's grades don't indicate need and girls with good grades can and do have ADHD.
Only a psychiatrist can diagnose ADHD.	Pediatricians, psychologists, neurologists, psychiatrists, and other mental health and medical personnel all diagnose ADHD.
Psychologists prescribe medication.	Only medical doctors such as pediatricians, neurologists, and psychiatrists, or nurse practitioners prescribe medication.
An equal number of boys and girls are diagnosed with ADHD.	In childhood, more boys than girls are diagnosed with ADHD but by adulthood the ratio is 1:1.
Most of the behavior of girls with ADHD is willful.	Girls with ADHD are not always able to behave consistently, independently, and predictably.
ADHD is a societal fad and will go away.	ADHD has been recognized since the mid-1800s but has been called by different names.
ADHD and ADD are the same thing.	ADHD is an umbrella term that is used in the DSM-5 criteria in place of ADD, a term found in previous DSM editions.

ADHD is a broad term that has evolved through the years. You may be familiar with ADD and ADHD because that was how individuals were classified during the 1980s. As research and education evolved, the most recent version of the DSM-5 classified ADHD as an umbrella term that has different subtypes. A girl can be diagnosed with either ADHD, Predominantly Inattentive Type (formerly ADD), Hyperactive-Impulsive Type, or a Combined Type. Few professionals use a general type of Other Specified or Unspecified ADHD. If your daughter was diagnosed with one of the above types, do you know which one? As seen in Figure 2, in this book we use the general term ADHD to include all types.

If your child was diagnosed with ADHD using the DSM-5 classification, then current diagnostic criteria require that your daughter presented with symptoms before age 12. She must have presented with several inattentive or hyperactive-impulsive symptoms in two or more settings. There should have also been ". . . clear evidence that the symptoms interfere with, or reduce the quality of, social, academic, or occupational functioning" (APA, 2013, p. 60). In addition, the clinician should have diagnosed your daughter with mild ADHD, moderate ADHD, or severe ADHD. Given some subtle changes in the DSM-5 ADHD diagnostic guidelines, many professionals believe it is more lenient and may result in more children diagnosed with ADHD.

Try to Become More Understanding and Patient

Through our experiences, we've learned that changing your girl's behavior often means changing your behavior as well. If you know she has ADHD, then respond differently to her behavior. That doesn't mean you will let your daughter "get away with things," but you will need to learn to respond in a way that doesn't escalate the situation or reinforce a negative behavior, but rather, teaches her how to respond more appropriately. When Jim gets upset or frustrated with his daughter and son, he tends to point his

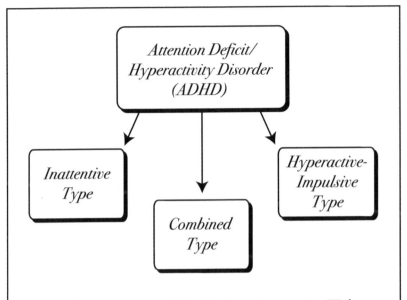

Figure 2. The many types of ADHD. From *Raising Boys With ADHD* (p. xiii) by J. W. Forgan and M. A. Richey, 2012, Waco, TX: Prufrock Press. Copyright 2012 by Prufrock Press. Reprinted with permission.

index finger at them and shake it up and down as he scolds. Jim became so frustrated at himself that he was determined to stop this automatic response. One day he decided to write the letters "u" and "p" on the edge of his finger. When he got upset and pointed his finger at his daughter and son, Jim had an automatic visual reminder to have understanding and patience. This simple strategy worked to change his behavior so that he could teach his kids about the right thing to do rather than complain about what they did wrong.

Locate Support Personnel

Begin to locate different support personnel such as educators, counselors, and doctors who can serve as resources throughout the years. Part of raising a successful girl with ADHD is recognizing that it's very tough to try to do it alone. If she is going to be successful, then at the very minimum you must have her teacher's support. Thus, take extra time to develop a rapport with her teacher and help him understand your daughter's strengths and weaknesses.

If you are searching for a professional who specializes in ADHD, one of the most respected sources of information is Children and Adults with Attention-Deficit/Hyperactivity Disorder (CHADD). CHADD maintains a searchable professional database of ADHD experts that may help you with your daughter's ADHD. Additionally, there are local CHADD chapters throughout the United States, and you can check its website (http://www. CHADD.org) to see if there is a chapter in your area.

You may have to interview several professionals to locate the right professional match for you and your daughter. The important key here is not to give up too soon. We've seen many clients start counseling and then quit because the child does not relate well to the therapist. Often, the comment parents make is, "We've tried counseling and it didn't work." After probing deeper into the circumstances, we learn that it may not have been the right connection, and in counseling, a strong relationship makes all the difference.

Prepare for the Long Haul

If your daughter is diagnosed with ADHD in preschool or elementary school, this is likely to be a lifelong disorder, and she (and you) are going to need support. The duration of ADHD was one area that Jim underestimated when his child was diagnosed with ADHD. Jim and his wife remember saying to each other during their son's first- and second-grade years, "Surely we won't be dealing with these types of behaviors in fifth and sixth grade." To their surprise, when fifth and sixth grade came around, they still had to address the issues in their child. ADHD was here to stay.

Realize that you and your daughter are going to have really good periods and really rough patches and that meaningful change will gradually occur. Remember that maturation sometimes results in improvement in boys with ADHD because their hyperactivity seems to lessen with age, but girls often have more problems during the teenage years—possibly because of increased estrogen and other hormonal fluctuations (a theory still under study). Dr. Ellen Littman explained this theory as such, "We now know that the brain is a target organ for estrogen, where it impacts cognition, mood, and sleep. For many girls, behavioral issues blossom around puberty, as estrogen levels increase" (p. 19).

At times you may feel like you've taken one step forward and two steps backward, so it helps to reflect and see just how far you've come. That's why completing the Dynamic Action Plan, which is integrated into most chapters and found at the end of the book, is useful. It documents 5 years of growth and serves as a written plan that shows her progress.

Why Seek a Professional Diagnosis?

Have you ever asked yourself, "Why seek a professional diagnosis?" Let's face it: You can build a house without a set of plans. It may take a lot longer, cost a lot more, and have hidden problems, but it can be done. So why start treating your daughter for something you suspect but haven't confirmed?

The diagnosis serves multiple purposes. First, it may provide parents with a sense of understanding, which is often accompanied by relief. Parents may be relieved to know their child really does have something fundamentally different about her mind. The diagnosis also can help parents shift their mindset about their child. When your daughter is mature enough to understand the diagnosis, sharing information with her can bring a sense of relief and an understanding of how she can better handle the difficulties she is experiencing.

Second, the diagnosis may provide you and your daughter with access to school services. Most public and private schools require a professional diagnosis or an evaluation to provide any formal accommodations. Accommodations are adjustments such as extra time to complete tests or homework, seating near the front of the class, or frequent breaks. Furthermore, as girls with ADHD prepare to take college entrance exams, a diagnosis and a complete evaluation report by a qualified individual are required to receive accommodations. Prepare yourself, because at the low end of the scale these evaluations cost close to $1,000 and the price goes up from there. Even though this is a hefty expense, we explain to our clients that it's an investment in their daughter's future for her well-being and for generations to come.

Third, the diagnosis allows you, if you desire, the option of trying medication. Not all parents want to try prescribed medication with their child. If you decide to do so, you must have a proper diagnosis before obtaining a prescription. Some medical doctors will write a prescription based only on their own examination of your child without a psychologist's written report. We recommend both a psychological and medical evaluation of your child before pursuing medical treatment. Both the psychologist and the pediatrician are important members of your daughter's team. One of the secrets to success is that the stronger the team, the more thorough and accurate the diagnosis.

The Importance of Ruling Out Co-Occurring Disorders and Other Deficits

Part of the reason for seeking a diagnosis is to make sure it is ADHD and not attributable to other disorders, which can look like ADHD and require very different treatment. These include learning disabilities like dyslexia or dysgraphia, depression, anxiety, Conduct Disorder, or Oppositional Defiant Disorder. Many of the symptoms for these disorders overlap with ADHD, making them very difficult to differentiate. Furthermore, many times a child will have more than one diagnosis, called co-occurring or comorbid disorders. A careful review of your daughter's history and a comprehensive psychoeducational or neuropsychological evaluation is often required.

Ariel was constantly out of her seat in kindergarten, going from table to table or getting up to use the bathroom. Her teacher tried everything to keep Ariel focused on classroom activities, but nothing worked. The teacher encouraged Ariel's mother to have her evaluated for ADHD to see if medication would help her focus. Ariel was starting to lag far behind her peers in identifying her letters and numbers and in all aspects of emerging reading and math skills. Ariel's mother decided to address the academic problems first. She hired a tutor, who also noticed that Ariel could not sit still. The tutor had experience with fidgety children, so she utilized lots of different strategies to teach Ariel the letters and sounds. As Ariel began acquiring skills, her activity level decreased significantly. Six months later, she was reading short sentences and her hyperactivity had completely disappeared. Obviously, her problems stemmed from her academic deficits and not ADHD.

Children with significant anxiety can be so preoccupied with their discomfort that they cannot focus or interact appropriately with peers. Others may have their own agendas where they want to do what they want to do at all costs. Where it might initially appear that their behavior is driven by impulsivity, it may actually be Conduct Disorder or oppositional behavior. A wise and thorough clinician can determine the root of the problem and arrive at an accurate diagnosis.

More About ADHD and Co-Occurring Disorders

Here is more worrisome news about raising a girl with ADHD. If you daughter has ADHD, then she has a higher risk for having co-occurring disorders, which could be academic, emotional, or behavioral in nature. The Milwaukee Longitudinal Study indicated that the risk of a girl diagnosed with ADHD requiring special education services was more than 50% (Hinshaw et al., 2012). The most commonly co-occurring disorders for females with ADHD are learning disabilities, depression, anxiety disorders, Conduct Disorder, and Oppositional Defiant Disorder. A longitudinal study conducted by Biederman et al. (2010) indicated "a strong association between ADHD and lifetime risks for antisocial, mood, anxiety, developmental, and substance dependence disorders at the 11 year follow up" (p. 416). Results differ from study to study, but one constant concern is the paucity of studies devoted to following girls over time, which is necessary to differentiate the most effective treatments for the different types of ADHD. The Berkeley Girls ADHD Longitudinal Study (Hinshaw et al., 2012) showed higher rates of suicide attempts and self-injury than the group without ADHD but no higher rates of eating pathology, substance use, or driving behavior. Suicide attempts were highly concentrated in girls with ADHD-Combined Type (Hinshaw et al., 2012).

The importance of this information is to alert you to be aware of additional problems that could require immediate attention and intervention. The biggest mistake parents make is ignoring problems and hoping they will go away. The best course of action is to recognize them, get early intervention, and develop an ongoing plan to mitigate their impact. Why act early?

> Early intervention is the insurance that non-adaptive coping patterns will not become entrenched, and that co-existing symptoms will be less

likely to develop secondary to ADHD. Above all, the earlier that identification and intervention can begin, the less damage will be done to a girl's developing sense of self. (Nadeau, Littman, & Quinn, 1999, p. 229)

Sluggish Cognitive Tempo

Sluggish Cognitive Tempo (SCT) is an emerging area of research. Although this concept did not appear in the DSM-IV or 5, research by Russell Barkley (2012) and others has identified a newer concept that is closely related to ADHD, Predominantly Inattentive Type. Children with SCT often have behaviors such as sleepiness, a flat affect, slow processing speed and reaction time, lack of focus, memory difficulties, and daydreaming. Children with SCT are often distracted by their own thoughts and may be viewed as daydreamers. Like children with ADHD, Predominantly Inattentive Type, these children often have co-occurring disorders including anxiety, depression, and social difficulty. Stay tuned for more emerging research on SCT.

After the Diagnosis

After learning your daughter's diagnosis, consider doing these three things. First, give your daughter a big hug, tell her you love her, and silently embrace her differences. Second, allow yourself time to grieve for any shattered dreams, because in your mind you may have pictured a perfect life for her and now ADHD has clouded your view. Third, begin to educate yourself about ADHD so that you can advocate for your girl and teach her to self-advocate. Your daughter needs you to be strong, to be her voice when she is weak, and to encourage others to treat her fairly. Without you, your girl can be at a great disadvantage in school, sports, friendships, gatherings, and life. You are a source of encouragement and support that is invaluable and can help your daughter keep her challenges in perspective. Even though you will become discouraged and frustrated at times, you love your daughter—and she loves you. Your hard work will pay off, and you'll feel rewarded.

Questioning the ADHD Diagnosis

Even after the ADHD diagnosis, some parents question the validity of their daughter's diagnosis. We're often asked, "How do you determine if she is exhibiting age-appropriate girl behavior or behavior that is unusual and reflective of ADHD?" You can probably arrive at an answer on your own, but you need to consider these four questions to know if your daughter's behavior is unusual:

◊ How is your daughter perceived by peers, especially girls?
◊ Have your daughter's behaviors, including her inattentiveness, been a continuous problem or a response to a temporary situation?
◊ Do the behaviors occur in several settings or only in one place, such as the playground, classroom, or home?
◊ How intense is your daughter's behavior during this time or how much does it interfere with her functioning?

Think about how your daughter is viewed within the social arena of other girls her age. The research tells us that girls with ADHD are rejected more often by both girls without ADHD and other girls with ADHD. Thus, don't discount her if your daughter tells you that other girls are mean and don't like her. Early elementary peer rejection is a strong predictor of problems your daughter may face during the teen years, including anxiety, depression, eating disorders, and suicide. As written by Kari Dorsett, a licensed social worker, in a 2013 *Attention* article,

> My sweet daughter got along great with many older individuals, such as teachers, and was won-

derful with younger kids. She had multiple real-life skills, a strong work ethic, accumulated hundreds of hours of community work, and was a wonderful artist and singer. Yet, she was continually dealing with friendship issues. She might have a good friend for a short time, but would invariably say or do something that would alienate her. Often we didn't know exactly what the infraction was; she would just be shut out or excluded once again.

Many times the rejection seemed almost unbearable. Although she never completely gave up her efforts to fit in with other girls, she could never quite successfully navigate the complex female relationships and the "mean girl" minefields. (para. 15–16)

The second question was, "Have your daughter's behaviors, including her inattentiveness, been a continuous problem or a response to a temporary situation?" If it's truly ADHD, your daughter should have been dealing with the same problem or problems for a period of 6 months or more. Thus, the professional who evaluates your daughter will ask questions to differentiate between ongoing problems and short-term problems like those created by changes such as divorce, death of a family member, teacher conflict, or peer problems, because these types of situations create temporary instability.

Nina, the parent of Juanita, came to us near the end of the school year because her daughter had a terrible third-grade experience. Her mother's intuition had warned her in second grade that something was amiss, and now she finally decided that something must be wrong. Through comprehensive testing we identified that Juanita had ADHD and especially had difficulty with shifting her attention. When something was "sprung" on her, she would likely have a major meltdown. Strategies were developed to help her learn to manage shifting in order to anticipate change better. Like many girls with ADHD, Juanita performed better in situations that were highly structured, as compared to situations that were more unpredictable. As a result of the evaluation, her parents created clear house rules that everyone agreed upon so that Juanita could predict the consequence of her behavior. This helped Nina take some of the emotion out of disciplining Juanita.

The third question was, "Do the behaviors occur in several settings or only in one place, such as the playground, classroom, or home?" ADHD permeates all areas of your daughter's life, so she may experience difficulties at home, in school, during Girl Scouts, at sleepovers, and at family gatherings. In preschool or kindergarten, other girls might find her too bossy. Your daughter's school problems may ebb and flow like the tide, but an intuitive parent senses when her problems are reappearing. Your daughter's ADHD may emerge anywhere and at any time. She may hold herself together better in school, but her true colors are displayed at home with demands, bossiness, and frustration. This difficulty is often what leads parents to call us for an evaluation.

The fourth question we asked you to consider was, "How intense is your daughter's behavior during this time or how much does it interfere with her functioning?" If your daughter's mood or behavior drags on and is so severe that no one wants to (or is able to) get near her for an extended period, that's a severe problem. When you consider the frequency, duration, and intensity of her behavior, it may become clear that a potential problem exists. Like one client told us, "When she has a bad day, it's a spectacularly bad day!"

A smaller group of parents suspect from an early age that their daughter is having behaviors related to inattention or hyperactivity. These parents either may be in the teaching or psychology profession, have other children with behavior difficulties, or may be alerted to the differences they see by friends or doctors. Megan told Jim that while her daughter was in the pediatrician's office for a checkup the doctor stated, "I've noticed that she doesn't stop moving or talking. We should consider ADHD." Eventually both groups of parents, those who have been pretty sure all along and those who are recently coming to terms with the diagnosis, reach a point when they understand their child's behaviors are related to ADHD. At this point, they begin to learn more about what ADHD means.

How Long Does ADHD Last?

Most researchers agree that ADHD lasts a lifetime. "Numerous longitudinal studies now support the conclusion that ADHD is a relatively chronic disorder affecting many domains of major life activities from childhood through adolescence and into adulthood" (Barkley, 2006, p. 40). Longitudinal studies have reported that ongoing interventions are necessary to maintain any treatment gains. It is clearly a chronic condition requiring ongoing treatment and monitoring, even into adulthood. Studies have reported that young adults in their 20s don't always recognize the degree to which their ADHD still remains when filling out self-reports. On the contrary, parents' reports of these same young adults show clearly that ADHD is still interfering with their daily living. It's not until many women with ADHD are in their 30s that they begin recognizing how their ADHD is still a major factor. The impact of ADHD on adults is currently the topic of many studies.

The important perspective is to have hope that your daughter's ADHD may decrease during puberty but to recognize that it may not. Regardless of the outcome, stand ready to give her the support she needs.

Is ADHD a Gift?

The answer to this question is generally no. Most of the time ADHD is not a gift. We've worked with many girls and women who struggle in school, with relationships, and with self-image because of their ADHD. On the other hand, we have worked with women who have come to appreciate their ADHD. Of course, ADHD varies by individual.

Whether or not your girl's ADHD contributes to success or failure is influenced by many factors including her temperament, attitude, resiliency, home life, and available supports. There will be countless times when your daughter's ADHD seems far more like a burden than a gift. Many people you encounter won't understand her and you may feel like they are judging you and your daughter. You'll hear comments like these:

◊ "She's so emotional."
◊ "She's a strange one."
◊ "She's too bossy."
◊ "She marches to the beat of her own drum."
◊ "She's too sensitive."
◊ "Girls don't like her."
◊ "Something's wrong with her."
◊ "She's so demanding."

The list goes on and on, and you can almost certainly add to it. So when *can* ADHD become a blessing? When your daughter's natural talents are harnessed in the right direction, ADHD can be a gift at any age. For some girls, it can involve having intuition that others lack; being able to see the big picture; participating in many extracurricular activities; excelling in art, music, or academic subjects that interest her; or interacting successfully with people, especially older or much younger children. Many believe that ADHD can be a gift when individuals with ADHD have perspectives that others lack and a high energy level that enables them to accomplish many things.

You understand your daughter with ADHD best, so think about her natural talents. What are they? Your insight will help you identify her strengths. Ask yourself these types of questions:

◊ What comes naturally to my daughter?
◊ What does she enjoy spending time doing?
◊ What makes her smile and laugh?
◊ What type of career do I picture for her?

The girls with ADHD whom we work with in our practices are usually described as being social, spirited, loving, sensitive, or reserved. These positive qualities should not be overlooked and can become huge assets when she is an adult. However, your nurturing will likely be required to help develop these qualities. Thus, the time and money you spend on building her strengths are investments in your daughter's and your family's future. You are filling her with positive thoughts and building her self-confidence, which will help her feel successful. For example, when Jim's daughter considered a career in dentistry, he purchased a book and read sections with her. They talked to dentists about pros and cons of the profession. You can buy books on topics your daughter enjoys, talk with experts, attend seminars, and take field trips. We know your child's strengths will carry her through life. School is the only place where we are expected to perform well in *all* subjects, but that's not the case in life. If your child is a C student in math, then perhaps take the viewpoint that it's satisfactory and instead of spending hours working with tutors and attending learning centers in an attempt to mold her into an A-level math student, spend time increasing her reading and writing talents.

Girls with ADHD often have strengths in many areas. Reflecting back to the beginning of the chapter, which words described your daughter? Now that you've identified some of your daughter's strengths, build upon them. Consider making a list of her talents and special qualities and posting it where you both can be reminded of them. Provide various opportunities for your daughter to develop these strengths as well as discover new hidden talents. Your girl has gifts that can take her far and help her have a happy and satisfying adult life. It's our job as parents, guardians, and families of girls with ADHD to nurture those talents.

What May the Future Hold?

We certainly don't have a crystal ball, but in our experiences, we find the parents who take time to read books, learn new skills, and support their daughters with ADHD have daughters who grow into independent and satisfied women. As a whole, girls who have parent or adult support fare better than those who don't. The time you invest helping your daughter will pay off in future dividends. While raising your daughter, keep these points in mind:

◊ Don't back too far away if she tries to push you away.

◊ Consider money spent on ADHD treatments as an investment in your family's future.

◊ Continue to provide just enough support that she knows you are there, but don't enable her to become dependent.

◊ Make sure you are not inadvertently reinforcing negative behaviors by allowing her to get what she wants when engaging in inappropriate behaviors (e.g., pestering, arguing, throwing tantrums).

◊ Try not to give in or take the path of least resistance and do things for your daughter that she can do for herself.

◊ Continue to have one-to-one time that allows you to develop your relationship and talk about her hopes, dreams, and desires.

◊ Know her friends.

◊ Help her set goals for the future such as attending college or trade school. The Dynamic Action Plan can help you with goal setting.

Explaining ADHD to Others

If your daughter has ADHD, should you tell other people? Do you worry about people judging your parenting skills and your daughter? Are you concerned with her having a label? Will her ADHD prohibit her from getting a job? These are some of the issues parents ask us about, and they are questions that don't always have easy answers.

The sooner you can quickly explain ADHD to family, teachers, and key people, the sooner you will help forge a road to success. If you're comfortable, you can have a heart-to-heart conversation with the person about your daughter's ADHD, but sometimes those kinds of talks just aren't possible. Figure 3 is a sample letter you might use to explain your daughter's diagnosis to loved ones. Rewrite it, insert your daughter's name, and customize it so it has the right feel for the recipient and for your situation.

Depending on your family dynamic, you might choose to discuss your daughter's diagnosis in person with her siblings, share it with them in a letter, or some combination of the two. Figure 4 is an example of how you can explain ADHD to siblings.

Figure 5 is a letter that one of our clients gave to their daughter's third-grade teacher before the school year started. It highlighted her strengths and potential areas of weakness and also offered suggestions of Individualized Education Plan (IEP) accommodations that helped. It's important to start the school year advocating for your daughter and letting the teacher know how to best work with her. We encourage you to send an e-mail or write a letter like this. Often it's helpful to personally meet with your daughter's teacher either before the first day of school or within the first week of school.

Dear _____ ,

This isn't an easy letter to write, but it is an important one—and you're a very important person in (insert daughter's name)'s life. Not long ago I took _____ for a series of tests and activities to find out how she learns best, and whether there were any areas of concern. The psychologist gathered input from me, from _____'s teacher, and from observing _____. Based on the evaluation results and the input from everyone, he/she concluded that _____ has Attention Deficit/Hyperactivity Disorder or ADHD.

There are a lot of myths about ADHD, so I wanted to make sure you have good, solid information about it. ADHD is a medical condition and one of the most well-researched childhood disorders. It is not a fad or an excuse for bad behavior or lack of motivation. Her brain is wired very differently from most other children's, which means that while she's a bright girl, she'll have to work much harder than others her age. Learning does not always come easily to her.

Many of our daily struggles are related to her ADHD. _____'s ADHD behaviors occur in school, at home, and with friends. This is why life is tough for her. She never gets a break from having ADHD. We've learned that _____'s brain is actually understimulated in the areas that maintain focus, deal with frustration, and apply what she knows consistently, predictably, and independently. This is why _____ can focus on something she really likes but has such a hard time focusing on things that don't interest her. It also explains why she can be so inconsistent in her behavior. It's all related to ADHD.

We are now using strategies at school and at home to try to minimize the effects of _____'s ADHD to help her and the whole family. It's a long road ahead and we all need your support along the way. There will be ups and downs as we teach _____ how to deal with ADHD. Please try to be as understanding and patient with _____ as you can. That's what I'm doing, and each day is a work in progress.

I have a lot more I can share, and I hope we can talk about _____ more soon.

Figure 3. Letter to family members. Adapted from *Raising Boys With ADHD* (p. 19) by J. W. Forgan and M. A. Richey, 2012, Waco, TX: Prufrock Press. Copyright 2012 by Prufrock Press. Adapted with permission.

Dear _____,

   I want to share something very important with you. You know that (insert sister's name) has a hard time when she gets frustrated or upset. You've seen her get mad and say mean things or even hit you. She doesn't want to behave that way, but her mind works differently. She knows what she should do but can't always make the right choices. She reacts before she thinks things through.

   I took _____ to a doctor, who said she has Attention Deficit/ Hyperactivity Disorder or ADHD. This is something she was born with, and no one person or thing caused it. Lots of people have ADHD, even famous people. Some people even think Albert Einstein may have had ADHD. It's something that _____ is learning to deal with, and so are we. We are working with her teacher at school to make sure she does well there.

   At home we're going to be trying some things to help _____ and everyone get along together. It's going to take a lot of work, and there are still going to be blow-ups along the way, but we're on the right track. You can help by being patient with _____ and guiding her to make right choices. I'm always here for any questions you have, and if you can't think of any now, you can always ask me later.

Love,
Mom/Dad

Figure 4. Letter to siblings. Adapted from *Raising Boys With ADHD* (p. 20) by J. W. Forgan and M. A. Richey, 2012, Waco, TX: Prufrock Press. Copyright 2012 by Prufrock Press. Adapted with permission.

Explaining ADHD to Your Daughter

You need to tell your daughter about her ADHD. You want her to understand ADHD, but you don't want her to use it as a crutch or an excuse for failing to behave or achieve her potential.

The Younger Child

We believe you can provide an age-appropriate explanation of ADHD to elementary-aged children. You may find it easier to explain by reading a children's book about ADHD to your daugh-

Dear Teacher,

We are pleased that Tara has you for a teacher this year and look forward to a great school year. Each year I give Tara's teacher a letter to explain her strengths and weaknesses and offer my two cents about how to help her in your class.

Tara has a caring heart and loves to help others. She is an only child and loves to help me around the house. If you give her responsibilities that allow her to help you she'll work extra hard for you. Simple things like allowing her to pass out papers, erase the board, or put items up on a bulletin board thrill Tara. Her second-grade teacher allowed Tara to read books to kindergarten students and this boosted her self-confidence. I believe the better bond Tara creates with you, the more she will put effort into learning because she will want to please you.

Tara was diagnosed with ADHD, Predominantly Inattentive Type at age 6 and memory is one of her weaknesses. We've known this since about age 3 because she had difficulty remembering colors, letters, and names. This has hindered learning and has made it especially hard for her to memorize math facts and spelling words. You can help Tara by following her IEP accommodations and allowing her to use a math fact table and by reducing the number of spelling words she must memorize each week. There are many more accommodations listed on her IEP that I attached to this letter. Tara also has a very hard time with writing narratives, and teaching her a writing formula or series of steps seems to help her.

I'm fortunate to be a stay-at-home mom and want you to know I am here to help you in any way. I'm available if you need a classroom volunteer or room mom. I hope this a great year for Tara.

Sincerely,
Stephanie G.

Figure 5. Letter to teacher.

ter. Reading books helps your daughter identify with the book's character and realize that she is not alone with her ADHD. A book also becomes a nonthreatening way for you to have a simple conversation about school and behavior. Because children's books go in and out of print, you'll need to check with your local library or search online for recent books. These are a few books currently available to explain ADHD to a younger child:

◊ *The Adventures of Phoebe Flower: Stories of a Girl With ADHD* (Barbara Roberts)

◊ *Putting on the Brakes: Understanding and Taking Control of Your ADD or ADHD* (Patricia O. Quinn & Judith M. Stern)

◊ *Shelley, The Hyperactive Turtle* (Deborah M. Moss)

◊ *Otto Learns About His Medicine: A Story About Medication for Children With ADHD* (Matthew R. Galvin)

◊ *The ADHD Workbook for Kids: Helping Children Gain Self-Confidence, Social Skills, and Self-Control* (Lawrence Shapiro)

The "Tween" or Teen

If your middle school or teenage daughter has recently been diagnosed with ADHD, you'll handle it a bit differently. Ideally, the person who officially diagnosed her will provide an age-appropriate explanation of her ADHD. This is a brief way we explain it to our teenage clients:

> Jasmine, the testing you completed with me showed that you have quite a few strengths, and some of them include (*fill in the blank with her strengths*). The testing also showed there are some things that are much harder for you, compared with other girls your age. For example, you mentioned that it is difficult for you to (*fill in the blank: e.g., keep your mind on important facts when reading, keep your materials organized, easily hold back your anger, etc.*). This difficulty is related to Attention Deficit/Hyperactivity Disorder or ADHD. Have you heard of ADHD? The testing process confirmed that you have ADHD. What this means is that you are smart, outgoing, creative, and hardworking, but because

of the way your mind is wired, you have difficulty with (*fill in the blank*). This difficulty is not going to stop you from being successful in school; it won't stop you from going to college or technical school or having a good career. You can be successful, but you are going to have to work harder than many people your same age. It also means that you may need more support, like having a counselor, coach, or person to help guide you. You and your family may consider trying different treatments to help you. The important thing for you to remember is that you can't use your ADHD as an excuse not to do well in school. As I already said, you can be successful, but it takes hard work. Your future is bright and your family will help you along the way. What questions do you have?

If the professional you worked with did not explain ADHD to your daughter, you can provide the explanation, and books can fill in the gaps. Here are resources you can share with your teenage girl:

◊ *Attention, Girls!: A Guide to Learn All About Your AD/HD* (Patricia O. Quinn)
◊ *The ADHD Workbook for Teens: Activities to Help You Gain Motivation and Confidence* (Lara Honos-Webb)
◊ *The Girls' Guide to AD/HD: Don't Lose This Book!* (Beth Walker)
◊ *Help4ADD@HighSchool* (Kathleen G. Nadeau)

Once your daughter understands her ADHD, she can begin to learn to work through and around it. An age-appropriate explanation provides relief to many girls and affirms that they are not broken, weird, or sick. The explanation and label can help put boundaries around your girl's weaknesses so she can move forward with an attitude of hope and optimism.

Points to Consider

1. Have you accepted your daughter's ADHD as a disability?
2. Do you need to seek further evaluation or support for any co-occurring disorders?
3. How will you explain ADHD to your daughter?
4. Review your self-assessment responses to decide if there are any areas where you still need to learn more.

Action Steps to Take Now

1. Remember that your daughter probably has a fragile self-image. What are areas where you can offer genuine encouragement?
2. Begin to establish a support system for yourself by enlisting the help of caring professionals (e.g., counselors, physicians, and teachers), researching support groups, and continuing to read and learn about ADHD.
3. Think about your daughter's strengths and needs and complete Step 1 in the Dynamic Action Plan.

Chapter 2

Treatment Options
for ADHD

**SELF-ASSESSMENT:
Where Am I Now?**

Each self-assessment helps you reflect on your daughter and your parenting practices and is a preview of the chapter's content.

1. When I consider treatment for my daughter's ADHD, I . . .

    a. have a good treatment plan in place.

    b. am researching and considering what's best for her.

    c. have tried them all and nothing worked.

    d. am so confused by conflicting information.

2. My daughter's doctor is . . .
   a. aware that she has ADHD and has recommended options.
   b. unaware that she has ADHD.
   c. understanding and has referred me to another specialist.
   d. I don't have a regular medical provider.

3. When considering my family . . .
   a. we have clearly specified rules and consequences.
   b. we have unwritten rules and expectations.
   c. we have no rules.
   d. we need to create family rules.

4. When considering my daughter . . .
   a. I strive to provide her with decision-making choices.
   b. I make the majority of choices for her because she's a child.
   c. I've never considered the value of providing her with choices.
   d. When appropriate, I give my daughter choices.

5. The words I use with my daughter . . .
   a. are mostly encouraging.
   b. are mostly discouraging.
   c. are a mix of positive and negative.
   d. don't have any effect on her.

From the day your daughter is born, she begins attending, learning, and picking up information from her environment. If she doesn't attend long enough to take in, process, and store information, then her development will be negatively impacted. Likewise, if her behavior results in persistently negative interactions with those around her, her self-concept will suffer. As parents, we must make sure she receives adequate treatment and support for her ADHD.

From our work with children with ADHD, it appears that their behavior breaks down when the demands placed on them exceed their ability to complete the requested task. Your daughter may impulsively tell you she hates you, shut down and withdraw, or purposefully try to push buttons when she is overwhelmed. A recent study done by Stephanie McConaughy and colleagues (2011) showed that 15%–55% of children with ADHD "exhibited 'clinically significant' impairment in academic performance and 26–85% exhibited 'clinically significant' impairment in social behavior, depending on the measure" (p. 221). When your daughter can't perform, she'll let you know in a good or bad way. Your child is fortunate to have a parent like you who is concerned enough to research and learn about the best treatment options.

You know that the subject of ADHD treatment is a highly charged topic. Strong opinions run the gamut from those who believe medication is the only truly effective treatment to those who only use natural, holistic interventions to those who support a combination of medication, environmental modification, and behavior therapy. We believe there is no one "golden nugget" treatment that fits every girl and that a combination of treatments works best. It is important to keep in mind that the impact of ADHD continues into adulthood, requiring ongoing monitoring and treatment as necessary—just like any other chronic condition.

With regard to medication, some professionals question the influence of the drug companies who manufacture the various medications. We are not medical doctors and can only speak from our own personal and professional experience and our review of the literature, which shows that medication can be very effective and necessary for some girls. Later in this chapter, we present information from well-respected medical doctors, a pediatrician and a psychiatrist, who have years of experience treating children with ADHD. The medication decision for your daughter needs to be grounded in solid input from medical personnel, teachers, and others working with her, as well as your own perspective and sense of what is best for your daughter. It is important for you to learn about treatment options to sort out fact from fiction.

The CHADD (2011) website recommended a multipronged approach to dealing with ADHD, including:

◊ parent training;
◊ behavioral intervention strategies;
◊ an appropriate educational program;
◊ education regarding ADHD; and
◊ medication, when necessary.

Starting Point

Kim was concerned and went to her pediatrician to have her 8-year-old daughter assessed for ADHD. After the doctor reviewed the behavioral rating forms, she diagnosed Kim's daughter with ADHD. When Kim called us, she said she was in a state of shock and asked what she needed to do to help her daughter. She felt confused and did not know what to do first. Should she put her daughter on medication? Should she tell her daughter's teacher? Should she tell her daughter? Kim was weighed down by her questions. She feared the future but was hopeful that the ADHD diagnosis provided answers to her daughter's struggles.

Many parents who seek treatment for their daughter begin with their pediatrician, especially if their daughter has a long-standing relationship with him or her. Pediatricians have strong knowledge of developmental sequences and see children of various ages on a daily basis. However, one thing to keep in mind is that your pediatrician is seeing your daughter in an individualized setting where little is required of her—very different from school, with other children, noise, and demands to complete tasks that may be uninteresting to your child. When concerns arise, some pediatricians refer to school psychologists, clinical psychologists, neuropsychologists, neurologists, developmental pediatricians, or psychiatrists. Pediatricians are often interested in knowing the level of your daughter's intellectual and academic functioning, as well as her executive functioning skills, in order to rule out learning problems as the root cause of the behavior. Most parents are very confused about the roles of the different specialists, so a brief overview is included in Table 2.

Most pediatricians can effectively treat a child with mild to moderate ADHD. A developmental pediatrician would be a good choice if your daughter also has complicating developmental issues such as autism spectrum disorder. A neurologist may be recommended if there are any concerns about brain functioning, such as seizures or tics. A psychiatrist should be consulted for complicated cases where there are accompanying problems with anxiety, mood, or oppositional behavior. All of the above have gone to medical school and also can prescribe medication. A nurse practitioner usually works under the direction of a doctor and also can prescribe medication.

Clinical psychologists, neuropsychologists, and school psychologists approach ADHD from the educational, as well as the neurobiological, perspective. They focus on the impact that the behavior and ability have on learning and general life adjustment. Their training involves using various assessment measures to provide information on the child's functioning. In addition to making a diagnosis, psychologists often rely on assessments to provide an overall picture of the child in terms of her intelligence, academic strengths and weaknesses, and processing abilities. Psychologists do not prescribe medication but often work closely with medical

Table 2
Roles of Professionals in Treating ADHD

Specialty	Training	Function
Pediatrician	M.D. or D.O., general practitioner	Oversees wellness of children, diagnoses medical conditions, and prescribes medication
Developmental Pediatrician	M.D. or D.O., specialist in developmental issues	Is consulted for anomalies in development, diagnoses medical conditions, and prescribes medication
Neurologist	M.D., specialist in neurology and brain	Is consulted for neurological problems, diagnoses medical conditions, and prescribes medication
Psychiatrist	M.D., specialist in mental disorders	Is consulted for behavior/mental health issues, diagnoses conditions based on DSM-5, and prescribes medication
Nurse Practitioner	Advanced Practice Registered Nurse (APRN)	Works under the direction of a doctor and prescribes medication
Clinical Psychologist	Ph.D. or Psy.D.	Diagnoses conditions and provides therapy, can't prescribe medication
Neuropsychologist	Ph.D. or Psy. D.	Diagnoses conditions, often does testing, can't prescribe medication
School Psychologist	Master's, specialist, Ph.D., or Psy.D.	Provides testing and consultation regarding problems that impact education, can't prescribe medication
Licensed Clinical Social Worker	MSW or Ph.D.	Diagnoses conditions and provides therapy, can't prescribe medication
Behavioral Therapist	Master's or Ph.D.	Provides behavioral therapy, can't prescribe medication

Note. From Raising Boys With ADHD (p. 28) by J. W. Forgan and M. A. Richey, 2012, Waco, TX: Prufrock Press. Copyright 2012 by Prufrock Press. Reprinted with permission.

personnel who can. Some psychologists also provide counseling for the individual and the family as well as behavioral therapy.

A psychologist would be a good place to start if you are unsure about the role your child's intellectual functioning plays in her behavior. For example, it is not unusual for gifted children to get into trouble at home and school because they are curious about how things work or their boredom causes misbehavior as they seek out stimulation.

Claire was a bright and precocious kindergartner who presented as a challenge for her teacher. She came across as an intelligent, talkative, and bossy young girl who was used to running the show. She called out correct answers, demanded attention, and breezed through her assignments so quickly that she distracted others during down time. The teacher recommended IQ testing to help determine her intellectual ability and correct classroom placement. After testing, the school psychologist reported that Claire's IQ was in the gifted range and recommended a full-time gifted class. After consideration, her mom agreed and Claire's new placement resulted in a better fit to meet her advanced intellectual ability.

If you are concerned about the possibility of a learning disability or processing problems, a psychologist can evaluate your child's intelligence, academic skills, and processing capabilities. For example, a child may appear to be inattentive when in reality, she is not capable of doing the schoolwork she has been given and feels completely lost in the curriculum. Or a child who is not processing language may appear to have attention issues while in actuality she is not following the instructions.

Lilly was a 5-year-old who attended a private preschool. Her mother was concerned that Lilly might have ADHD, Predominantly Inattentive Type, so she brought her to us for a comprehensive evaluation. After testing Lilly's language, memory, attention, auditory, and visual processing, we determined that she had memory weaknesses and auditory discrimination issues that presented as if they were ADHD. Our recommendations included individual tutoring using the Lindamood-Bell auditory discrimination program and working memory training. Lilly's mom followed through and these early supports helped provide treatment matched to Lilly's need.

Licensed clinical social workers and behavior therapists may provide therapy such as cognitive behavioral therapy, behavior modification, or family therapy. Sometimes behavior therapists work in conjunction with the classroom teacher, providing support in implementing behavior management plans designed to increase a student's motivation to comply with teacher requests and complete assigned tasks. Neither social workers nor therapists prescribe medication.

When Jim evaluates a child and diagnoses her with ADHD, he and the parents discuss medication as one possible treatment option. Before recommending medication, he has parents consider these three questions:

1. How is her self-esteem? If your daughter's self-esteem appears low, then her ADHD may be impacting her daily functioning and a medication trial may be warranted.

2. How is her school performance? Is she failing classes? Does she detest going to school? Do you receive frequent calls about her troubles from school staff? Does she say other kids don't like her? If she is having major school issues, a medication trial may be needed.

3. How is your home life? Does your daughter's moodiness seem to put everyone in a bad mood? Are you constantly being embarrassed by her behavior? Is her ADHD causing relationship stress? If your home life is super stressful, then a medication trial may be warranted.

Jim's discussion centers on the parents' answers and the severity of the difficulties. The more severe your family's and daughter's difficulties, the stronger the possibility a medication trial is warranted. What a trial means is that she will try it for a few weeks and we will see how she responds, not that we are committing to keeping her on ADHD medication for the rest of her life. If she starts to feel better about herself, her grades improve, and home becomes calmer, then continue with the medication. But if she has negative side effects or it doesn't seem to help, then stop after consultation with your doctor. This is how Jim and his wife approached using medication for their child, and the benefits made it worth continuing.

What the Research Says

In 1999, the National Institute of Mental Health (see NIMH, 2009) released the Multimodal Treatment Study of ADHD (MTA), a study that looked at the benefits of various treatment options for nearly 600 children ages 7–9 across the country. The treatment options included:

◊   medication only,

◊   medication in conjunction with therapy,

◊   therapy only, and

◊   community care—the control group that was generally treated with lower doses of stimulant medication.

The outcomes of the study were (Pliszka & AACAP Work Group on Quality Issues, 2007):

1.   Stimulant medication alone was more effective in treating ADHD than behavior-modification therapy alone.

2.   The two groups of children receiving medication and those receiving medication plus behavior therapy fared better over a 14-month period than did the control group that was receiving routine community care including lower doses of medication and those receiving intensive behavioral therapy and no medication.

3.   The follow-up study in 2004 showed no clear advantage to medication only as reported in the earlier study.

A follow-up (Grady, 2010) showed that the initial presentation of symptoms predicted later functioning better than the type or intensity of treatment. Thus, this large-scale research study showed long-term benefits to using a combination of medication and behavior therapy.

At a symposium at the 2013 CHADD national convention (Hinshaw et al., 2012), more recent longitudinal studies, including the Montreal Study, Milwaukee Study, and Berkeley Girls ADHD Longitudinal Study (BGALS), were discussed. Findings showed continued impairment from ADHD into adulthood and the need for ongoing monitoring and intermittent intervention. Treatment in childhood had little or no effect on the outcome in adulthood. The Milwaukee Study particularly highlighted the adolescent years as a critical time for intervention.

The NIMH also funded the Preschoolers with ADHD Treatment Study (PATS), which involved more than 300 preschoolers who had been diagnosed with ADHD. The study found that low doses of the stimulant methylphenidate were safe and effective for preschoolers but that the children were more sensitive to the side effects of the medication, including slower than average growth rates (NIH News, 2006). Therefore, preschoolers should be closely monitored by their doctor while taking ADHD medications.

Although there are some dissenting views, most physicians consider Ritalin, the drug studied in the MTA, to be effective, safe, and to have relatively few side effects. As reported by DuPaul (2007), "Numerous studies have shown methylphenidate and amphetamine compounds to improve classroom attention, behavior control, and peer interactions as well as to enhance productivity and accuracy on academic tasks and curriculum-based measurement probes" (pp. 185–186). One client explained how medication helps her seventh-grade daughter with ADHD and said,

She has to take her medication every day because without the meds we argue like cats and dogs and don't get along. If we start to argue with her off the meds then she'll tell me I don't like her unless she is on meds—that I don't like her personality unless she is on medication. Truth is, nobody can stand to be around her without medication because she argues, carries on, and is mean.

Treatment Is Not All About Medication

One thing to keep in mind is that ADHD is a very complex disorder with very diverse presentations and is often accompanied by other conditions such as anxiety, oppositional behavior, and/or depression. When these conditions are present, they should be addressed either through counseling, behavioral therapy, medication, or a combination of several treatment strategies. Medication does not have to be your only choice for treatment. Studies have shown that therapy in combination with medication can result in the need for lower doses of medication (Dawson, 2007). Pelham and Fabiano (2008) found in their research that treatment does not have to center around medicine when behavior modification strategies are taught to children, parents, and teachers. There is general consensus that while medication addresses symptoms, it doesn't address specific impairments such as planning, organization, and social skill deficits. Therefore, we recommend you work with a professional who can see your daughter's complete picture and help you choose the best treatment for her unique needs.

Treatment Should Match the Need

Various studies have shown that if the correct match is made, then less intensive treatments can be as effective as more intensive ones. The goal of much of the current research is to predict which types of interventions will produce the most effective results in different types of ADHD. In other words, you want to identify your daughter's main challenges and then match them to the most effective treatment.

In our experience, it's often helpful for parents to work with a psychologist, psychiatrist, or other professional who understands ADHD treatment. Because we consult with parents from across the United States to help them help their children, we'll explain how we prioritize treatments and match them to needs.

When parents work with us, one of their first tasks is to complete background paperwork. During this process, we gather the big picture about the girl with ADHD and her family. The paperwork includes developmental history, age of diagnosis or suspected diagnosis, all past medications, current medications, associated therapies, counseling, evaluations, and if available, medical treatment records.

It is important to gather her past and current school records including any Individualized Education Plans (IEPs), 504 plans, progress reports, report cards, referrals, and teacher notes about your daughter. During this process, we are trying to identify what types of school support, if any, are in place.

If the child is older or a teen, we gather her input through surveys and behavioral rating scales. Some psychologists overlook this part, but we believe it's critical to obtain her input because she is the consumer and a central piece to this big puzzle.

We will have thoroughly reviewed this history before the first conference and will use that opportunity to clarify any questions. Individual evaluations, such as intelligence, academic, and/or process testing, may yield valuable information. Through this process we can identify the most important needs for the girl with ADHD. We delve into treatments that are aligned with parents' needs so that they don't waste valuable time, money, and energy doing things that don't work well. Throughout the meeting, we work with the parents to complete the Dynamic Action Plan so they leave with a specific plan.

Consider Tina, a working single parent, and her daughter, Carmen, a ninth grader in high school. Carmen was diagnosed with ADHD in third grade and since that time had been on and off medication. She was not a stellar student but earned mostly grades of B, C, and an occasional D. Carmen was not taking medication and in the months leading up to our appointment, her grades were slipping. Tina felt like she had to be on Carmen's case all the time. In addition, Tina was concerned because Carmen was choosing friends who were not known for good grades.

When we met, our process identified Carmen as having serious emotional issues with depression, anxiety, and feelings of inadequacy. Thus, she was surrounding herself with people who had an equally poor self-concept because it helped her feel less inadequate. Priority needs for Carmen were to address her anxiety and depression, so plans were made to meet with a psychiatrist and mental health counselor. Carmen also did not have well-developed study skills, so part of her plan was to learn how to sort and prioritize the quantity of information her teachers gave her each day. At the end, plans for future visits were confirmed, and while there was still a lot of work ahead, Tina and Carmen left with guidance and, most importantly, hope for the future. A blank Dynamic Action Plan, similar to the one we created for Carmen, is in Chapter 7 and is discussed throughout the book.

Bottom Line

The bottom line is that one type of treatment does not work for all children. Because each girl has unique characteristics, her treatment needs to be comprehensive, customized, and carefully monitored. Although researchers have documented that certain treatments work for the majority of children with ADHD, there are always exceptions. You should work with a professional who takes the time to understand your daughter within the context of her family and school and then selects treatments that work for her and you.

Our review of research has revealed that most practitioners believe that stimulant medication is safe when prescribed and monitored by a doctor. Although promising, the research is less clear on documenting the effectiveness of other treatments, including behavioral therapy, neurofeedback, diet, and treatment for allergens if the child happens to be allergic. Pelham and Fabiano (2008) have noted a number of studies that show the value of behavior-related therapies and parent training. There are other, less well-known studies that appear to document some benefits of modifications to diet and some emerging studies citing the benefits of neurofeedback and working memory training.

As an informed parent, it will be up to you to consider the big picture—any additional problems in academics, executive functioning, language, and emotional or behavioral functioning that your daughter may have in addition to ADHD, as well as family stressors. It is important to keep in mind that medicine in general seems to be going in the direction of very individualized treatment protocols for many types of medical conditions, and ADHD is no exception. Much research is underway about specific areas of the brain impacted by ADHD, as well as studies of the effectiveness of treatments and combinations of treatments. It will be up to you and your physician to decide what treatments or combinations will prove the most effective for your daughter.

Advice From Doctors

Because we are not medical doctors, we asked Dr. Tommy Schechtman, pediatrician, and Dr. Marshall Teitelbaum, child, adolescent, and adult psychiatrist, both in the Palm Beach, FL, area, to write about medication and ADHD.

A Pediatrician's View

We posed two questions to Dr. Schechtman:

Question 1: What questions should parents ask their pediatrician when they come in for a visit? Dr. Schechtman recommends that parents ask their pediatrician five important questions, and he also explained the importance of asking each question:

1. **What are the risks if I decide not to treat my child?**
    Everything we do in medicine should be based on constantly assessing the benefits of treatment versus potential side effects of our therapeutic interventions. Although most parents are appropriately concerned about the short-term and long-term side effects of medication, what often is not asked is, "What is the risk of not treating my daughter?" Not treating ADHD when it is evident can be risky. This can have a negative impact on academic performances, self-esteem, motivation, future success, and emotional stability. ADHD permeates into several areas of one's life and can impact not only your child's performance in school but, due to the impulsive nature of these individuals, can also adversely affect their social skills and personal relationships. In addition, more studies show that those who go untreated have a higher propensity to self-medicate later in life. This can take the form of substance use or addiction. Most importantly, without treatment we are depriving the child of the opportunity to meet or exceed her own expectations. When

we do treat a child, we afford the child the ability to achieve her optimal success both in school and in life. When we treat a child, we do not change who she is or who she wants to be, but rather provide her with the "toolkit" to maximize her potential, whatever that potential is.

2. **Are there comorbidities?**

Comorbidity is the simultaneous appearance of two or more diagnoses. For example, one might meet the diagnostic criteria for ADHD and anxiety. There are several comorbidities that may appear in any individual diagnosed with ADHD. There are several other conditions that can co-occur with ADHD. The common ones include: anxiety, depression, OCD, a tic disorder, sleep disturbances, learning disabilities, and Oppositional Defiant Disorder. Some comorbidities happen alongside the diagnosis of ADHD and are separate from it. Some comorbidities are caused by the ADHD and may go away, or the symptoms may disappear when the individual is adequately treated for ADHD. When there is a separate or underlying issue in addition to the diagnosis of ADHD, this is a more complicated issue and requires a different approach to address all of the presenting issues.

3. **What happens when my child does not respond to medication?**

If your child appears to not be responding to the medication prescribed, there are several possible explanations. First of all, this may indicate that the right dose has not been achieved yet. This may require that the medication be titrated up to reach optimal clinical effectiveness. Secondly, this could indicate that this is not the right type of medication. There are two forms of medication to consider in the treatment of ADHD, stimulants and nonstimulants. Stimulants have been shown to be the most clinically effective and are commonly used as a first course of treatment. If your child is experiencing severe mood changes or increased anxiety, for example, this may be an indication that there is a separate comorbidity at play that needs to be addressed and treated in addition to or separately from ADHD.

4. **How are you going to monitor my child's progress?**
   It is important to have routine periodic visits with your child's physician while she is regularly taking any form of medication. It is always important to monitor the child's growth and development as well as her vitals throughout the course of treatment. Also, we should never expect "perfect" results, but neither should you accept "good" results. Your doctor should be constantly monitoring and assessing your child's progress. Each child responds differently to different medications, and your child's regimen needs to be custom tailored for her in order to achieve "great" results.

5. **On what evidence are you basing the ADHD diagnosis?**
   Oftentimes a diagnosis of ADHD is made or assumed by an individual who is untrained or unqualified to do so. When it has been suggested to you that your child may have attention issues, make sure you address this from a comprehensive approach. Although there are several national standardized tests (e.g., Vanderbilt, Connors) for ADHD, these are not perfect assessment tools. There are not any blood or imaging (x-rays) tests or physical exam findings that help with the diagnosis. The diagnosis is one of exclusion (ruling out other neurological, physical, and psychological disorders), and one of profiling of commonly associated symptoms (e.g., lack of focus and short-term memory, poor organizational skills, impulsivity). The diagnosis needs to be made by a qualified and experienced mental health professional and/or a physician. However, because ADHD can permeate so many areas of one's life, it is

recommended to seek the service of both. Ideally it would be best if these professionals had access to each other so that there could be the best coordination of treatment.

Question 2: As a medical doctor, how do you explain to parents how stimulants work?

Many parents are confused about how stimulants work for their already hyperactive or distracted child and they are apprehensive of using them. This is a complex decision and understandably a difficult one to make. Parents rightly should seek all of the answers they need to make a confident decision. Part of having that confidence is partnering with a physician and mental health provider who can educate you and walk with you through the diagnosis and treatment process. We try to explain the mechanics of the use of stimulant medication for the treatment of ADHD in very simplistic terms. Very simplistically, the ADHD brain craves being stimulated, due to deficiencies or developmental issues. That is why children are so easily distracted or appear to be hyperactive. These are the ways the brain is attempting to get the stimulation it needs. When we can satisfy the brain's craving through medication, the brain can then focus on the material at hand (e.g., the teacher lecturing, the book they are reading, the test they are taking). ADHD does not affect one's ability or intellect. Take, for example, a child who wears glasses. We can all agree that wearing glasses does not affect the student's ability to read or her intellect. When she removes her glasses she has not lost the ability to read nor has her IQ dropped, but she can no longer read the words on the page. Her glasses are the tool her eyes need to focus on the paper she is reading or object she is looking at. In the same way, stimulant medications are a tool used to help the individual focus on the task at hand.

A Psychiatrist's View

We also posed two questions to Dr. Teitelbaum.

Question 1: What medications are most likely to help girls dealing with ADHD?

The first question is truly sorting out what the primary symptoms causing interference in the girl's life are. Once this is clarified, it is easier to come up with appropriate treatment plans for both pharmacologic and nonpharmacologic approaches.

Girls are *more likely* than boys to have symptoms that are more problematic on the attentional and organization spectrum of the disorder without the same degree of impulsivity issues. This often makes the process of diagnosis slower, in spite of perceived lesser life interference without the frequency of the behavioral manifestations that lead to earlier interventions. In other words, if a child is up from the seat, interrupting, walking around the room and disruptive in class, the parents hear from the teacher quickly. If the child is more distracted, daydreaming, and disorganized, and often even more so if above-average intellect, the teacher doesn't see the issues nearly as quickly, or often misinterprets them. These aren't necessarily signs of being lazy, having other learning disorders, or of family problems. Unfortunately, these issues cause just as much difficulty for a girl as impulse control issues such as hyperactivity do. These issues cause fewer behavioral problems, but lead to tremendous risks for lesser esteem and self-confidence, higher anxiety and risk for depression, and lesser educational and career achievement if not addressed adequately. I have yet to find a good reason beyond ADHD for why a child would complete homework, often with much time and family conflict, and then commonly forget to hand it in!

If there are biologically associated diagnoses present, such as Obsessive-Compulsive Disorder (OCD), autism spectrum disorders (ASDs), a chronic tic disorder (including Tourette's syndrome), bipolar disorder, or the new DSM-5 diagnostic categorization of disruptive mood dysregulation disorder (DMDD), then consideration has to be given toward the potential risk of using an ADHD medication in combination with the related condition. If there are behaviorally-associated comorbid conditions present, such as Oppositional Defiant Disorder, Conduct Disorder traits, and/or low self-esteem/depressive disorders, then a more aggressive measure such as using medication becomes practically essential. However, the decision-making process becomes trickier with girls who are struggling with eating disorders, such as anorexia nervosa, binge eating disorder, and bulimia nervosa, or other body-image issues. These difficulties are far more prevalent in adolescent girls than boys. There are also a variety of OCD presentations that overlap with body image and eating issues that are more likely to occur in girls.

ADHD and its related comorbidities present differently in different individuals. For instance, I've found that adolescent girls being seen in psychotherapy for anxiety issues, depression, family conflict, and low self-esteem are often raising concerns about issues with disorganization and poor focus while being told otherwise by their parents and even clinicians. Although many boys are resistant to getting help as teens, many of these girls are practically begging for it, finding that nobody is listening. It appears that families are commonly more accepting of the psychotherapy idea with girls, but not wanting to advance treatment any further. I often will have the same girl return for treatment after turning 18 years old and while in college struggling, knowing that she now has the final say in her treatment. Contrary to popular belief in the media, college students are not always simply looking to seek drugs unethically. Clearly, if I've seen someone in the past and/or have family corroboration of symptoms, it makes me more comfortable, however.

This makes a cookbook approach impossible. The specific symptoms of ADHD in concert with the other medical problems and risks affecting the given person need to be blended to come up with a rational treatment plan. If there is anticipation of near-term disturbance of behavioral, social, or academic functions, the ADHD symptoms have to be addressed immediately. The goal is to avoid the future consequences for what happens if these problems are allowed to evolve, such as lower school and/or career achievement, significant anxiety problems, higher risk for legal or substance abuse problems, more relationship challenges, higher risk of personality disorder development, and more injuries, ER visits, moving traffic violations, and likely even undesired pregnancies. This doesn't even begin to cover what the early adult years can be like, including as a parent and often trying to intervene with her own children who are at higher risk of having this very heritable condition. In other words, we must equally worry about the potential risks of both the treatments and of the underlying medical problem left unregulated or inadequately regulated. There are a number of ADHD medications available, which I will summarize below.

ADHD medications are primarily categorized into two groups, stimulants and nonstimulants. The FDA-approved nonstimulants are Strattera (atomoxetine), Intuniv (long-acting guanfacine), and Kapvay (long-acting clonidine formulation). These options are typically slower to take effect and less potent, although they can be used in combination with stimulants if necessary to augment treatment. All except atomoxetine are based on alpha-2 agonist blood pressure medications that have been used for years off-label to treat ADHD, but over recent years longer-acting versions have come out on-label and with greater ease of use (as the prior ones often required three to four dosages per day). The alpha-2 agonists can be helpful with tic disorders, thus assisting when this genetically linked condition is part of the equation. Given the potential for blood pressure effects and tiredness, they have to be increased slowly, and after having been used for a sufficient length of time, *have to* be reduced gradually to avoid a sudden rise in blood pressure. This is a particular concern for children passing between different households, especially if one parent tries to avoid medication use. Atomoxetine works by way of blocking uptake on the neurotransmitter norepinephrine. It may have some weak antidepressant properties, potentially being helpful with depression but being a bit more risky if bipolar disorder is suspected. Any of the medications described above can be of value if a stimulant is not considered a safe medical option or if the necessary adequate dosage of stimulant medication is not tolerable. It is common for a nonstimulant option to work well as an augmentation tool along with a stimulant that may not alone be sufficient or well-tolerated at the required effective dose. In addition, the FDA-indicated nonstimulant medications are unlikely to reduce appetite. This can make one of the above options more desirable as a first-line choice in the presence of an eating disorder.

The stimulant medications are the more well-known FDA-approved ADHD treatments. This class is predominantly broken down into two types, those related to methylphenidate (i.e., Ritalin) or amphetamine (i.e., Adderall or Dexedrine). They all tend to cause appetite suppression, but for most it can be managed well with the appropriate interventions.

Methylphenidate-based medications include shorter-acting (usually no more than 4 hours) and longer-acting (upwards of 8 hours). The shorter-acting medicines include methylphenidate (Ritalin) and dexmethylphenidate (Focalin). The longer-acting methylphenidates include Concerta, Ritalin LA, Metadate CD/ER, Ritalin SR, Daytrana, and Quillivant XR, along with the related dexmethylphenidate, Focalin XR. Daytrana is a patch that goes on the hip, rotating sites daily to lessen the risk of skin irritation. It can allow for better morning symptom management if applied while a child is still in bed, and can allow more active management of the wear-off time based on when it is removed, regardless of the time it is applied (i.e., if you have a teenager who likes to sleep in on weekends). Concerta, Ritalin LA, Metadate CD, and Focalin XR are medications with delivery technology that increase the likelihood of ongoing benefit throughout the day. Concerta may last longer for some, although Focalin XR may kick in faster. Quillivant XR is a liquid long-acting version that has the advantage of being used when a child doesn't swallow pills and, more so, when an atypical strength is most suitable (for example, the strength can be adjusted simply by adjusting the number of mL provided). There are some who find that the level of appetite suppression is less intense when using dexmethylphenidate XR/Focalin XR. The times of day that require better medication coverage need to be kept in mind when using these. There are commonly practical applications to consider, such as cost and insurance limitations. Even though higher tech medications, such as Concerta and Adderall XR, are now available in generic formulations, they are not necessarily cheaper. For those who prefer branded options, there are also generic formulations that are actually the same (for example, Watson Labs generic Concerta is provided by the original branded manufacturer).

Shorter-acting (up to 4 hours) amphetamine-based medications (admit it, the name is scary) include Adderall (mixed dextro- and levo-amphetamine salts), Dexedrine (dextroamphetamine) and ProCentra (liquid dextroamphetamine), with ProCentra being useful at times for kids who cannot swallow pills. Longer-acting versions include Adderall XR, Dexedrine Spansule, and Vyvanse. The longer-acting medications are more likely to allow better full-day coverage, with Vyvanse being the longest-acting on the average (up to 13 hours). Vyvanse is a prodrug, meaning it is turned into its active product (lisdexamfetamine into dextroamphetamine) only after the digestive system starts to break it down.

As I'm prone to reminding parents, nonschool hours are often as or more important, as these can be times of higher risk. Driving while distracted can be a major danger, for instance, and the GPA is irrelevant when someone is in the emergency room. For adolescent girls, the risks can be even greater if distracted, whether it is while walking alone and zoning out or hyperfocusing on a smartphone. The more the distraction, the more likely the person is to be a target. Unfortunately, there is still a tendency to believe that the predominantly inattentive/nonhyperactive subtypes of ADHD don't require routine management. Being the butt of "blonde jokes" for their lack of attention or for seeming "ditzy" or "spacey" to others is very damaging for girls' self-esteem, and can also cause reduction of expectations and motivation. In addition, impulsive actions, such as placing certain verbal or picture postings on public Internet sites, can lead to significant and long-lasting shame and embarrassment.

There are a variety of other medication classes still being researched, as well as medications that are frequently used for off-label treatment of ADHD. It is always of the utmost importance that the risks for both medically treating and not treating ADHD be fully explored to help dictate the appropriate treatment course.

Question 2: How do you know when to stop using ADHD medications with your daughter?

This is often quite challenging to decide, as it is hard to potentially take this risk with a girl who is doing well. There are many considerations. First, if she's on a faster-acting medication such as a psychostimulant, have there been days of missed dosages, and if so what transpired on these days? If your daughter had a miserable day with the original symptoms of ADHD seen prior to medication initiation, in all likelihood the medication needs to be continued. If the child has been doing really well for an extended time, it is usually wise to reassess the medication need at least annually, and usually at a time when it would be the least problematic if reduction causes symptom recurrence. For instance, stopping her medication just prior to final exams or some other type of big event would be silly. Often, lowering the dosage sometime when there is less going on at school, and possibly with the teacher's awareness, makes it easier to assess the efficacy. Other times, it can be less risky to reduce when school is out, although if the main issues of ADHD are on the inattentive (versus impulsive) spectrum, then it can be more challenging to evaluate. For younger girls, summertime challenges often include difficulty getting summertime academic pursuits, such as summer reading, addressed. Also, there is a tendency for more parent-child conflict when symptoms aren't adequately addressed.

The most important issues have to do with whether the symptoms of ADHD are still there, which is usually the case to at least some degree for the majority of affected individuals, and what ways the residual symptoms are still interfering. A child who has problems with socialization or behavior when off of medication is likely to have a variety of problems if taking an extended medication break over the summer, for instance. If a child is either having no further life interferences without medication or is having minimal enough disturbance that it can be addressed in other ways (i.e., organizational coaching, psychotherapy, etc.), then it may be reasonable to stop medication. There are many girls who don't have significant impulse control symptoms who may be able to use medication on a more as-needed basis, such as for driving, summer projects or jobs, organized activities, or other related focused actions. Some may need routine treatment but at a lesser dosage. The process becomes trickier when reaching the age of driving, however.

More importantly, even if the medication is working wonderfully for the ADHD symptoms, if you daughter is becoming too focused on weight loss the medication will likely require reassessment by your treating clinician, and quickly!

It is hard being a parent. It is even harder when you have a child with ADHD, as often you do not get the support of others like you do with a child with most other medical problems. However, it is your responsibility to make the decisions that are in the best interest of your child, regardless of whether they are easy or popular. I often compare the condition to severe allergy or vision problems, as none are thought of as immediately life-threatening, but the quality of life and potential risks going forward, if the condition is ignored, can be severe. If the medical issue is interfering with your child's life, then it is your responsibility as a parent to make decisions, even those that you do not like. It has to be kept in mind that the child is not choosing to have ADHD (i.e., be distracted, disorganized, and/or hyperactive). Take advantage of all of the resources that this modern society has to offer!

Thanks to Drs. Schechtman and Teitelbaum for sharing their valuable insight with us. We acknowledge that it's not often that parents are afforded the time during their daughter's doctor's visit to hear this type of information because many doctors are pressed for time. And even if we had the time to hear this from a doctor, it would be too much to quickly take in, so it is nice to have an explanation in writing to read and reference as needed.

Cautions About Medication

Parents have a myriad of concerns about medication, including decreased appetite, impact on growth, medication dependency, and recent concerns about heart problems. We had these concerns ourselves, and from our experiences as parents, we acknowledge that medications did impact our son's sleep, appetite, and moods as the drug wore off. Jim and his wife grappled with the medication's side effects and ultimately concluded that during the early elementary years, the gain they saw was worth the discomfort of the side effects. As their son became a teenager, he did not want to continue taking the medication. When asked why he said, "I just don't need it anymore; I can concentrate on my own." After a discussion about the pros and cons, they decided to allow him to attend school without taking medication. He fared well for almost 2 years without taking the medication.

If your child is or may soon be taking medication, an honest discussion with your doctor is important so he or she can explain the cautions and help you feel comfortable with your decision. There's no doubt that you have already been influenced by the media, family, and friends, so it is important to know that you have considered the best available advice and made the best decision for your daughter. Ask your doctor some of the insightful questions discussed in this chapter. Finally, if you choose medication, be assured that there is much research to back up its benefits and safety when it is prescribed judiciously and carefully monitored by you and your physician.

When to Stop Medication

When meeting with parents, we ask them to consider the following points before deciding to stop ADHD medication:
◊ Is she mature enough to try going without medication?
◊ Are the benefits of medication worth the side effects?
◊ How are her grades?
◊ How is her school and home behavior?
◊ What is she saying about how it helped?

◊ What is she like when the medication wears off?

◊ If she stopped now, would she have to start again later?

◊ What does the medical doctor say about stopping?

We suggest that you consider these and your own points. During this process, one thing we typically advise parents against doing is stopping medication just because their daughter puts up a fuss when it is time to take her medication or if she complains that she doesn't want to take it anymore. These alone are not valid reasons to cease treatment. We recommend that there be a medical reason or several compelling reasons to stop.

Your Daughter's Diet

There is no question that children with and without ADHD will benefit from a well-balanced diet of proteins, fats, and carbohydrates, as well as adequate vitamins and minerals. The natural foods movement has been gaining momentum for all people. However, there is significant controversy about the role of diets in children with ADHD. There are proponents of elimination diets and/or supplementation with nutrients as treatments for ADHD, neither of which have wide research support but have anecdotal support. If you choose any of these elimination or supplementary diet approaches, it will be important to first discuss it with your pediatrician. The National Resource Center on ADHD (2008) provided a discussion of complementary and alternative treatments and warned readers that "the FDA does not strictly regulate the ingredients or the manufacturer claims about dietary supplements. Go to the FDA web site to learn about existing regulations" (para. 27).

The Feingold Diet, developed during the 1960s by Ben Feingold, a San Francisco allergist, focuses on eliminating "artificial flavorings, preservatives, dyes, and other additives, as well as food containing naturally occurring salicylates (such as oranges, apples, apricots, berries, and grapes" (Armstrong, 1995, p. 72). However, most studies have not verified the effectiveness of the diet, even though anecdotal reports indicate some children with sensitivities to these substances have benefited from it. We don't recommend this diet.

If you feel that your child may be sensitive to food additives, you might want to keep a log of food your child is eating and note adverse effects. Many doctors recommend 2 weeks on and 2 weeks off for any substance you are checking for sensitivities. Monitor any specific behavior changes in your daughter during that time and report them to your doctor or other professional. Below is excellent advice on nutritional supplements and dietary interventions from Dr. Judith Aronson-Ramos, a developmental and behavioral pediatrician in south Florida.

A Top 10 List of Alternative Medicine Guidelines

The following guidelines are intended to support families in their search for safe and scientifically validated approaches to the use of nutritional supplements and dietary interventions.

There is a wealth of information available on "complementary and alternative medicine" (CAM) in bookstores, on the Internet, in health food stores, and in the popular press. It can be confusing to sort through all of this information. It can often be contradictory, and it is difficult to know what is based on sound research and valid evidence.

There have been numerous claims made regarding the use of various alternative approaches in treating learning, behavior, and psychiatric problems in children. Even though a substantial body of research does exist, very often families and their physicians are unaware of the research. Studies have shown that quite often people rely on advice from friends and family, popular news shows, manufacturer advertisements and claims, and health food store personnel to guide them in their search for reasonable and effective alternatives.

To help families, I would like to offer a "top 10 list" of pointers useful in evaluating any potential nutritional or dietary intervention. As physicians, we take an oath that states: "Do no harm." In the realm of "natural" and "alternative" products, this still applies. A natural product has the same potential to be harmful as does a standard medication or procedure. The purported health benefits of many supplements and the actual contents of these products are not yet evaluated by any nationally recognized independent agency. You can never be sure what you are actually taking. There are also risks of contamination with heavy metals and other toxic substances. This must be understood when choosing to try different supplements and nutritional products.

1. **Know yourself and your child.**

    Don't begin a diet or nutritional plan you or your child will not be able to successfully follow. Be realistic. Be reasonable. There are isolated examples of diets that have cured diseases (e.g., gluten free for celiac disease, the ketogenic diet for seizures, etc.). However, in general, diets are very difficult to prove or disprove, and scientifically sound evidence is lacking for many of the popular diets. If a family is committed to trying a particular diet, and proper supplements are used to prevent nutritional imbalance, a diet can be tried for a reasonable period of time. In general, 4–6 weeks of a dietary intervention should be sufficient to judge whether or not there is a beneficial effect.

2. **Know exactly what you are taking.**

    Dietary and nutritional supplements comprise an essentially unregulated industry. The Dietary Supplement Health and Education Act (DSHEA) enacted by the federal government in the late 1990s stipulates that botanical (herbal products) and other dietary supplements are not "drugs" and are there-fore not held to the same regulatory standards as drugs. This means that any product sold on the market does not need to demonstrate evidence of both safety and efficacy. Companies can make statements that do not have to be proven by scientific research. (This is why products carry the label, "This statement has not been evaluated by the FDA.") Additionally, what the bottle states and what is actually in the product may vary. There are, however, several good independent laboratory groups that perform third party testing on products, and the results are available to consumers. (Examples include Consumer Labs and The Council for Responsible Nutrition.) These organizations do not receive financial support from companies making the products they are analyzing. This is essential to prevent a conflict of interest that could bias results. Products that pass their analyses can be labeled with their seal of approval. Be sure you look into the validity of "certifying" groups. Keep the following points in mind: who pays for their research, if there are financial links to specific industries or companies, and who serves on their scientific advisory boards.

3. **Know where to get good information.**
   The federal government created the National Center for Complementary and Alternative Medicine (NCCAM) in 1997. This is a branch of the National Institute of Health. Its website has a tremendous amount of information available to consumers and professionals. This agency provides information about products that may be harmful, as well as potentially dangerous interactions between supplements and medications.

4. **Know what is affecting what.**
   Oftentimes when children are placed on a diet or given a supplement, there are many different variables changing at once. In this setting, it is impossible to know what products were or

were not effective. A reasonable stepwise approach will allow you to better evaluate what is truly making a difference. Some practitioners will state certain products need to be given in combination to have an effect. Be wary if the list is long and costly.

5. **Know the difference between self-interest on the part of a practitioner and good clinical practice.**
   When the person recommending a product is also selling you that product, beware of conflict of interest and ethical issues.

6. **Know when to stop.**
   There are an unlimited number of diets and products to try. Constantly jumping from one thing to another can be a time-consuming pursuit.

7. **Know what is based on good scientific research and what is not.**
   All "studies" are not equal. A good, valid study is well designed, published in a reputable journal, and others have duplicated the results. With the Internet, families can do their own research if they know where to go. Information can be shared with the professionals involved in your child's care. If done in the spirit of mutual understanding, a good professional will not be defensive. Some helpful websites include the following (of course you may find others in your own research): http://www.quack watch.org; http://www.jointcommission.org; http://www.fda. gov/medwatch; http://www.childrenshospital.org/holistic.

8. **Know what is reasonable.**
   As the old adage goes, if it sounds too good to be true, it probably is. Do not rely solely on the advice of those individuals actually selling you products. It is imperative to do your own research or consult with practitioners involved in your care.

9. **Know what the significant side effects and precautions are for anything your child takes.**

   Potential side effects and drug interactions may not appear on product labels. It is important to do some research and be sure of the safety of any products you give your child. Remember that the liver metabolizes many products, and children may be particularly vulnerable to toxic metabolites at different ages. Always keep the poison control center hotline on hand; in the event of an accidental ingestion, call 1-800-222-1222. In the case of a serious or concerning side effect noted from taking a supplement, you should immediately go to your nearest emergency room. Take the bottle of the product in question with you. The following websites have extensive information on product safety and product interactions: http://medicine. iupui.edu/flockhart (continuously updated information on liver metabolism and different drugs and supplements); http:// dietary-supplements.info.nih.gov (impartial information provided by the Office of Dietary Supplements, a branch of the National Institutes of Health).

10. **Know what tastes good!**

   If you find something tastes terrible, don't expect your children to take it. Similarly, there are times when a product does not appeal to your taste buds but may be delicious to your child. Be persistent and resourceful to find a product that will work; often there is a solution.

Thanks to Dr. Aronson-Ramos for allowing us to reprint her valuable tips on evaluating nutritional and dietary interventions. These tips and more can be found on her website: http://draronson ramos.com.

Neurofeedback/Biofeedback

Neurofeedback (also called EEG biofeedback or biofeedback) is a type of brain exercise or training and is an alternative treatment for ADHD that is gaining some research validity. In a 2009 meta-analysis study, Arns and colleagues concluded that neurofeedback had a large effect size for inattention and impulsivity and a medium effect size for hyperactivity. A 2011 meta-analysis by Lofthouse and colleagues included 14 neurofeedback studies and reported a large effect size for inattention and moderate effect size for hyperactivity-impulsivity. The researchers concluded that neurofeedback is shown to produce positive effects but that more studies still need to be conducted. These analyses imply that neurofeedback may help your daughter more if she is inattentive or impulsive and less if she is hyperactive.

In addition to these meta-analyses, many neurofeedback studies have been conducted by researchers outside of the United States. Within the United States, some studies report positive results for using neurofeedback to treat individuals with ADHD. Readers interested in the specific neurofeedback literature are referred to the work of Monastra and colleagues (Monastra, 2004; Monastra et al., 2005; Monastra, Monastra, & George, 2002), as they provide a good starting point. It was reported in some of Monastra's (Monastra et al., 2002) studies that EEG biofeedback was a promising treatment for ADHD when used as part of a multimodal treatment approach of parent counseling, EEG biofeedback, and stimulant therapy but that more research was needed. In their 2005 study, Monastra and colleagues concluded:

> Although it is clear from the outcomes of each of the published cases and controlled studies of EEG biofeedback for ADHD, that significant, beneficial effects have consistently been reported in patients/ families who volunteered to receive this type of

treatment, additional controlled, group studies (with random assignment to treatment condition) are needed in order to promote a clearer understanding of the number of patients and degree of improvement that can be anticipated in clinical practice. (p. 108)

The premise behind how neurofeedback works is that a person's brain rhythms are either working too fast or too slow. Thus, neurofeedback training helps a person modify her brain's rhythms or electrical activity. While participating in a neurofeedback session, the girl's brain rhythms are recorded using EEG technology. Depending on the neurofeedback practitioner, she either has electrodes attached to her scalp or she wears a special cap that contains electrodes. These electrodes record brain activity as she engages in a computer-based activity that teaches her how to alter her brain rhythms. The goal is to teach her how to become aware of and modify her brain rhythms that translate into improved behavior and schoolwork.

Working Memory Training

Working memory training programs are emerging alternative treatments for children with ADHD because working memory is a core component of most models of executive functioning, an area consistently shown to be problematic for children with ADHD. Many researchers have supported the importance of working memory in a child's ability to remain attentive (Alderson, Rapport, Hudec, Sarver, & Kofler, 2010; Kofler, Rapport, Bolden, Sarver, & Raiker, 2010).

Working memory training programs have received varied reviews in the research literature. Melby-Lervåg and Hulme (2013) examined existing working memory studies and created a meta-analysis that analyzed and summarized the current state of working memory training. They reported that working memory training has a positive effect on tasks similar to those utilized in the training. For example, if a child trains on repeating numbers backward, she can improve on that task. There was less evidence to support if working memory training had a positive effect on academic tasks such as reading comprehension or arithmetic. The researchers reported that working memory training *alone* cannot be recommended as a treatment for ADHD or dyslexia.

Of the available working memory programs, we believe Cogmed Working Memory Training has the most independent research supporting its effectiveness. At this time, there are numerous independently published research studies that provide evidence regarding the effectiveness of Cogmed Working Memory Training to help children with ADHD improve working memory and behavior (Holmes et al., 2009; Mezzacappa & Bucker, 2010; Rief, 2008), improve word reading, and improve reading comprehension in children with special needs (Dahlin, 2011).

The Cogmed Working Memory Training program is an Internet-based computer software program that the child completes at home with her parent along with weekly check-ins and monitoring with a coach. Cogmed is a 5-week, 5-day-a-week program and each session ranges from 35–45 minutes. As the child finishes each working memory activity, her performance is recorded within the Cogmed software. The software is self-adjusting so that the child works within her instructional zone. A quality assurance coach checks in with the parent once a week, reviews the child's performance, and offers suggestions for improvement. After the child completes the 5-week regimen, there are regular booster sessions and follow-ups from the coach. In our personal experiences, we have found that Cogmed helps younger children and those children whose working memory is moderately, but not significantly, impaired.

Allergies and ADHD

If your daughter has or you suspect your daughter has ADHD, then we recommend a comprehensive medical evaluation. For example, if a girl has allergies, they can affect her concentration, memory, or ability to focus. Many parents are concerned about allergies to red food dye. A medical doctor can take a thorough history in order to determine if allergies could be involved. If you or your doctor strongly suspects your daughter may have allergies, then blood work will be requested to make a diagnosis.

In our experiences, having blood work done is the preferred procedure for allergy testing. Because of a person's testimony, Jim spent considerable money and had his son tested for allergies using a nonmedical practitioner who did not use blood work as part of the procedure. The testing involved simply holding onto a vial of a substance, such as wheat. If the practitioner could push down the child's raised arm, he or she was considered allergic to the substance. Then a holistic procedure was performed along with a 24-hour elimination period. Jim had his son tested for a couple of substances and saw no difference. Due to his wife's diligence, they discovered their son could not tolerate soda and after eliminating that from his diet, his stomach problems went away.

We believe some children have real allergies to certain foods, dyes, or food ingredients. We find some children benefit from limited amounts of wheat—having a gluten-free diet. Gluten causes some children to feel very lethargic and have difficulty concentrating. Other children have accompanying gastrointestinal problems that cause feelings of sickness. When we work with parents who have this concern, we often refer them to a nutritionist. For those who want to try to eliminate gluten on their own, we recommend you do substantial research, because gluten is found in some foods that you may not suspect, including soy sauce and many salad dressings.

Counseling

Because of the often co-occurring issues, many girls with ADHD obtain help working with a counselor or mental health therapist. Counseling helps girls learn to understand themselves and their ADHD. Medication alone won't teach your daughter the valuable life skills she'll need for success, so that's why counseling can be an effective treatment. Because each girl is unique, your daughter will have her own specific needs. What skills does your daughter need help in developing?

In our experiences, parents typically seek counseling when they feel like they have done everything they know how to do, yet there are still problems. When your daughter's challenges reach crisis level, it may prompt you to reach out for a professional's support. We receive frantic phone calls from parents who want to "do something" to help their daughter. As school psychologists, we become the "do something" as parents turn to us for parenting guidance. To have the most benefit, counseling usually involves you, your daughter, and the immediate family.

There are various counseling methods. We prefer using cognitive behavioral therapy because it presumes that a girl's thoughts, not external events or people, cause her feelings and behaviors. Thus, we try to change her behavior by changing her thoughts. Cognitive behavioral therapy has a solid research base and is short term, goal oriented, and instructive. During counseling, girls are taught how to identify and express concerns, problem solve, and apply what they learned. The sessions involve learning to take responsibility and make measurable steps toward achieving the desired outcome. As part of the counseling process, parents also learn how to change their thoughts and behavior, because in many cases, both the parents and girl are skilled in pushing each other's buttons.

We receive feedback from parents and girls that this type of counseling is usually helpful for making meaningful life changes. For instance, Maria was a teenage client with whom we worked to help her overcome self-defeating thoughts. She had a negative outlook on herself, school, and life that lowered her self-esteem and academics. Maria approached each situation from a negative, rather than positive, perspective. For example, if Maria's mom told her they were going to a nearby water park, then one of Maria's first thoughts would be that the lines would be so long that she'd spend most of her time standing around waiting. Maria's mom, Beatrice, continually reminded Maria about how negative she was, but it really never seemed to resonate with Maria. Through cognitive behavioral counseling, we concentrated on helping Maria recognize how often she thought negatively. We gave Maria a simple click-counter to hold for an hour. Each time she had a negative thought, she was to click the counter. In one hour, she had up to 39 negative thoughts, and even she was surprised at this number. We helped her learn positive self-talk to suppress the automatic negative thoughts. Over time she was able to reduce the number of automatic negative thoughts to less than 10 per hour. This improved the quality of life for Maria and her family.

A secret to making counseling work for you and your daughter is finding the right match between your daughter and her counselor. Therefore, you should interview several counselors to help determine if he or she is the right pairing. After several meetings with the counselor you have chosen, ask your daughter questions such as, "How do you like the counselor? Do you feel like he or she listens and understands you? Are you becoming comfortable talking to him or her?" Likewise, ask the counselor if your daughter is expressive, open, and honest. From this point, you can make the decision to stay or find another counselor. These are questions to ask when choosing a counselor for your daughter:

◊ What is your philosophy toward helping make meaningful change?

◇ What type of counseling is used?
◇ Is there a specific curriculum?
◇ How long does the average client remain in counseling?
◇ What are common causes for leaving?
◇ What is the most common age range of girls you counsel?
◇ How are parents and/or family involved?
◇ Does the counselor communicate with teachers or school staff?

From our experiences, you may have to try more than one counselor to find that right fit. Despite your best efforts at researching and interviewing, a particular counselor may not seem to "click" for your daughter. Counselors understand this, so you don't need to feel bad if, after a few sessions, you have to leave. Simply tell the counselor you appreciated his or her help but will be moving on. We recommend you don't stay with a counselor just for the sake of "doing something" or because that person is on your insurance plan because, simply put, counseling will not work if it's not the right fit.

To summarize, counseling is a proven way for your daughter to learn important life skills for managing her ADHD and building a skill set for life. Some consider it time consuming and costly, but it can help give your daughter a new outlook on her life. Jim worked with one family in which the mother was strongly in favor of counseling for her daughter, Karen, but the father was very skeptical because, in his words, "It's a waste of money." Jim's background knowledge about the family indicated that they frequently took their children to Disney World from very young ages. Jim said, "Why did you start taking Karen to Disney World at such a young age when today she probably doesn't remember those early trips?" He replied, "To give her a foundation and experiences that I never had as a kid." Jim closed with, "From an early age, and even though she can't remember specifics, you've given Karen opportunities that have shaped who she is today. Why stop now?" The father thought for a few seconds and agreed to try treatment.

Coaching

Coaching involves assistance with tasks such as organization, scheduling, goal setting, and time management. Teenagers and adults with ADHD are the most likely candidates to find success with coaching. Coaching is often more action oriented than counseling. The coach will often assist the person with ADHD in breaking down tasks into short-term goals and will check in frequently to see how the person is progressing toward those goals.

Nancy Ratey and Susan Sussman have established the National Coaching Network and a formalized curriculum for coaching adults with ADHD. Many of their strategies can also be used in coaching children and teenagers with ADHD. Their plan involves self-evaluation to assess strengths and weaknesses, including whether the person responds to visual or auditory reminders, and the creation and monitoring of a plan to manage needed changes (Ratey, 2008).

Parent Training

Let's admit it: You are busy providing for your family and yourself, so at the end of the day you may feel like you've given so much that you don't have much left. As parents of our own kids with ADHD, we've been there too and have felt like we are running so hard just to keep life in the balance that we are spent. Like our kids', our own energy ebbs and flows; therefore, we've had to prioritize what we can do to help our kids. You are certainly doing the right thing by reading this book.

Dr. Phyllis Teeter (1998), author of *Interventions for ADHD: Treatment in Developmental Context*, suggested that parent training will be essential, especially to increase the likelihood that your child will comply with your rules and structure. She discussed three major parent-training programs from Barkley, Patterson, and Forehand and McMahon. All three "incorporate techniques to improve parent-child interactions, to decrease noncompliance and to facilitate family communication patterns" (Teeter, 1998, p. 155). The overall benefit to parent training has been difficult to document through research studies, but our experience has been that it is always of some benefit when parents can improve their skills, even in one area. How many times have you wished for just one skill that would make you feel like you had some impact on your daughter's behavior?

If you like to learn by watching or listening, Jim has an online parent support system that teaches parents skills for helping their boy or girl with ADHD. Although his program is not research based, it was created based on 14 years of helping parents and raising his own son with ADHD. Jim designed the program for busy parents so that when you have a few minutes of free time, like on a lunch break, you can log in and watch a video between 3–20 minutes long and learn techniques for helping your child. This program is on his website at http://www.JimForgan.com.

Another online parent training program we also mention in the preschool chapter was created by CHADD, the largest ADHD nonprofit organization. It provides 14 hours of ADHD training that was created by parents for parents. You can purchase the program and complete it online at home. Alternatively, CHADD offers the program in person through local chapters, so visit its website (http://www.chadd.org) if you'd like additional information.

General Behavior Strategies

In upcoming chapters, we will discuss behavioral techniques that have proven successful with various age groups. We will stress the importance of structure, predictable and consistently administered consequences, an environment engineered for success, and positive support for all age groups. Listed below are specific behavioral strategies you may also want to implement that we have found useful with our sons and clients. As parents, we set these boundaries to protect our children.

Establishing Clear, Firm Boundaries

One of the secrets of effectively parenting girls with ADHD is to provide clear and firm boundaries for what types of behaviors are and are not acceptable in your home. If you don't establish what is and is not acceptable behavior, she will take advantage of you and her siblings, and you will find yourself yelling at your children and feeling like they don't listen or respect you. This is often when we receive calls from our clients seeking help—as one exasperated client confided to Jim, "She is making home life a living nightmare."

Here's what we recommend. Create this plan with your spouse or other adult(s) in the home who will be helping to implement the plan. You want everyone on the same page and consistent.

1. Identify and write down your five most important house rules.
2. Write down the consequences for not following the rules (e.g., first infraction, second, third).
3. Schedule a family meeting.
4. Discuss the rules and consequences and clarify expectations.
5. Implement the new plan.

When deciding on your five most important rules, try to keep them short. For example, rules in Jim's home include: no cursing, no name calling, keep hands and feet to yourself, no talking back, and complete assigned chores. His consequences include a verbal warning, time in your room, loss of privileges (e.g., video games, phone, computer, driving), and grounding.

As you sit everyone down for the family meeting, structure the conversation by saying something similar to this:

> This is an important meeting and the first of many like this. You may have noticed that things have not been running so smoothly in our family lately, and there has been a lot of yelling and arguing. It's time to get our family back on the right track. It's time for everyone to learn responsibility, so we came up with these new rules. We've always had family rules, but they might not have been so clear. Now we've clearly listed them along with the consequences of not following them. Let's discuss them together so we are all on the same page. We believe these will help our home run smoother and get everyone feeling better.

By having this type of talk and agreement with your family, you have just removed some of the emotion that will occur the next time you discipline your daughter or other children. The clear consequences help you remain neutral because everyone has agreed upon the rules and consequences. So if your daughter decides to talk back, you can confidently state the warning and inform her that the next infraction results in a loss of a privilege. Expect your daughter to test you on the new rules and consequences for two reasons. First, she is impulsive and she will know the rule but won't consider it before acting and breaking the rule. Second, she wants to test you to find out if you are serious about enforcing the rules. Most parents we work with notice that their child's behavior temporarily gets worse before it becomes better, so don't despair if you find this with your family. This plan will work, but as we've stated before, you must be consistent in using it and following through.

Using Behavior Plans

Behavior charts and plans also work to help shape your daughter's behavior when used consistently. In our experiences, parents are challenged to maintain and monitor the plans over time. Most parents start out strong and then fizzle out within a week or two. Although it's beyond the scope of this book to provide in-depth information on behavioral charts and plans, we do want to explain the basics of using behavior plans at home.

During Jim's son's early elementary school years, he used behavior plans. Although he did not use them continually throughout the year, he faded them in and out as needed. Behavior plans work well for children who do not yet have the natural ability to self-monitor their own behavior. Behavior plans help kids with ADHD who have little internal self-control because the behavior plan provides external control.

Jim used the behavior chart again when his son was in the seventh grade because his grades were falling and his behavior became problematic. As seen in the chart in Figure 6, the middle school day was divided into seven class periods. Jim and his wife decided the two primary areas where their son needed improvement were in his effort and behavior. After explaining the chart to their son and obtaining teacher assistance, the behavior chart began on a Monday. After each class, Jim's son would bring the paper to his teacher, who would circle how he performed in class. As a reward for earning a 4 or 5, he received gaming time at home. He received 10 minutes of game time for each 5 and 5 minutes of game time for each 4. Likewise, if he earned a 1 or 2, reward time was subtracted. Although this system took time to monitor, this external control was used for 3 months and helped him improve his grades and behavior.

	Effort				Behavior			
	Did not work	Worked but did not get at least half done	Put forth the effort but did not finish	Finished what was expected of me	Had to leave class	Distracted others; didn't stop with redirect	Required redirect but responded	Had a good class
	1	2	3	4	1	2	3	4
Rotation #1								
Rotation #2								
Rotation #3								
Rotation #4								
Rotation #5								
Rotation #6								
Rotation #7								

Figure 6. Sample behavior chart.

Providing Choices

Which do you prefer, reading a book or watching the movie? Getting a gift of jewelry or going on a nice vacation? Receiving a gift card or being surprised with nice clothes? People like choices, and the same holds true for girls with ADHD. As parents we found that our kids usually responded better when presented with two choices. For example, we've given choices such as, "You can do your homework now or in 30 minutes," "You can wear these clothes to school or these clothes," "You may choose to have a birthday party at our house or grandma's house," and "Would you like to clean that one thing up now or clean all of this up when we get home?" Giving your daughter choices does not excuse her from the task.

Think about what providing choices does for her. First, it helps her learn to problem solve. For instance, if she is presented with the choice of cleaning the bathroom on Saturday before or after she checks Facebook, then she must think about the benefits. If she completes the task before her computer time, then she does not have to think about it and can enjoy social networking later. Even though this seems like a simple decision, it requires her to apply problem-solving skills.

Next, providing choices helps your daughter learn to make decisions. Some girls become indecisive because choices are made for them. As parents we should provide our daughters with age-appropriate decision-making opportunities. If choices are made for her as a child, then your daughter may mature into a young adult who relies upon others to make decisions for her. She may be easily swayed into unhealthy habits or relationships.

Finally, giving your daughter choices can help empower her and make her feel valued. We worked with one family who allowed each family member to take turns deciding on the restaurant for a weekly family dinner. Another family took turns choosing the game for family game night. Simple choices like these allow your daughter to feel comfortable making decisions that influence others. After presenting a workshop for parents, Jim had a mom approach him who agreed with giving girls power through choices. She had five children, one of whom was a girl, and she intentionally gave her frequent opportunities to make choices that influenced her brothers. This mom's philosophy was that in the business world it's tough for women to compete with men and that from an early age her daughter needed to become strong at putting up with boys' complaints resulting from her choices.

The main points to remember are that you want your daughter to learn to problem solve and to make her own good choices. In order to do that, she needs three things from you: opportunity, instruction, and helpful feedback. You can get started today.

Words

Regardless of which treatment type you choose, the words you use with your daughter influence the outcome of treatment. Your words and the words of your family have the power to hurt or help her ADHD. So how are you using your words today? Are you using words to tell your daughter how special she is to you, how she is improving, trying, putting in effort, and making you proud? Or are your words harsh, critical, and condescending?

For a moment, reflect on the significant adults during your childhood. What positive words did they say to you? Now think about the negative words that they said to you. If we asked you to create a side-by-side list of these words, would you remember and list more positive or negative words? Hopefully you had many more positive words said about you than negative ones. Now fast forward and think about your daughter when she's the same age you are now. How many positive words would she remember that you said about her? Is today the day you need to start talking to her differently?

You've heard of the self-fulfilling prophecy, which says the words you say, hear, and think determine how you become. Words are so powerful that if your daughter hears you tell her she is dumb, a loser, and good for nothing, then it is likely she'll grow into that role. On the other hand, if you want your daughter to grow up feeling loved, cherished, important, capable, and special to you, tell her this. As you read this you may be thinking of someone in your daughter's life whom you need to approach about his or her communication with your daughter and its effect on her. As you read in a previous section, if one of your house rules is not to put others down, then start enforcing it, because it applies to children *and* adults.

These words also influence your daughter's self-esteem. Our self-esteem is a reflection of how we believe others view us and how we view ourselves. Having healthy self-esteem is important for helping your daughter make it through life, because when she is teased by other girls, she needs to have the strength not to let it permanently affect her. Throughout each chapter we offer ideas for building up your daughter's self-esteem.

Figure 7 is our list of positive words or phrases that you can use to build up your daughter. Because we work with many bilingual clients, we listed them in English and Spanish. Just for fun, try using them in both languages!

Ambitious Ambisioso	Expressive Expresivo	Kind Bondadoso	Remarkable Increible
Appreciative Apreciado	Extraordinary Extraordinaria	Leader Leder	Smart Inteligente
Astonishing Asombroso	Fantastic Fantastico	Love Amor	Special Especial
Awesome Impresionante	Generous Generoso	Motivated Motivado	Successful Exitoso
Caring Cuidadoso	Hardworking Trabajador	Organized Organizado	Sunshine Mi sol
Compassionate Compasivo	Helpful Util	Outstanding Destacado	Tremendous Tremendo
Determined Determinado	Humble Humielde	Patient Paciente	Truthful Verdadero
Energetic Energetico	I'm proud of you. Estoy orgolloso de ti.	Phenomenal Fenomenal	Unique Unico
Enthusiastic Enthusiasmado	Incredible Increible	Proud Orgulloso	Winner Ganador
Exceptional Excepcional	Inspired Inspirado	Radiant Radiante	You're the best. Eres el major.

Figure 7. Words to praise your daughter.

Points to Consider

1. When deciding on treatment, have you matched her needs to the type of treatment?

2. What choices do you provide your daughter in her day-to-day life?

3. Which supplemental treatments or behavioral strategies do you need to research?

4. Review your self-assessment responses to decide if there are any areas where you still need to learn more.

Action Steps to Take Now

1. In the Dynamic Action Plan, complete Step 2 to create the vision for her future. (Remember, the Dynamic Action Plan can be found in Chapter 7.)

2. Decide which professionals need to be involved in helping your daughter reach her full potential.

3. Determine which topics need to be the subject of further research for you.

4. Decide on one behavioral strategy you can apply or try again.

5. Make it a point today to say one positive statement to your daughter.

Chapter 3

Infancy and Preschool

Each self-assessment helps you reflect on your daughter and your parenting practices and is a preview of the chapter's content.

1. When I think about my preschool-age daughter, I . . .
   a. am confident her diagnosis is accurate.
   b. am concerned she may be misdiagnosed.
   c. may need to seek a comprehensive evaluation.
   d. am still considering my next step.

2. When I think about the support I need to help my girl, I . . .
   a. know all I need to know.
   b. am researching different supports.

    c.   have matched my need to the right type of support.

    d.   am confused by so many options.

3.   When considering my girl's preschool, I . . .

    a.   know it's the right fit for her.

    b.   am content, but not satisfied it's the best fit.

    c.   know I need to locate another school.

    d.   need to schedule a meeting to talk to the director about my girl's needs.

4.   When I consider my daughter's preschool teacher(s), I . . .

    a.   know they love my child like their own.

    b.   believe they tolerate my child.

    c.   am not sure if they understand her uniqueness.

    d.   need to talk to the teacher about my child.

5.   When engineering success for my daughter at home, I . . .

    a.   need help understanding the symptoms of ADHD.

    b.   need to work on structuring her day.

    c.   should be more consistent when disciplining her.

    d.   am barely holding things together and cannot take on another task.

Infancy and Preschool

Diagnosing ADHD in preschoolers is always approached with great caution, especially in girls. Many fewer girls than boys are diagnosed at this young age because their symptoms are usually not as clear-cut. In addition, the diagnostic criteria for ADHD was developed on primarily male samples and favors boys and their presentation of the disorder. Compared to boys, girls are more likely to be inattentive than hyperactive.

You may suspect that your daughter is different from her peers in how long she can stick with one activity, how emotionally reactive she is, and/or how demanding she is of your attention. She may be even more physically active than most. Even though she may be wearing you to a frazzle, her behavior may not warrant a diagnosis. In fact, statistically it is unlikely that your preschool daughter will be diagnosed with ADHD, but given how important preschool is in a child's life—the time when her self-esteem is beginning to develop, as well as her concept as a learner—it is important to be aware of developmental milestones, your daughter's progress, and how she compares to peers. If she does have deficits in areas like the amount of time she can remain on one task, organizational skills, social abilities, or impulse control, keep learning about things you can do to help her develop the skills she may be lacking. It is much easier to help her develop good habits now than change unproductive ones down the road. One simple way to promote good habits is to reinforce her positive behaviors. With positive reinforcement, children are more likely to continue good behavior.

It is important to remember that organization, thinking before acting, and being able to sustain attention are all developmental by nature, meaning that behaviors can occur within a range of ages and still be considered within the normal range. Parents often wonder how it is possible to distinguish typical behavior appropriate to the developmental stage from atypical ADHD behaviors and how long it should take their daughter to progress through developmental stages. Dr. Russell Barkley (2000b) reported that a majority (57%) of 4-year-olds may be rated as inattentive and overactive by their parents. However, the majority of these children improve within 3–6 months. Even among those children who received a clinical diagnosis of ADHD, only half maintained that diagnosis through later childhood and adolescence. He noted that when the "pattern of ADHD lasts for at least a year, ADHD will likely continue into later childhood" (p. 91). The lesson that we can take from this information is that the severity of ADHD symptoms and length of time they last predict which children will show a chronic course of ADHD.

In looking at your daughter's behavior, think about the following:

◊ Does her behavior negatively impact her success with peers and/or adults on a consistent basis? Think about how frequently she interrupts, is aggressive, doesn't listen, or insists on having her own way. Do you find that other children don't want to play with her?

◊ How does her behavior compare to other girls of her same age and similar temperament? (Remember that even a period of months can mean big developmental leaps, so comparing your daughter to girls very close in age is important.)

◊ Does her behavior occur in more than one setting—at home, preschool, or in play groups?

◊ Are there other life events that could be contributing to the behavior, such as the birth of a new sibling, divorce or separation, death of a pet or loved one, or a move?

◊ Could the behavior be caused by other conditions, such as a language delay, allergies, memory weakness, deficits in fine motor skills, or another developmental delay?

When Is a Comprehensive Evaluation Warranted?

A preschooler who puts herself in danger by being overactive, distracted, or impulsive and who has difficulty with daily activities such as eating, communicating, playing with friends, attending preschool, and interacting in the community merits a comprehensive evaluation. The chances of a child like this growing out of this level of behavior without intervention are slim. The more knowledgeable you are about the disorder, the more you can help your daughter.

Lin is a beautiful little girl who darts from one activity to another, like she cannot fully take in one thing before her racing mind pulls her to the next. In fact, children find it hard to follow her in play because she is always jumping up and running off to something else without inviting them to join. If not carefully supervised, she never puts away toys before yanking out something else. She is engaging and friendly with adults. In fact, she demands almost constant adult attention and interaction except when she is coloring, her favorite activity. Parents are beginning to see that she is losing favor with her peers because of her delayed social skills and erratic play skills. She is invited less and less often to homes to play. Her teachers are beginning to notice that she is having difficulty becoming more independent and following the routine of the classroom. They often question whether or not Lin is actually listening to them. Although Lin may not clearly be a candidate for a comprehensive evaluation, which would include a thorough developmental history, reports and/or ratings of her behavior in different settings, and a neuropsychological and/or medical examination to rule out other conditions, she should have some intervention and careful monitoring to assist her in developing executive functioning and social skills.

Awareness and early detection enable you to have a better understanding of your child's behaviors. The preschool years are an important window of time in development. Your daughter will need you to be her advocate and safety net as she explores her world and adapts to the structure of a preschool setting.

ADHD has been diagnosed in children as young as 2 and is the "most common mental health diagnosis for children ages 3 to 5," according to the *Harvard Mental Health Letter* (Harvard Health Publications, 2007, para. 1). It is being recognized at earlier and earlier ages for several reasons. More is known about the condition, and children are beginning "school readiness activities at earlier ages" in preschool programs (Wolraich, 2007, p. 9). These programs bring new demands in terms of compliance, attention and focus, and behavioral control. It can be a time of great stress for parents as they struggle to find answers and interventions for their daughter's behavior or find and locate an appropriate preschool, all while managing their own personal and professional lives. Parents often tell us that parenting preschoolers with ADHD has been one of their biggest challenges but also a time of great satisfaction as they watch their children mature.

Prenatal Issues

As noted in an earlier chapter, it is important to put aside any parental guilt if your daughter has or appears to have ADHD. The latest research reported in *The Lancet*, a British medical journal (Williams, 2010), has shown that children with ADHD have a larger number of DNA segments that are either duplicated or missing, known as copy number variants. Genetically based neurological characteristics, including less activity in the frontal regions of the brain (especially those areas that inhibit behavior, resist distractions, and control activity level) and differences in the effectiveness of neurotransmitters, have been suggested. Although home environment plays a role in improving or worsening a child's temperament, it does not cause true ADHD. Because it is genetic, it is possible that you or your mate have ADHD.

In addition to the genetic link, risk factors can be increased by (Barkley, 2000b; Goldstein, 1999):

◇ prematurity and significantly low birth weight;
◇ prenatal exposure to alcohol, tobacco, and illegal drugs;
◇ complications of the fetus that interfere with normal brain development;
◇ excessively high lead levels; and
◇ postnatal injury to the prefrontal regions of the brain.

Developmental Issues: Birth and Beyond

According to the Perinatal Collaborative Project (discussed in Barkley, 2000b), some features in the early development of children predict a greater risk of development of ADHD, even though the risks are reported to be low. These risk factors include (Barkley, 2000b):

◇ smaller head size at birth,
◇ amniotic fluid stained by meconium (intestinal material from the fetus),
◇ signs of nerve damage and/or breathing problems after birth, and
◇ delays in motor development.

Developmental Sequences

Educating yourself about what to expect at different age levels is important for any parent, especially if you have a bouncing bundle of energy on your hands. These characteristics have been shown to be common in children later diagnosed with ADHD (Bailey, 2009):

Infancy (0–12 months):
◇ Very high activity level, constantly moving
◇ Little interest in cuddling
◇ Low frustration tolerance, impatient, and highly demanding of caretakers
◇ Intense reactions to stimulation
◇ Highly attention seeking

Toddler (1–3 years):
◇ Difficulty maintaining attention for even several minutes
◇ Distracted by noise or visual stimuli

◇ Poor eye contact
◇ Ability to pay attention to things she is really interested in such as video games
◇ Excessively active
◇ Lack of interest in quiet activities
◇ Difficulty regaining control when excited
◇ Highly impulsive and risk taking
◇ Accident prone
◇ Difficulty sleeping, either falling asleep and/or waking early

Preschool (3–5 years):
◇ Can't sit still
◇ Little interest in quiet activities, such as looking at books or listening to stories
◇ Limited task persistence, changing tasks every few minutes
◇ Inconsistent attention skills, especially between preferred and nonpreferred activities
◇ Weak social skills
◇ Behavioral problems, disobedience, and engaging in unsafe behaviors
◇ Very talkative
◇ Constant motion, such as running without looking
◇ Clumsy or poor coordination
◇ Difficulty waiting a turn
◇ Aggression, such as hitting other children or grabbing items from them
◇ Highly emotional

Consideration of Wide Variations in Normal Developmental Sequences

Developmentally, many children begin acquiring the ability to inhibit behavior at 3 years and can voluntarily direct their attention to a nonpreferred task at 4 years (Wendling, 2008). The ability to use language to guide behavior, called self-speech, assists with self-control and "is critical for tasks involving motivation, task persistence, multistep directions, and motoric responses" (Nussbaum, 2012, p. 89). However, the developmental sequence can vary widely and still be considered to be within the normal range. Gender differences have been widely documented. Girls are generally more advanced than boys in meeting many developmental milestones, especially in language, fine motor skills, and the ability to sit and engage in quiet activities.

Preschool girls are much more prone than boys to enjoy sedentary activities such as coloring and looking at books, but girls can still be very distractible and have many competing thoughts while engaging in those quiet activities.

Again, it is important to understand that attention and focus are developmental in nature and do not occur at the same time for all children. Developmental readiness determines what a child is able to do at any point in time. It cannot be rushed. One parenting secret to successful preschool years is to educate yourself about developmental stages and what you can realistically expect at various ages, taking into account gender and developmental differences. There are many good books available about what to expect during your daughter's development.

Importance of Ruling Out Other Causes of Behavior

As a preschooler, your daughter will be very busy asserting her independence and may be exuberant as she explores her surroundings. A hallmark of the "terrible twos" is disruptive behavior, especially when your daughter is overtired or overstimulated. These characteristics and a number of other developmental issues make ADHD difficult to diagnose in preschoolers. These include an overlap between symptoms of ADHD and other conditions, differences in parenting skills and childhood experiences that could exacerbate the condition, variations in parental tolerance for behaviors, and especially the wide range of normal developmental sequences.

A cautionary factor for physicians and psychologists in diagnosing ADHD in preschoolers is that symptoms can mimic other conditions such as anxiety, depression, behavioral disorders, hearing or vision problems, sensory issues, developmental delays, language processing problems, or lead exposure. It is important to rule out other factors, especially if that knowledge leads to effective interventions.

For example, Sienna had fine motor delays resulting in difficulty cutting and coloring in a preschool setting. She quickly lost interest in activities that she could not complete successfully. When tasks were adjusted to her skill level, her willingness to engage increased. Her lack of interest was related more to a mismatch between her skills and the task requirements than an attention problem.

A good clinician must look at the root cause of the behaviors and rule out other conditions. This is complicated when more than one disorder is present. Research suggests that up to 45% of children with ADHD have at least one other psychiatric disorder such as Oppositional Defiant Disorder, bipolar disorder, anxiety, or an autism spectrum disorder.

Emily threw a tantrum every morning when she had to separate from her mother. She would not make eye contact with her teachers, did not interact with other children, often looked at objects out of the corner of her eye, became upset if routines were changed, and often appeared to be daydreaming or in her "own world." Her preschool teachers encouraged the parents to have her evaluated for ADHD, Inattentive Type. However, after a thorough investigation, Emily was determined to have an autism spectrum disorder. Testing showed that her social language skills were very delayed and sensory sensitivities made her very uncomfortable in a large classroom setting. She had difficulty establishing joint attention, reading social cues, and communicating with age-appropriate social language skills. She needed a structured classroom with social skills infused throughout the day and qualified for a special education preschool program offered through her school district.

The root of any behavior must be looked at carefully and thoroughly. An evaluation by a developmental pediatrician or a neuropsychologist may be necessary to rule out conditions whose symptoms might overlap with ADHD.

Anna had language delays and difficulty in processing auditory information. Her preschool teachers complained that she did not follow directions, but roamed around from place to place in her classroom rather than working on the assigned task. A thorough language evaluation revealed that Anna did not process or understand many of the directions from her preschool teachers, who gave primarily auditory directions. When auditory directions were paired with visuals, such as cue cards to remind her of expected behavior, and a visual schedule to structure her day was developed, her rate of on-task behavior increased significantly.

In addition to developmental differences and symptom overlap with other conditions, life experiences and parenting styles can also cloud the picture. This doesn't mean that parenting causes ADHD. Rather, chaotic conditions can impact a child's behavior, causing her to have more disorganized behavior, mimicking ADHD. In addition to lack of a secure, structured environment, studies have shown that the manner in which parents respond to a difficult child can impact the course of those behavior problems. In terms of parenting style, a negative and critical style of management has been shown to predict the continuation of behavior problems into later years. Even parents who take a more positive approach can inadvertently reinforce inappropriate behaviors by giving in and allowing the child to get what she wants following the behavior or by providing too much attention to the negative behavior.

Preschool Issues

Preschools are very different settings from home and from most daycares. They have much more structure and more demands. Placing your daughter with ADHD or symptoms that would suggest ADHD in a preschool setting could bring additional stress to both you and your child. It is commonplace for boys with ADHD who are oppositional or aggressive to be kicked out of daycares and preschools, but it's not so likely to happen with girls because their behavior is usually less disruptive. When selecting a preschool for your daughter the main secret to success is to find a school that is the right fit. As you talk to preschools, be honest if you have concerns about your daughter's behavior to determine if they have had success in teaching children like her. For example, if she is a daydreamer, do they make efforts to keep her engaged or do they just allow her to play by herself and entertain herself with her imagination?

Time spent researching the right fit between a preschool and your daughter could pay big dividends and enhance her self-esteem. You want to avoid early experiences of failure because of the stress that brings to you and your child. She is building her sense of self-esteem as a capable learner and participant in the educational setting from these early ages. Your choices may be limited according to your geographical location, but it will be important to find the best fit that you can.

Helpful Questions in Your Preschool Search

Philosophy. What is the school's mission statement and philosophy? Your goal is to find a school that seeks to understand a child's strengths and build from those rather than focusing on the negative. Preschool is only the beginning of a long educational experience, so having it begin in as positive a way as possible is critical. Some questions to consider might be:

◊ What are the teacher's expectations for what your daughter should be doing at her age? How do those expectations match her skill set?

◊ How adaptable is the program in accommodating individual needs? For example, if a child becomes too stimulated, is there a quiet space where she can go and regroup but still be supervised?

◊ What rate of success has the school achieved in successfully engaging girls who are inattentive and difficult to engage? How parent friendly is the school? Does it allow parent volunteers in the classroom? How does it communicate with parents and how often?

Physical set-up. Some questions to consider about the physical set-up of the preschool include:

◊ Is the environment inviting, colorful, warm, and comfortable?

◊ Is it well equipped with colorful materials to develop language, fine motor, early literacy, and math skills?

◊ What is the ratio of preschoolers to staff? Girls with inattentiveness and ADHD-like symptoms function much better in small-group or individualized settings than in large-group activities.

Daily routine. Some questions to consider about the preschool schedule and routine include:

◊ Do children follow a structured schedule that is consistent?

◊ Does the teacher explain and model each desired behavior and practice until all students know exactly what is expected from them, including how to walk from place to place in line, sit in circle time, and raise a quiet hand to get the teacher's attention? (Some of these may be long-term goals.)

◊ Is movement throughout the day a key feature?

◊ How long are children expected to sit still?

Curriculum. Some questions to consider about the curriculum at the preschool include:

◊ Do they use theme-based units of study that focus on concepts (such as community helpers) as well as social skills? For example, the social skill of being a good friend could be taught through literature, songs, games, and role-playing.

◊ What kinds of continuing education do the teachers receive to enable them to keep up with trends and "what works" with children? For example, girls with ADHD typically do much better at the beginning of the school year when things are new and fresh for them. They become easily bored, often resulting in an increase of problem behaviors and daydreaming. A proactive preschool would be alert to those patterns and program activities to avoid boredom such as bringing in new, exciting educational materials periodically.

◊ Does the curriculum involve hands-on activities?

Behavior management. Some questions to consider about the preschool's behavior management style include:

◊ What are some techniques the teacher will use to gain and keep attention? Does she use frequent visual and verbal cues, maintain close proximity to active children so she can intervene quickly, and provide frequent feedback (Rief, 2008)? If you daughter "zones out" frequently, can the teacher effectively bring her back to the group with minimal attention to the problem? Does she try to figure out what might be effective for individual children? For example, if your daughter can't sit still in circle time, could she be given an instrument to play while classmates are singing or a job to do, such as assisting the teacher, to redirect her attention in a positive way?

◊ What are their disciplinary techniques? How is time-out used and how often? If time-out does not prove effective for your daughter, what alternatives will be considered? Remember, if you daughter is placed in time-out often, she will miss learning opportunities.

Safety. Some questions to consider about your daughter's safety at the school include:

◊ How closely are children monitored for safety?
◊ If the children go on field trips, what is the procedure for making sure no child is left behind on a bus or at an event?
◊ Are the play areas enclosed?
◊ Is the overall facility secure?

Importance of Structure

As in the home setting, consistency and structure are critical for your daughter's success. It is important for her teacher to be very clear about the expectations and boundaries for her behavior, consequences, and rewards. The preschool structure should allow for the teaching of good school-related habits such as staying in an assigned space, following a routine, organizing a workspace, following teacher directions, cooperating with classmates, waiting for a turn, and cleaning up after completing a task.

Jim's son started out attending a Montessori preschool. Things seemed to go pretty well for about 3 months, and then the teachers started having conferences because he was often "wandering about." He would go from area to area but not really complete any of the lessons, thus interfering with the other children's work. Jim and his wife decided that the Montessori program was not structured enough, so they moved him to a preschool with a traditional schedule. This was the right fit and helped because the class's daily schedule was more structured with a series of short activities, as compared to the more open schedule of the Montessori school.

Teacher Characteristics

A preschool teacher who is firm but loving is important for your daughter. Energy and creativity are important, as well as a love of children and knowledge of their developmental differences. A teacher who is highly organized, is intuitive about behavior, and has situational awareness will assist a girl with ADHD in acclimating to her new situation. It will be important for the teacher to be effective in communicating concerns and positive accomplishments with you so you can work together as a team.

Think back to the questions you can ask when finding a preschool for your daughter. You should talk to your daughter's potential teacher so you can get a feel for her personality. You don't want a teacher whose demeanor is totally soft spoken and flat because your daughter can take advantage of her. On the other hand, you don't want a teacher who is gruff and intolerant. It's best to try to observe the teacher in action, even if it means scheduling a time to return another day.

Considering Retention

Occasionally preschool staff may recommend having a girl repeat a year of preschool. Before that decision is made, there are many factors to consider. These include birth date, physical size, social maturity, fine motor skills, and progress in her current setting. Many parents of girls and boys who have August or September birthdays decide that holding them back and having them repeat a year of preschool before entering kindergarten allows them to mature and be more ready for the academics presented in kindergarten. The important consideration is to try to determine if an additional year would make a significant difference in performance. Try to project ahead and think about how this retention would impact her as an elementary school student, a teenager, and a college student.

If you are still not sure, take your daughter to a local school psychologist and have some educational testing done. For an investment of a few hundred dollars or less, a good psychologist can help you determine your daughter's readiness for elementary school. When we test preschool students for readiness, we often use the Wechsler Preschool and Primary Scale of Intelligence-IV, an IQ test designed for young children, and school readiness tests, such as the Woodcock-Johnson III Tests of Achievement or Kaufman Test of Educational Achievement-II. With each year that passes, it becomes harder to retain a student. Our advice is that if you are in doubt, then get it checked out.

When More Support Is Needed

As a parent, it is easy to take a wait-and-see approach, deny the existence of problems, or postpone action. Monitor your daughter's behavior, attention, and adjustment carefully. Early intervention services can be very valuable to your child, so you will want to keep your eyes open to her needs. You don't want her to go for years with untreated symptoms that may cause difficulty with learning and social relationships and result in low self-esteem.

When more support is needed, you should consider a preschool designed to handle developmental delays that interfere with a child's functioning in a typical preschool environment. These delays would cover a wide array of conditions, including behavioral, speech and language, gross and fine motor, and intellectual delays. These preschools are usually offered in conjunction with community agencies and the public school. Federal law requires that school districts provide early identification and intervention services for children with disabilities severe enough to impact their functioning. If you think that your child's symptoms are severe enough, contact your local school district to find out how to access an evaluation and possible specialized preschool services. There will usually be a screening evaluation and then a more in-depth evaluation (if needed) to determine if your daughter qualifies for these services. Infants and toddlers may qualify for services, and preschoolers (ages 3–5) may qualify for services through the Individuals with Disabilities Education Improvement Act (IDEA). See Chapter 6 for more discussion of legislation governing disabilities.

Maria's parents were at their wit's end because she was not successful in her daycare center. Her preschool teachers complained that she was often grabbing toys from other children, intruding in other children's play without asking, running from place to place, and throwing tantrums if her needs were blocked. Her parents had tried reasoning, rewarding, and punishing—all to no avail. After a thorough evaluation, including a cognitive assessment by a school psychologist, an in-depth speech language evaluation by a speech-language pathologist, an occupational therapy assessment, and a developmental history, Maria was determined to be eligible for a special needs preschool program that focused on behavioral goals along with emerging academic skills. The classroom had a low pupil-to-teacher ratio, additional assistance from a classroom aide, and a highly structured behavioral management program where behaviors were taught and reinforced. In addition, she had occupational therapy to help improve her deficient fine motor skills, which were impacting her ability to hold a pencil, cut, and color. Maria had her ups and downs but eventually improved in her ability to follow directions, stay in her assigned area, and keep her hands and objects to herself. Without that early intervention, Maria would have encountered much more difficulty in elementary school.

As noted previously, an evaluation by a developmental pediatrician, neurologist, psychiatrist, school psychologist, clinical psychologist, or neuropsychologist might provide instructive information and give you more direction. For example, if a child is determined to have fine motor delays or sensory issues that impede her performance, then occupational therapy might ameliorate some of her difficulties. If she has delays in pragmatic or social language that impact her social skills, then language therapy and social skills groups might provide much-needed assistance.

Some school psychologists and clinical or neuropsychologists use an evaluation tool called A Developmental Neuropsychological Assessment (NEPSY) to help diagnose ADHD in preschool-age girls. It is a test that measures your child's neurological development. This assessment can be used with children of preschool age, and it contains tests of attention. If your child's pediatrician recommends you try medication but you want a second opinion, find a psychologist who uses the NEPSY. If your preschool-age child really has ADHD, it should show up in the NEPSY test scores and therefore provide a quantitative measure helpful in diagnosing ADHD. It also removes some of the subjectivity of parent and teacher rating forms.

If the preschool girl's NEPSY attention scores are average and at expected levels, then ADHD may not be present, but it's important to interpret these scores within the context of all available data. Even if the parent and teacher rating forms scores are high for observing ADHD behaviors, it may be more of a behavioral issue than a true attention issue. Because most professionals consider ADHD to be a neurological disorder, we would argue that a true ADHD disorder should have shown up in the neuropsychological testing scores. Thus, we would use the average neuropsychological test scores as the basis to recommend behavior therapy as a first intervention. As mentioned previously, 57% of preschoolers may be rated as inattentive and overactive by their parents, but the majority improve within 3–6 months.

Medical Intervention With Young Girls

The challenges of managing a young girl in a structured educational setting may prompt your daughter's preschool teacher to encourage you to try medication. The use of medication in young children with ADHD requires careful consideration of the severity of the behavior balanced with the side effects from medication. Be certain to read the valuable insight from a psychiatrist's view of medication for girls included in Chapter 2.

Most pediatricians recommend medication for young girls only when behavioral interventions implemented with fidelity over time and parent training have proven to be ineffective or when the child is exhibiting dangerous behavior. There are uncertainties over the long-term effects of medication on children's developing neurological structures. There are significantly fewer studies on preschool children than on older children and none that we know of to date on the effects of medication solely on preschool girls.

As reported in the *Brown University Child and Adolescent Behavior Letter* ("Pharmacological . . . ," 2009), a review of four decades of research showed "that methylphenidate (Ritalin) has a greater evidence base than other medications, psychosocial interventions, and alternative treatments in the short-term treatment of ADHD in preschoolers" (p. 4). A National Institute of Mental Health study (Wolraich, 2007) found that the effectiveness of methylphenidate was more limited in preschoolers than in older children. Other studies have shown that preschool children can be more sensitive to side effects of medication, including irritability, insomnia, and weight loss (Bower, 2006).

However, the Food and Drug Administration (FDA) only recommends amphetamines (e.g., Adderall, Dexedrine, Vyvanse) for children as young as 3, according to Dr. Mark Wolraich (2007), professor of pediatrics at the University of Oklahoma. It is widely believed that the difference in the FDA recommendations for amphetamines versus methylphenidate "has more to do with the regulations that were in place when the FDA approved the medications than they do with how much evidence there is about how well amphetamines work or how safe they are in preschool-aged children" (Wolraich, 2007, para. 3). As cited in the *Brown University Child and Adolescent Behavior Letter*, doctors "have to balance exposing children's rapidly developing brains to psychopharmacological agents against the potentially damaging consequences of not treating the disorder" ("Pharmacological . . .", 2009, para. 3). It is very clear that if medication is used, then it should be closely monitored by medical personnel.

A review of the literature indicates fewer studies on the effects of various treatment approaches for ADHD in young children compared to older children. There are even fewer studies comparing the effectiveness of alternative treatments to pharmacological treatments. Alternative treatments include specific diets; supplements, especially herbal; biofeedback; parent training; and behavior therapies.

Some studies indicate that elimination diets (e.g., additive-free, sugar-free, carbohydrate-free) have shown some promising evidence. Some clinicians believe that diets higher in protein and lower in carbohydrates and sugars provide a more stable sugar level and prevent meltdowns based on metabolic problems, which might exacerbate ADHD. (See the section on diets for ADHD in Chapter 4: The Elementary Years.)

A study of 135 preschoolers over a 5-year period released in 2007 and published in the *School Psychology Review* indicated that preschoolers with ADHD may require "more behavior therapies and less medication" (as cited in Breaden, 2007, p. 5). The September 2007 issue of the *Harvard Mental Health Letter* (Harvard Health Publications) suggested that "parent training and specialized day care should be considered before resorting to stimulant medication" (p. 1).

Home/Community Issues:
Being a Proactive Parent

You know your child better than anyone else. If she has ADHD, then continue to educate yourself to have a thorough understanding of ADHD and how your child's daily interactions are affected. The diagnostic criteria are the same for young children as for older children. If your child is diagnosed with ADHD as a preschooler, her developmental changes can be large, so you will want to get her reevaluated when she enters elementary school. Observe your child's presentation of the following characteristics of ADHD at home and determine ways you can assist her with:

◊   excessive activity,
◊   poor attention to tasks,
◊   impaired impulse control and inability to delay gratification,
◊   deficits in memory or storing information to use in guiding behavior in the future,
◊   difficulties with regulating emotions and motivation,
◊   diminished problem-solving ability,
◊   delayed development of internal language, and
◊   greater variability in quality of work.

Be a detective in determining ways your daughter's characteristics affect her daily life and try to provide supports when you can to help her work around and grow in her deficit areas. At all times, remember that some behaviors may not be completely within your daughter's control. Everyone knows ADHD can carry long-term risks. As a proactive and informed parent, you will want to intervene as early as possible. Dr. Russell Barkley (2007) stated that even though ADHD is not *caused* by "how parents raise a child, how parents *respond* to and *manage* a child may contribute to the persistence of ADHD" (p. 86). He indicated that parents can make the problem better or worse by their response to the child.

Consistency and structure are critical for your daughter's success. It is important for you to be very clear about expectations and boundaries for her behavior, consequences, and rewards. Jim and his wife structured their home routine to help their son when he was a preschooler, using a behavior and reward chart that had a place to write the expected behaviors and a spot to place either a happy, sad, or neutral face if he followed the behaviors. They explained the chart to him and reviewed it daily. For example, one rule was, "No screaming at Mom or Dad." Each day he could earn a reward if he had a certain number of happy faces. This was a concrete way to teach him responsibility and help him learn about the importance of self-control.

Whether your daughter has been diagnosed or is suspected of having ADHD, there are a number of things you can do to help manage her behaviors in the home and community.

Engineering Success

Understand the Symptoms of ADHD

Applied knowledge can be a very powerful ally in creating success. A few things we recommend you do to learn more about ADHD include:

◊ *Seek out parent training in effective management and discipline.* Contact your pediatrician, community agencies, or school district for information. Behavior modification techniques, including immediate consequences, praise, ignoring negative behavior that is not dangerous, and teaching replacement behaviors, can be very effective. CHADD has a well-respected parent training program called Parent to Parent.

◊ *Learn what management tools are effective with your child.* Distraction is often effective if you see your daughter starting to get upset.

◊ *Be positive and focus on strength areas.* If your daughter is creative and innovative, provide items that will encourage that talent. If she enjoys helping others, try to engineer those opportunities. Try to praise your daughter several times a day for things she is doing correctly.

◊ *Create an environment that promotes success.* If your daughter is accident prone, put away items that can be easily broken. If she has trouble cleaning up toys, provide an organizational structure. Placing pictures on shelves or drawers can help in cleanup. If she has trouble transitioning from one activity to another, use a kitchen timer to count down the time before she has to switch activities, or give verbal warnings. Timetimer (http://www.timetimer.com) is a visual timer that allows the child to see time remaining.

Structuring Her Day

◊ Provide a structured environment with adequate opportunities for activity and rest. Meal times, naptime, and bedtime should be consistent. Some children benefit from having a visual schedule that shows their daily routine or a visual cue card to prompt certain behaviors.

◊ Prepare your daughter in advance when a change in schedule is unavoidable.

◊ Provide plenty of time for physical release throughout the day, including playing outside or engaging in some energy-releasing activity.

◊ Keep your daughter busy in productive activities. Idle time may create problems. Limit television and video game time and avoid those with violence. The American Academy of Pediatrics (n.d.) suggested that children younger than 2 years old should not watch entertainment on screens such as TV, DVDs, computers, video games, or videotapes. The AAP cited the rapid development of children's neurological structures during the first 2 years of life, noting that children learn more effectively from interaction with humans than screens. Limit television and video game time to no more than 1 to 2 hours a day in older children.

◊ Plan ahead for times when long periods of sitting will be required, such as when traveling in a car. Bring snacks, games, books, electronics, and videos (if she is older than 2) to keep her occupied.

◊ Be prepared to remove your daughter from highly stimulating activities if she becomes easily overwhelmed. Children frequently need some quiet time.

Managing Behaviors

◊ Make sure you know what behavior you expect of your daughter in different situations. Discussing expected behavior beforehand is often helpful.

◊ Practice how you would like to respond when she misbehaves in situations to avoid overreacting.

◊ Be as consistent as possible. It is always important to muster the energy to follow through on directions and consequences. If not, you will likely pay for it later. Consistency enables your daughter to know exactly what you expect and to be clear about the rules. Behavior cues used consistently by parents and caregivers, as well as by teachers, can be critical.

◊ Monitor your daughter's activities closely for safety if she is impulsive. Cover electrical outlets and lock up cleaning products and other dangerous items. If your daughter is a climber who enjoys getting into kitchen cabinets, provide a cabinet at floor level just for her that contains items of interest.

◊ Some behavioral problems can be avoided by providing distractions if you see that your child is getting upset. Suggest a walk or sing a song (Alexander-Roberts, 2006).

◊ Use time out judiciously. Some experts estimate that time out should include 1 minute for each year up to 5 years of age. Time out can often begin at 2 years of age (Alexander-Roberts, 2006).

Teaching and Learning

◊ Keep eye contact with your daughter, especially when giving directions. If necessary, gently hold her chin so she is looking right at you to ensure she is listening. (Caveat: Be alert to situations in which holding her chin could set up a power struggle. Sometimes it is better to avoid eye contact in dicey situations so as not to challenge or antagonize.)

◊ Keep directions clear and simple. Children with ADHD are especially unreceptive to long directions or conversations. Keep directions to only one step until you are sure your child can handle two-step directions.

◊ Provide repeated practice for new skills, especially social skills like sharing a toy. Children with ADHD seem to learn through experience and practice rather than by observing social cues.

◊ Don't assume that your daughter understands cause and effect. Specific training in identifying cause and effect relationships in stories, movies, and real-life situations can be helpful.

◊ Ensure that the environment is free from distracting stimuli when engaging in a teaching activity. Children with ADHD are less able to screen out competing stimuli than other children.

◇ Allow fidget toys or items that may help the child sit and focus—for instance, when a book is read. Fidget items are things that keep the child's hands busy and serve to calm her. These can be favorite toys such as small dolls, a stuffed animal, or a squishy, sensory toy. Websites such as http://www.addiss.co.uk are good sources of fidget toys.

◇ Use as many senses as possible when teaching a new skill. For example, when teaching the names of fruits, allow your daughter to draw them, touch them, smell them, and taste them. Interactive learning will be the most productive.

◇ Give her a head start on learning to focus and develop some internal limits on behavior. As noted above, a kitchen timer or Time Timer can be used to help your daughter extend the time she can focus on one activity.

Support for Parents

There is no question that parents of children with ADHD are under much more stress than parents of children without ADHD. Mothers of children with ADHD generally report more self-blame, social isolation, and lower levels of self-esteem about their parenting skills than other parents (Barkley, 2007). Until your child is 8 or older, the divorce rate is higher for parents of children with ADHD (Wymbs et al., 2008). If you have more than one child with ADHD, then of course your stress level will be even more elevated. Your daughter's behavior is baffling and often disruptive to the entire family. You may feel you are constantly on guard and never have time to yourself. Even finding a babysitter who can handle your daughter effectively may be difficult if she is very active and defiant.

Realize that time away from your daughter is important to allow you to regroup and keep a positive attitude. The search for a competent babysitter who understands your daughter will be well worth it. Find someone who is willing to be educated about her condition. Oftentimes, your daughter will respond more positively to someone who is willing to engage in high-energy or creative activities while keeping in mind the importance of safety. If money limits your ability to have a babysitter, try to exchange babysitting duties with another parent who understands ADHD and its management techniques. You want to avoid putting your daughter in situations that could be damaging to her self-esteem.

Remember that you are human and will lose your patience from time to time. Build in little breaks that will make this less likely to happen. Finding a parent support group may be helpful if that group is positive and focused on sharing what works and new techniques and trends. A support group of parents of children who have ADHD can be aware of and share information on local resources and services. To find support groups, check the Internet, local colleges or school systems, or pediatricians or other health professionals. CHADD, an organization for children and adults with ADHD (http://www.chadd.org), may have a chapter in your area.

As noted previously, parent training specific to ADHD children is available through CHADD-sponsored Parent to Parent programs. More intense and specialized training, such as Parent Child Interaction Training, may be available in your community. Keeping up with the latest research can be helpful. Type "childhood ADHD" or "ADHD in preschool" into an Internet search engine to find the latest research findings.

Assistance With Siblings

In addition to the challenges in preschool and in the community, your daughter with ADHD will, of course, bring her difficulties into the home. Her difficulty with listening, impulsivity, and organizing her own behavior will inevitably create conflict with siblings. Brothers and sisters are often jealous of the additional time parents must spend with a child with ADHD. They may actually see the child with ADHD as lucky and envy her. You must walk a fine line in helping other family members have some understanding of ADHD behavior while still treating the child as a full and integral member of the family.

We often recommend books to help parents explain ADHD to siblings. Books often allow for an open discussion within a supportive context and for children to identify with the issue or character. We recommend these three books: *Learning to Slow Down and Pay Attention: A Book for Kids About ADHD*; *Cory Stories: A Kid's Book About Living With ADHD;* and *My Brother's a World-Class Pain: A Sibling's Guide to ADHD/Hyperactivity.*

Don't be afraid to use the help of a professional psychologist or counselor to learn problem-solving approaches. The same parenting style that works for one child does not always work for another. Jim and his wife took two parenting classes that were offered at a local preschool. One class was called Conscious Discipline, and the other was Redirecting Children's Behavior. In one class, Jim learned a strategy to help him not to overreact to his son's behavior—STAR, or taking time to Stop, Take a deep breath, And Relax. Jim placed paper stars at strategic places around the house to give himself and his wife a visual reminder not to overreact.

Utilizing problem-solving approaches to difficulties can often result in positive resolutions to many problems. Family and behavioral therapy can often be helpful in establishing a cohesive family bond. Remember that it is often very difficult for a girl with ADHD to hold her behavior together in school and community settings. Her behavior may disintegrate in the home setting, where she feels safe. Providing a quiet place where she can regroup without trampling on the rights of other family members will be important.

In our private practices, we teach parents to physically get on their daughter's level when they are talking to her. When standing, parents tower above their daughter. When talking to, disciplining, or teaching her, parents should kneel, sit, or bend down to look her in the eye. This simple technique has an amazing effect in getting active or inattentive girls to actually listen and understand.

A second technique we teach parents and siblings of active and emotional girls is to lower one's voice as the girl's voice gets louder. Energetic preschool girls often are loud and have lots of drama with their play and voices. An effective strategy is to talk softer and get down to a whisper as your daughter gets louder. Inevitably, your daughter will take your cue and start to whisper too.

A third strategy that often works well for preschool-age girls is teaching parents and siblings to make a game of things. Preschoolers usually enjoy games, and their competitive nature fits well with playing racing games. For example, when cleaning up toys, Mary Anne would often race her daughter to see who could pick up the most toys the fastest.

Self-Esteem

Self-esteem is a collection of beliefs a person has about herself. It begins developing in toddlerhood and continues throughout life. It fluctuates, because it is often based on interactions with others and opportunities for success. It can be defined as pride in one's self or self-respect.

Self-esteem in preschoolers is in its early, developmental stages. The preschool girl with ADHD has likely heard hundreds, if not thousands, of redirections from her parents, teachers, caregivers, and classmates. She is likely bombarded with many more negative than positive comments. All of these redirections and negative comments can take a toll on your young daughter's self-esteem.

Preschool-age girls with low self-esteem may say things like "I'm a bad girl" or "Stop it, me. Be quiet." They may hear this from their classmates and even some teachers and parents. You may even overhear your young daughter say these things when she is angry or frustrated at herself. If your daughter makes negative comments about herself, give her a hug and reassure her that you love her just the way she is. You can admit that her behavior sometimes frustrates you but that you still love her very much. Tell her that there is nothing she can do to make you stop loving her. Each night when you tuck her into bed, make it a nightly ritual to tell her how much you love her.

Strategies to Increase Self-Esteem

Helping your daughter develop a "can-do" attitude must be based on opportunities to accomplish realistic tasks. Don't expect more from her than she is capable of giving. Her frustration tolerance may be limited, so patience will be required.

Giving honest, accurate feedback will help her as she develops her view of herself. Do not compare her to other children, especially siblings. More than likely, she will be making her own comparisons.

Providing a safe, secure environment for her, both at home and at school, will enable her to be able to take risks as she strives to accomplish tasks. Give her chances to make some of her own decisions and help her learn to solve problems.

Most preschool-age girls with ADHD love it when adults read out loud to them. Books are a great resource to help build the self-esteem of preschool girls. A few books we recommend to our clients with preschool-age girls include *I'm Gonna Like Me: Letting Off a Little Self-Esteem* and *Love You Forever*. Reading books like these with your daughter helps her identify with the character, learn how the character solves a problem or develops a new behavior, and then apply that solution to her life. Books provide a nonthreatening and peaceful way to teach your child and build self-esteem.

Begin by asking your daughter to sit on your lap or right next to you so you can both see the pictures. As you read the book aloud, use an animated voice. Help your daughter identify with the character by pointing out similarities between her and the character. Look for positive things that are related to the character and your daughter in addition to troublesome behaviors.

There are additional activities you and your preschool daughter can do to help build self-esteem. One way is to provide your young daughter with an age-appropriate journal. One of our colleagues, Dr. Janet Mentore Lee, wrote a kid's journal called *The Daily Doodle: A Journal for Children Ages 4–7*. Dr. Lee describes her journal as a way to help kids feel reassured, validated, and supported. Each page of the activity book is a writing, scribbling, or doodling prompt that will help your child express her inner thoughts, feelings, and coping skills. Depending on her developmental level, you can help her write words or letters. *The Daily Doodle* provides prompts and is a great way to collaborate, create, and connect with your child, critical components to a parent-child relationship and building self-esteem.

Another activity you can do with your preschool daughter is to help her create a self-portrait. A large piece of butcher paper or many copy-sized sheets of paper taped together work well. Place the paper on the floor and ask your daughter to lie on top of it. Use a pencil or marker and then trace the outline of her body. Tell her you'd like to work with her to make a self-portrait. Use her and your favorite art supplies, which could include crayons, paint, ink, chalk, and so forth. Place a small mirror within reach and encourage her to look at it frequently. Help her by drawing in her ears, eyes, and mouth, and allow her to color her features. Comment about her beautifully colored eyes, nice hair, wide smile, or strong arms. When the project is completed, hang it up in her room. You could even take her picture next to it and tell her you are going to e-mail it to relatives, share it with friends, and brag about how cool she and her portrait look. An alternative to the life-size portrait is just to draw the shape of your daughter's head on paper and then allow her to color in her facial features.

Regardless of the activity you complete with your daughter, it's important to reinforce how much you love her and enjoy being with her. Try not to stress too much if she is wiggly while you read or squirms as you trace her outline. You have to keep the mindset of having fun and reinforcing her positive qualities. As a parent of a preschooler with ADHD, Jim always tried to strive for a ratio of five positive comments to one negative comment, but he rarely achieved it. To encourage himself he even bought a small counter to keep in his hand and click as he said positive comments. This helped for a while as he tried to change his mindset toward saying more positive comments.

Points to Consider

1. It is important to remember that organization, thinking before acting, and being able to sustain attention are all developmental by nature, meaning that behaviors can occur within a range of ages and still be considered within the normal range.

2. Time spent in researching the right fit between a preschool and your daughter could pay big dividends and enhance her self-esteem.

3. As a parent, it is easy to be in denial about problems and postpone action. Be proactive.

4. You will walk a fine line in helping other family members have some understanding of ADHD behavior while treating the child as a full and integral member of the family.

5. Review your self-assessment responses to decide if there are any areas where you still need to learn more.

Action Steps to Take Now

1. Develop a stronger relationship with your daughter's preschool and ensure that her needs are being addressed. Use the questions in this chapter if you interview prospective preschools for your daughter.

2. Become a detective in determining ways your daughter's characteristics affect her daily functioning, and try to provide supports when you can to help her work around and grow in her deficit areas.

3. Recognize your child's temperament or pattern of personality characteristics. Structure her environment to enhance chances of good behavior.

4. Seek out parent training in effective management and discipline.

5. Try some of the tools we suggest in this chapter such as using books, becoming a STAR, changing tasks into games, or getting down to her level when you talk.

6. Be positive, notice, and compliment the positive things your daughter does.

Chapter 4

The Elementary Years

SELF-ASSESSMENT: Where Am I Now?

Each self-assessment helps you reflect on your daughter and your parenting practices and is a preview of the chapter's content.

1. When I think about my elementary-age daughter, I . . .

    a. feel she is doing the best she can considering her ability and the effects of her ADHD.

    b. question whether she is becoming increasingly overwhelmed in her classroom.

    c. am concerned she is missing instruction because she is daydreaming too much.

    d. am more concerned with her emotional/social standing than her academics.

2.   When I think about the support I need to help my daughter, I . . .

    a.   have not had time to really think about it.

    b.   am confused about all of the options.

    c.   have identified a cadre of people who can help me maximize her strengths and remediate her weaknesses.

    d.   am in the process of identifying the best people who can help her be successful.

3.   When I think about her elementary school, I . . .

    a.   am sure her educational needs are not being met.

    b.   question whether the right foundation for skills in reading and math are being developed.

    c.   feel that the school is doing a great job of helping her.

    d.   think I need to communicate more effectively with her teacher and the school staff to fine tune some of the supports that might help her.

4.   When I think about her teacher(s), I . . .

    a.   am sure they do not even know she has ADHD.

    b.   question whether they have knowledge about ADHD and effective interventions.

    c.   need to improve the level of communication with the teacher about homework, my daughter's progress, and upcoming longer assignments.

    d.   am very satisfied with her teacher(s).

5. When I think about my daughter's social skills in the school, community, and home, I . . .
   a. realize she is delayed in her social skills.
   b. see that she is increasingly becoming isolated and prefers to be alone.
   c. have noticed that she is not invited to birthday parties or sleepovers.
   d. see she is well-liked by adults and children.

The Elementary Years

Many ADHD diagnoses come during a child's elementary school years. So if you've skipped Chapters 1, 2, and 3 and turned directly to this page, you wouldn't be alone. (We just hope that when things settle down—as much as they ever do with an elementary-aged daughter with ADHD—you'll start again from the beginning.)

Here's what's happening: Your daughter's emotions are still developing, but she's probably way behind the curve of other kids her age. She may look like a little lady, but she's likely a bundle of raw emotions and feelings strung together in an almost primal way. Although her needs may vary, it is likely she will require lots of your time and patience in teaching her how to compensate for her deficits, especially her tendency to daydream or get lost in her own thoughts. You may need to spend extra time teaching her how to stop and think, rather than just react, because it probably will not come naturally to her. Or she may be so scattered, you will need to start at ground level in helping her develop some organizational skills. Perhaps her social skills require specific teaching and structured opportunities to practice what she has learned. Regardless, you'll need a ton of patience, because those times you'll need to do the teaching will be exactly the times you'll be most challenged by her behavior. To help yourself, remember to try the understanding and patience method as described in Chapter 2.

Your daughter is in school full-time now, and she'll likely be expected to master the same curriculum as all of the students around her. Both of you will need plenty of tools to meet this goal without lowering the bar for her academic success, and we'll spend a lot of time in this chapter sharing strategies that will help your daughter succeed in the classroom. Your daughter's teachers will be a critical part of her success, and we'll help you identify some of the characteristics of school settings where a girl with ADHD can flourish.

These are the years when your daughter is learning basic skills and work habits she'll use for the rest of her life. We're not going to sugarcoat it—these years can be tough. But there is tremendous satisfaction in knowing that all of the hard work, patience, and consistency you invest now will establish a firm foundation for your daughter.

We've been in the trenches, and we know that sometimes it seems like the struggles are never going to end. But take our word for it. One day, you're going to look back and say, "Wow, those years went by fast."

Going to School

Your daughter's elementary school career will be full of ups and downs. Each year, she will face new challenges and expectations. Her behavior and adjustment to school will be related to how well she can handle the increased demands on her organizational skills and coping mechanisms. For most students, ADHD impacts not only their focus but also their ability to inhibit behavior and their executive functioning skills (e.g., planning, remembering, and organizing). If your child responds impulsively, she does not have the luxury of planning ahead, thinking about what she has learned in the past, or delaying gratification (Barkley, 2000a). As girls move from preschool to elementary school, they will be called upon to be more independent, organized, and goal-directed—areas that are weaknesses for most children with ADHD. Barkley (2000a) stated, "The solution . . . is not to harp at those with ADHD to simply try harder," but to provide . . . "the sorts of cues, prompts, physical reminders and other captivating information that will guide behavior toward the intended goal" (p. 33).

Julissa was a mess. Her teacher said Julissa always had papers everywhere. None of the children wanted to sit at her table because she was always bothering them to ask what she should do next. Furthermore, the class received rewards based on their table's performance, and all of the children knew Julissa would lose points for her table. Her difficulty in being accepted by her classmates didn't stop there. At recess, none of the children wanted to play with Julissa because she was so unpredictable and usually insisted on everything her way.

Academically, Julissa was falling behind in all subjects, especially reading comprehension and math problem solving—two of the areas that required the most concentration and memory. Her parents didn't know how to help her when she got home because they could not read the scribbles in her agenda planner, and Julissa never knew what she was supposed to do. They actually dreaded picking her up from school, because she often had meltdowns in the car based on how her school day had gone. She would cry because none of her classmates picked her for their team and no one wanted to be her best friend. Julissa often said the very words that tear at a parent's heart: "Everybody hates me!" The saddest part was that they knew she was not exaggerating, because she was rarely invited to any birthday parties or to play at anyone's house. They had always known she wasn't the perfect, well-behaved child, but she had managed to fit in much better in kindergarten, first grade, and second grade than she had in third grade. It seemed that the other girls were maturing and leaving Julissa in the dust.

Problem-Solving Perspective Required

If you are like most parents of girls with ADHD, you will find that your daughter's elementary years will be filled with learning and new challenges for you as well. There will be little room for complacency. Just when you think you've figured out how to handle your daughter's difficulties and are experiencing a period of smooth sailing, a new problem will pop up. If a girl with ADHD is anything during these years, we've found that she is consistently inconsistent. In talking about kids with ADHD, Dr. Sam Goldstein (2004) said, "They know what to do, but do not consistently, predictably, or for that matter, independently do what they know" (p. 1).

We recommend that you adopt this stance: Look at every situation that arises as simply another puzzle with a solution. You and your daughter will fare much better if you keep that problem-solving perspective, because you never know when you will need it. Even when challenges come at you fast and furiously—and we know they will—we encourage you not to feel defeated by problems as they arise. Don't let your daughter feel beaten either. Instead, make sure she knows that together you're going to look at her capabilities along with resources that could be available to help her and then work to make things better. You are not going to ignore problems, because by now you probably know they won't go away unless addressed. As her world has gotten bigger, your team can also grow. You can turn to her teacher, her principal, her school guidance counselor or psychologist, her doctor, and trusted friends for help and support. Part of the problem-solving mentality is remembering that you don't have to have all of the answers yourself.

Elementary schools are not the same as when you were a student. Your daughter is faced with high-stakes testing, mandatory retention, curriculum that doesn't account for differing developmental levels, reduced opportunities for recess, and a complex social milieu that is often complicated by social media in the later elementary years. Don't despair. Some positive changes in education may actually make your daughter's life easier. Schools and teachers are much more knowledgeable about ADHD and how to effectively serve those who are impacted. Recently released research on girls with ADHD is making people, especially teachers, more aware of their struggles. Increased use of technology in the classroom is also a plus for most children with ADHD.

When you factor in her ADHD and the likelihood that your daughter may also have academic deficits, she is definitely going to need your involvement and support if she is to develop and maintain a positive attitude toward learning. It is well-documented that girls diagnosed with ADHD often have learning disabilities and lower performance on standardized testing. There will be increased demands on her organizational skills and persistence, often exceeding her capability. These are critical years for her when she is cementing her view of herself. Your goal will be to help her be as independent as possible while providing enough support to enable her to view herself as a capable learner. As her study skills develop, remember that it is much easier to establish good habits from the very beginning than to break bad habits. Educate yourself so you can make the best possible choices for her.

Emotional/Behavioral Developmental Milestones

Along the way, your daughter is maturing a little bit every day, albeit more slowly than children without ADHD. Girls with ADHD often have great difficulty with regulating emotions and with self-control. To keep tabs on your daughter's progress, try to have some awareness of when these developments occur in the general population. Based on research and child development theory, consider the following stages of development (Teeter, 1998):

◊ Ages 6–9: Self-control improves and more internal thinking develops.

◊ Middle childhood: Children are influenced by and use standards set by parents.

◊ Ages 7 and up: Self-talk guides behavior and enables children to take the perspective of others.

◊ Ages 6–12: Children become more adept at regulating emotional reactions to situations.

◊ Ages 10–12: Children are better able to control negative feelings and separate actions from feelings.

Melissa was a 10-year-old girl in fifth grade who had been diagnosed with ADHD and was taking medication. Rather than developing more self-control, her parents felt Melissa was displaying less. She would blow up at home at the slightest provocation and seemed constantly stressed. A visit to the doctor prescribing her medication ruled out the medication as the cause of her unpredictability.

Her parents were spending more and more time helping her with her homework but felt like they were presenting material for the first time rather than reinforcing what had been taught in the classroom that day. A conference with her teacher showed she was falling farther and farther behind in the classroom. Her teacher reported that she often looked confused and didn't know where to start on assignments. Unbeknownst to her parents, Melissa had recently been dropped from her group of friends at school, children she had been friends with since third grade. Her teacher reported overhearing insensitive comments Melissa had made to the other girls prior to the dissolution of their friendship and noted Melissa often wanted to "call the shots" during play. Now at recess, she would wander around aimlessly, as if she did not know what to do with herself. A conference with Melissa, her teacher, and her parents revealed that Melissa was miserable at school, constantly thinking about how sad she was rather than focusing on her schoolwork. Her parents realized Melissa was not yet able to take the perspective of others and needed assistance in refining her social skills. Fortunately, the school's guidance counselor had a small group focusing on social skills, which Melissa joined. All involved felt Melissa perked up and seemed to benefit from specific teaching about social skills. Her parents helped her identify other students in the classroom who might be good friends and made plans to establish play dates. When watching movies or reading books, they also tried to guide her in anticipating what other children might be thinking. As her social life became less rocky, her attention improved in the classroom and she was better able to control her emotions.

School Choices

Your choice of schools (and whether you have a choice at all) will depend upon where you live, your financial situation, and whether your local school district allows freedom to move from one school to another. In some cases, your local public elementary school may be your one and only option. If that's your family's situation, we encourage you to keep reading because what you learn here may help your school to become a more welcoming place for all children with ADHD, including your own daughter.

However, many communities offer a variety of choices—public schools, charter schools, and private schools. Some school districts have online or virtual schools in which students complete class work via the computer. Homeschooling is another option that we will discuss in Chapter 6.

It is critical that you select the type of environment that will provide the best learning opportunities for your daughter. Time spent researching your options will likely pay off and will certainly give you peace of mind that you did the best that you could.

Consider the overall philosophy of the school. Children with ADHD do better in schools with structure, good communication with parents, solid curriculum that matches instruction to the child's abilities, energetic teachers who utilize experiential learning and a variety of instructional techniques, high expectations for learners, and reasonable class sizes. It is important for the staff to have an understanding of ADHD as a neurobiological condition with deficits in impulse control and executive functioning, so they don't immediately attribute a child's problems to laziness and lack of motivation. When you're evaluating a school, we recommend you ask the following questions:

◊ Does the curriculum match state guidelines? In most states, you can go to your state department of education's website and access the curriculum for various grades. The new Common Core State Standards adopted by almost all states are available online as well (see http://www.corestandards. org).

◊ What is the average class size? Smaller is often better; 20 students or fewer is optimal.

◊ Does it appear to be a highly organized and structured environment?

◊ Do the students sit in desks or at tables? A highly distractible child usually does better at a desk.

◊ Does the school provide opportunities, such as tutoring, for extra help if a child lags behind academically?

◊ What kind of success rate has the school had for girls with ADHD?

◊ Is close supervision provided at all times, especially during transitions?

◊ What is the school's communication policy with parents?

◊ Is the school willing to accommodate your child's needs with strategies such as preferential seating, frequent cueing to task, or allowing movement as long as it does not disturb others?

◊ What is the behavior management plan? Is it proactive and designed to eliminate opportunities for misbehavior? Children with ADHD benefit from positive reinforcement, contingency management or a reward system, and being held accountable for their behavior.

◊ Does the staff make organization a priority and assist students in developing organization skills?

◊ Do they make it a priority to help every child feel connected to others in the classroom and try to foster friendships for children who are struggling in this area?

Teacher/Classroom Match Is Important

Once you have selected a school, a good plan of action may be to have a conversation with the principal and provide some information about your daughter to help the school make a good teacher match for her. Some teachers are much more effective than others in dealing with girls with ADHD. The ultimate decision will be up to the principal, who has to consider many factors. Teachers who are patient, have high energy, and are structured and loving but firm are usually most effective with children with ADHD. One confounding factor about these children is that their focus is often governed by their motivation, so it is key to have a teacher who tries to make learning interesting. Some families have the good fortune to find a teacher who is flexible enough to work with their daughter's built-in restlessness and distractibility while boosting her independence and self-confidence. Those teachers allow children to move about after tasks are complete, as long as it does not bother other students, and make it a habit to refocus children when attention wanders. Or they might allow a girl to stand beside her desk and work. Having a teacher who can appreciate your daughter for her strengths and not become too annoyed with her impulsivity, distractibility, or activity level will be invaluable.

Information for Your Teammates: Your Daughter's Teachers

The quality of your young daughter's education can have a direct relationship to her adult life, so these years are very important. In our practices, we have observed excellent teachers who know exactly what strategies work with girls with ADHD. As your daughter's most powerful advocate, you should have a solid understanding of instructional techniques that might help your daughter and share them with her teachers in a respectful way. More than likely, many of her teachers will already be implementing many of these strategies. You can develop your own personalized list of interventions that seem to help your daughter and share them with new teachers when appropriate. Your goal is always to establish a collaborative relationship, not to tell the teacher how to run his or her classroom. You might even want to incorporate some of these techniques during homework time.

Classroom Organization/Management

In an ideal world, your daughter's educational environment will include:

◊ a positive classroom environment where the teacher has an understanding of ADHD and is familiar with strategies to prompt your daughter to become an active participant in the learning process;

◊ specific classroom procedures established and practiced consistently. In kindergarten, children may need practice to understand how to stand in line, take turns, raise their hands, and wait to be called on before speaking;

◊ organizational skills taught and modeled throughout the school day, with assistance where necessary. Use of color-coded folders for each subject and a separate folder for homework can be very helpful;

◊ seating in a distraction-free area, close to the point of instruction but as far away as possible from air conditioners, high-traffic areas, bathroom access, and other active students;

◊ provision of a study carrel or separate area of the classroom where a child can choose to go and work when distractions become too great. In some cases, students have referred to these areas as their offices;

◊ work areas that are kept neat and free of distractions;

◊ placement of students with ADHD near positive role models;

◊ when possible, core classes that are scheduled early in the day. An optimal schedule for a girl with ADHD is to have lunch and physical education or recess at intervals that break up the day;

◊ achievement motivators that stress effort and persistence. In other words, the child is rewarded for doing her very best, not for producing an "A" result;

◊ concept of time out used as a chance to regain control rather than as a punishment;

◊ supervision, especially during transition times and lunch. Lack of structure allows for more social interaction where potential problems may flourish;

◊ allowance for movement as long as other students aren't disturbed. For example, the girl with ADHD may be allowed to get out of her desk to retrieve something, walk around the classroom, go to the restroom, or get a drink of water. Work by Rapport et al. (2008) suggested that activity may serve a purpose in helping students with ADHD to process information; and

◊ acceptable substitutes for motor behavior, such as allowing the student to squeeze stress balls or chew gum if permitted by the school, as long as these items do not become a distraction.

Behavior: Rewards and Consequences

Children with ADHD may require more relevant rewards and consistent consequences for behavior than other children. An individualized behavior plan using tangible rewards is sometimes necessary and can be developed by the teacher, a school psychologist, or a behavior specialist. Stickers, happy faces, or check marks can be redeemed for opportunities for extra computer time, to mentor another student, to be a teacher's helper, or to have lunch with a special teacher or administrator. Sometimes a response/cost plan, whereby a student can also lose something for poor behavior, works for some students and may be necessary for serious behavior. For example, if a student hits someone or causes a big disruption in the classroom, she might lose all of her points for the day or lose one of the privileges she had already earned. It is critical for rewards or consequences to be delivered as close to the behavior as possible. It's important to bear the following in mind as you implement this practice for girls with ADHD:

◊ Sincere verbal praise for specific behavior is invaluable as a tool for reinforcing the desired behavior. Make sure to "catch her being good."

◊ Students should be taught how to become independent learners and how to self-monitor their own behavior.

◊ Frequent visual cues between student and teacher help maintain optimal attention and behavioral control. A cue could be a special sign that only the girl with ADHD and her teacher know. This is a great proactive way to help a child.

Lesson Presentation

Teaching girls with ADHD sometimes requires a little bit more ingenuity (and a lot more patience). Respectfully ask your daughter's teacher to think of this list as extra tools for his or her toolbox:

◊ Give directions in short sentences, accompanied with visuals when possible. In the upper elementary grades, it is often helpful for a child to see what the finished product should look like before she begins working.

◊ Offer assistance breaking down longer assignments into manageable chunks. Some children are overwhelmed by the amount of information on a page and benefit from covering part of the page with a blank sheet of paper. When a child is overwhelmed, she often shuts down rather than attempting to start on a project.

◊ Establish eye contact with a child with ADHD before delivering key points of instruction. Watch for signs that indicate lack of comprehension, especially daydreaming.

◊ Provide frequent review and repetition of previously learned material.

◊ Understand the child's capability and provide lessons that are challenging without being frustrating.

◊ Hands-on, experiential learning is a favorite for children with ADHD. Their attention to task increases significantly when it is of high interest.

◊ Ignore minor inappropriate behavior (Parker, 2005).

◊ Provide warnings before transitions (e.g., "Five more minutes before science").

◊ Demonstrate proper behavior. Helping a girl compensate for social skills deficits can be very beneficial, especially in younger grades. Sharing and turn-taking can be especially difficult for young children with ADHD. Teachers can model behavior, reinforce appropriate behavior, and help the child initiate interactions.

◊ Use of computerized instruction as part of the curriculum is a positive way for most girls with ADHD to learn because it is stimulating and interactive.

◊ Target her learning style. Because children with ADHD can be incredibly focused on topics or activities of their choice, an effective motivator can be to allow them extra credit on selected topics with the project to be matched to their learning style. If a girl is talented verbally, then she might research something and present to the class. If she's creative and good with her hands, she might build a project instead.

Your Daughter's Peers

Outside of your family, your daughter's school offers the most important opportunities for her socialization, and elementary school is when your daughter should be making great strides in learning how to appropriately interact with others. During this time, it is common for girls with ADHD to have one of two problems:

◊ they may lack social skills appropriate for their age, and

◊ they may have the skills but may not stop and think before they act.

If your daughter is having problems with her peer group at school, it is important to know what is at the root of the problem. Is she insistent on being the boss? Does she have trouble following the verbal interactions of girls? Is she unable to read body language and pick up visual clues from others? Is her thinking so unorganized that she can't stay on topic? Does she withdraw from groups because she does not feel accepted? More than likely, her teacher can share information about her functioning in the classroom, and you can make observations on your own at birthday parties or other social outings.

Dr. John Taylor (2001), a clinical family psychologist, has classified children and adolescents with ADHD as having difficulty in many of the following areas:

◊ turn-taking in games and conversation,

◊ accepting criticism,

◊ losing in games or competitions,

◊ understanding and following instructions,

◊ honoring other people's "personal space,"

◊ resisting peer pressure, and

◊ disagreeing with others and solving problems.

If you have pinpointed some problem areas for your daughter in the above list, then you can go about helping her acquire those skills in a number of ways:

◊ Communicate with her teacher and solicit his or her help. Sometimes children need to be explicitly taught social skills; they don't acquire them by osmosis. Some schools have social groups run by a guidance counselor or school psychologist in which children are taught skills and have the opportunity to practice them using role playing. Some classroom teachers are excellent at weaving social expectations into their daily curriculum and setting up opportunities where children can interact successfully.

◊ There are a number of books written for children that highlight social skills through the use of stories that you can read and discuss with your daughter. This concept is called bibliotherapy. One of Jim's previous books, *Teaching Problem Solving Through Children's Literature*, contains book titles and specific lesson plans for each book that teachers or parents can use to help kids increase their social skills.

◊ There are also games, such as *Do Watch Listen Say* by Quill, and interactive CDs, such as *My School Day Enhanced* and

You Are a Social Detective by Social Skill Builder, Inc., that teach social skills interactively.

◊ Arrange play dates and provide opportunities for your daughter to establish relationships with other girls. Put time and effort into selecting the children and the activities to maximize opportunities for success.

Some teachers are very good at setting up social opportunities for awkward students and definitely go the "extra mile" to help students connect. Mary Anne has observed a teacher grabbing a basketball and encouraging a child who usually hangs on the sidelines to join in a game. Within minutes, other children were joining in. If situations can be set up where children can interact comfortably, little by little, their skills begin to grow.

Bullying

Unfortunately, bullying is often in the news and occurs in all schools, despite careful oversight and strict rules against it. Bullying almost always involves an imbalance of power and is defined as intentional, aggressive behavior directed toward another. It can take many forms, including physical and verbal attacks, and sending threatening messages via e-mail, text, or phone (cyberbullying—discussed in more detail in the next chapter).

With the exception of cyberbullying, bullying and intimidation have been around for ages and were previously viewed as part of the childhood experience. Research and current culture have pointed out the dangerous effects of bullying. It can make life miserable for the one being targeted, especially for those who are socially naïve and timid. When the victims internalize the bullying, their hurt can lead to anger, loneliness, withdrawal, lowered self-esteem, and depression. In the worst cases, it can lead to self-harm. It is important to talk to your daughter about bullying and make sure she can recognize it and has some tools to handle it.

The U.S. Department of Health and Human Services (n.d.) has a "Stop Bullying Now" campaign (http://www.stopbullying. gov) and offers the following tips for parents:

◊ Keep communication open with your daughter. Know the names of children she likes and doesn't like at school and why, find out if she feels left out at school, and encourage her to tell you if anyone makes fun of her.

◊ Explain that it is important to tell teachers or principals if she observes or is the target of bullying. This information is usually confidential and is not considered "tattling."

◊ Try to practice or role-play some strategies to use if she is bullied.

◊ Model good behavior for your daughter. Handle disagreements with your spouse, friends, or the school without resorting to aggressive, threatening behavior. Bullying is a learned behavior. In Mary Anne's school experience, children who are disrespectful and bully others have often observed similar ways of handling conflict within their home.

◊ Supervise your daughter so she is less likely to be in situations where bullying can occur.

◊ If you suspect she is being bullied, don't ignore it—get to the bottom of it and see that it is resolved.

Other important pointers for your daughter if she is being bullied include:

◊ Try not to show fear or anger, as this is often the reaction a bully is seeking.

◊ Maintain emotional control.

◊ Don't fight back by resorting to bullying.

◊ Calmly tell the bully to stop or simply walk away.

◊ Try to stay with a group of friends, as bullying is more likely to occur when alone.

◊ Don't bring expensive things to school that other children are not likely to have.

◊ If riding a bus, sit near the front of the bus, not in the back.

A Quick Look at Causes, Presentations, and Possible Solutions for Behaviors

As we have stressed throughout the book, no two girls with ADHD will be alike. Your daughter's ADHD may manifest itself in very different ways than another girl's. Scan the chart in Table 3 to see if you recognize any familiar behaviors. If you do, it will help you understand not only the likely causes but also suggest ways you might work with your daughter to overcome some of her challenges.

Callie breezed through kindergarten, first, and second grades. However, in third grade, her academic performance started falling behind her peers. Her school was departmentalized, so she had to travel to different teachers for math, reading, science, and written language. She could never seem to pack up her materials correctly and usually ended up stuffing all of the papers in her backpack. She missed turning in assignments because she couldn't find the papers. She was frustrated that all assignments seemed longer and more complicated, requiring more concentration and focus. Callie's teacher observed more daydreaming.

Callie experienced difficulty with reading comprehension, because by the time she finished reading the long passages, she had forgotten what she had read. When reading aloud, she often skipped over words that also impacted her comprehension. Writing also seemed overwhelming. Callie rushed through writing assignments and wasn't disciplined enough to effectively use planning

Table 3
Causes, Presentations, and Solutions for ADHD

Cause	Presentation	Possible Solutions
Faulty sense of time	• Always late and behind schedule • Doesn't get started on tasks • Misses deadlines • Doesn't start tasks promptly • Poor planning	• Use agenda or planner • Create a behavior plan • Break assignments down • Use prompts and reminders • Maintain a schedule
Impulsivity	• Acts before thinking • Doesn't consider consequences • Jumps from one task to another • Doesn't listen to others • Blurts out in class • Limited self-control	• Provide structure • Teach verbal rehearsal • Share stop/think strategies • Conduct role-playing
Inflexibility	• Trouble with transitions • Easily agitated • Uncooperative	• Give prior notice for transitions • Teach coping skills
Inattention	• Disorganized • Loses items • Unable to listen • Forgets task of moment • Doesn't store material in memory • Thinks of many things at once	• Teach self-monitoring • Create a designated place for items • Insist on eye contact • Use organization tools • Use memory strategies
Overarousal	• Fidgeting • Excessive talking • Constant movement • Easily stimulated	• Give student permissible movements • Use of fidget item • Provide calm areas • Ignore low-level behaviors

Note. From *Raising Boys With ADHD* (p. 112) by J. W. Forgan and M. A. Richey, 2012, Waco, TX: Prufrock Press. Copyright 2012 by Prufrock Press. Reprinted with permission.

strategies or go back and proofread. In math, she was resistant to showing her work on multistep problems.

Fortunately, Callie was already in a structured, predictable classroom setting with an enthusiastic teacher who was determined to figure out strategies to help her be successful. She worked with Callie's parents to establish weekly communication about her progress. Her parents agreed to have Callie empty her backpack every night and get all of the papers in their proper places. They helped her establish a designated place by the door where she could put all of her school items for the next day. At school, Callie was motivated to use a monitoring checklist, developed by her teacher, which was broken down by subject. She was placed on a reward system and was able to select her reward from a menu of reinforcers that she could earn dependent on her total number of points, which included additional time on the computer, opportunities to assist her teacher, and homework passes. She was required to self-monitor on the items shown in Table 4 with teacher oversight.

In Mary Anne's work as a school psychologist in the public school system, individualized behavior and/or self-monitoring plans are often developed for students. Callie's plan had its ups and downs, but her teacher was able to establish that she did not have academic skill deficits, but rather performance deficits. Everyone was motivated by Callie's progress—her teacher, her parents, and most importantly, Callie herself. Her situation shows that interventions in the classroom and at home are often multifaceted and require commitment from all involved parties, especially the child, in order to be successful. It is critical for interventions to be implemented when your daughter first starts having difficulty—not waiting until her self-esteem has been battered and she has dug herself into a hole where escape will be difficult.

Table 4
Self-Monitoring Chart

All Subjects	Good (2)	Fair (1)	Needs Work (0)
Did I have all materials ready and available?			
Did I catch myself daydreaming and bring myself back to my work?			
Reading			
Did I use comprehension strategies when reading?			
Did I reread if the sentence did not make sense?			
Writing			
Did I complete a brief diagram to organize my writing?			
Did I proofread all of my writing for complete sentences, punctuation, and capitalization?			
Math			
Did I follow a plan my teacher gave me to solve math word problems?			
Bonus points for kind deeds, extra work, or exceptional behavior:			

Note. From *Raising Boys With ADHD* (p. 115) by J. W. Forgan and M. A. Richey, 2012, Waco, TX: Prufrock Press. Copyright 2012 by Prufrock Press. Reprinted with permission.

Being a Proactive Parent/ General Home Interventions

Home plays a far more important role than just a place to do homework (which we'll cover in the next section). In fact, the expectations you set for your daughter at home are just as important to her success as anything that happens in the classroom.

In our practices, we recommend that parents extend the concepts of structure, activity, and discipline into their home. It's important that your daughter understand that school is not the only place she needs to maintain self-control, nor is it the only place where she can depend on a certain amount of structure and sameness. Some things to try include the following:

◊ Provide a structured home setting. Have a predictable schedule and try to stick to it.

◊ Try to avoid sending your daughter to school tired. She will have to expend so much energy to battle her ADHD during the day and will need some reserves.

◊ Help her establish some order in her room, especially for important things. Here you will have to choose your battles carefully. At the very least, she should have a specific place to keep her backpack, lunch box, or anything traveling with her daily to school. If her room isn't the place, choose somewhere else in the house for these essential items.

◊ Until she naturally is disciplined enough to keep order to her backpack, have her empty it every night and put all of the papers in their proper places.

◊ Provide a quiet, uncluttered homework center. Eliciting her help in selecting and creating the space might result in more compliant use. Many girls enjoy adding their own decorative touch to the space.

◊ Try to feed her a healthy, balanced diet that is not loaded with processed food.

Whether your daughter likes it or not, daily physical activity and some opportunities to relax and blow off steam and release some excess energy are important. At home, you might try the following:

◊ Make sure that she has ample opportunity for activity. If she tends to be sedentary, don't give up until you find an active outlet that she enjoys. Some parents find that children benefit from running or riding their bike *before* going to school in the mornings.

◊ Make sure your daughter is not overscheduled so she has ample opportunity for breaks, activity, and sleep. You want to strive for a balance—enough activities for exposure but not an overload.

◊ Try to avoid placing her in situations where the problems associated with her ADHD will be aggravated. Think ahead.

Never presume that because your daughter is in school, it's now her teacher's responsibility to see that she behaves properly. That job is yours as well. We do recommend that you establish a system for communicating with her teacher (whether it is via e-mail, notes in the agenda planner, or on a daily behavior log), so you can work as a team to steadily improve your daughter's focus and self-discipline. At home, try to put these practices in place:

◊ Work to understand the difference between willful acts of disobedience and behaviors that are the result of her ADHD and may not be under her control. Deal with them accordingly, because open defiance should have definite consequences. Impulsive actions or behaviors caused by her distractibility may provide teachable moments where you can help your daughter develop strategies for dealing with her ADHD.

◊ Try to make sure you are not inadvertently reinforcing her ADHD behaviors. For example, if a girl receives big pay-offs for impulsive behavior by getting what she wants or receives lots of attention for it, the behaviors will be constantly reinforced.

◊ Give directions in short, concise sentences, using prompts or visual reminders if memory seems to be an issue.

◊ Provide plenty of positive reinforcement and limit the negatives to the really important things. We definitely advise parents to pick their battles. Remember, your daughter probably gets plenty of negative feedback outside the home. There is a difference between being firm and being overly critical.

◊ Provide consequences within short order of the offending act. Providing them consistently is also key.

Homework

Be honest. Many of you would rather walk over hot coals than try to get your daughter to do her homework, wouldn't you? It's daunting for so many reasons. If your daughter has had a frustrating day at school, she will not look forward to sitting down at a desk again. Frequently, children with ADHD have weaker executive functioning skills and have great difficulty initiating activity, planning, and organizing. They honestly may not even remember what the teacher wants them to do. Our experience with children with ADHD is that they resist settling down to do homework and usually wait until the last minute. Procrastination can reach a new level on large projects, especially term papers and science projects.

For Jim's son, homework was, and is, a nightly battle. In Jim's experience, this is classic ADHD behavior. Homework requires sustained mental effort—and that's difficult for children with ADHD. Over time Jim and his wife have found that applying Grandma's Rule works. Grandma's Rule means you have to eat your veggies before you can have dessert. In other words, work comes before play. Thus, Jim's son has to complete his homework before he can engage in preferred activities. His IEP also includes a reduction in his homework load and receiving his homework early, so he can get started over the weekend. These accommodations help reduce frustrations.

Homework can be very stressful. The following guidelines have worked for our families:

◊ Establish ground rules and stick to them. For example, turn off the television and loud music, and don't permit your child to receive telephone calls or text messages during study time.

◊ Figure out the optimal time for homework in your household. Some children need a break after school, and others cannot be corralled after playing outside.

◊ Determine how long your daughter can work without becoming frustrated. Provide frequent activity breaks.

◊ Remember that she may have difficulty figuring out where to start and how to approach different tasks. Help her learn to prioritize tasks so the most difficult and important ones are done first. Guide her in making a plan and taking one task at a time. You may need to cut assignments into parts so she doesn't feel overwhelmed.

◊ Provide help when needed, but do not become so involved that your daughter is not independent—a very fine and tricky balance.

◊ Allow her to use the computer or iPad (with teacher permission) for producing written work.

◊ If homework time produces too much conflict that cannot be resolved, then consider the services of a tutor (if you can afford it or can find a college or high school student willing to volunteer his or her time).

High-Stakes Testing

In most states, standardized testing plays a role in a school's evaluation and sometimes in whether a student is promoted. These tests are usually 45–90 minutes long, often have a great deal of information on a page, and can be very tedious and boring— clearly not optimal for girls with ADHD. Accountability is critical in school systems, so it is important to help your daughter make the best of the situation. Many school districts have practice tests on the computer, an effective way for a girl with ADHD to learn. Take advantage of opportunities for your daughter to practice if they are available.

Work to learn more about what is covered on the test and try to incorporate some of those skills into your daily interactions with your daughter. For example, if fractions are on the test, involve her in measuring when cooking or when building a project. If she might be asked to make a prediction about what she thinks may happen in a story, then ask her to make a prediction when you are watching a television program together.

From time to time, a girl with ADHD has heightened anxiety because she recognizes that she has performance deficits. Try to be sensitive to that possibility and help her figure out coping strategies to use when she is anxious, such as breathing deeply or visualizing herself in a peaceful place. You and her teacher will walk a fine line between motivating her to do her best and putting too much pressure on her. If your daughter needs extended time or other accommodations related to her ADHD, a 504 plan or IEP can be considered (see Chapter 6).

Retention

Most studies have not shown benefits to retention. However, it is a decision that must be made based on individual circumstances, the educational environment, and advice from educators and others involved with your daughter. Some questions to ask are:

◊ Does your daughter's birthday make her one of the youngest or oldest children in the class?

◊ Would the retention be likely to produce long-term benefits? Surely the retention year would be easier for her, but what about subsequent years?

◊ Is she delayed in areas other than academics? What are her social skills like? What about her physical size and development?

◊ If she has siblings, how would that impact retention? If she would end up in the same grade as a sibling, sometimes that can cause conflict.

◊ What is the school's recommendation?

◊ If retention seems to be the best option, can you frame it in a positive way to your daughter?

Our experience has been that retention is easier on children than their parents. It is a complex decision that must not be taken lightly. Consideration should be given to repercussions for the retention year as well as its impact on the remainder of your daughter's school career.

Janie had been diagnosed with ADHD in second grade and had been responding positively to medication. However, she began struggling in third grade with all academic subjects. This was the first year the results of standardized testing could result in retention. Janie was so frustrated with the lengthy tests because she called them "boring" and was rarely able to finish them in the allotted amount of time. She was in danger of retention, and she knew it. That seemed to fuel her anger. Her parents were upset that recess was being withheld from Janie because she had not completed her work. They felt, and rightly so, that she needed an outlet for her energy.

Her family consulted with Janie's psychiatrist, who advised against any change in medication but recommended an evaluation through the school district to determine if Janie also had a learning disability. The results of the evaluation indicated that she had difficulty with sequential auditory and visual memory as well as deficits in processing speed. All of her academic skills were significantly below grade level, and her class work was at her frustration level. The school implemented intensive, research-based interventions targeted to her academic deficits. She made progress but did not reach her academic goals. Janie subsequently qualified for services with a learning disability and received some of her academic instruction in a smaller classroom setting at her instructional level. She received modification on standardized testing; what was especially helpful was extended time and frequent breaks. Without significant interventions, Janie might have been retained and her interest in school and her academic skills might also have continued their decline without specialized instruction geared toward her learning disability.

What to Do When There's No Progress

Even after diligent research, excellent communication, and support at home and school, your daughter may be struggling too much in her current setting. If you feel she is not learning and/or is miserable, it is important to be proactive. Schedule a conference with the teacher and ask for his or her honest assessment of the situation. Together, brainstorm additional strategies or accommodations that could work. If your daughter is on medication, consult with the prescribing doctor to see if adjustments are in order. If a change is made in medication, sign a release for the teacher to communicate directly with the doctor to provide firsthand information about the effects of the medication during the school day.

Inquire if the school has any additional resources that can be tapped. Is there a guidance counselor or school psychologist who could observe your daughter and provide feedback? Sometimes fresh eyes may look at a problem from a different perspective and come up with solutions. Consult with the principal, since he or she is the instructional leader of the school. Changing teachers or classrooms is usually not an option but could be explored.

If no workable solutions are forthcoming, you could explore the advisability of changing schools. This should not be entered into lightly, because stability is important. However, sometimes the school/student match just doesn't produce the desired results and could end up damaging a student's attitude toward learning. It is important to be cautious about just how much information you share with your daughter in these situations.

Time to Change Schools

How do you know when it's time to move your daughter to a different school? We know girls with ADHD have their ups and downs, but sometimes the bad times far outnumber the good ones. When this occurs, it may be a sign that it's time to change to a different school.

If your daughter is attending a private elementary school, there is always the chance that she may not be asked back for another school year. It can throw you into a tailspin if you are informed she can't return. You may feel panicked, disappointed in your daughter or yourself, or discouraged that you must search for another school. If this happens to you, and even if it appears to be your daughter's fault, we recommend that you not blame her. It won't help the situation and will certainly hurt her feelings, reinforce that she failed again, and decrease her self-esteem. Yes, you want to have a straightforward conversation about her work habits, effort, and behavior, but rarely is it 100% your daughter's fault. Emphasize to your daughter that when a private school placement—or any school placement, for that matter—does not work out, it is always a combination of factors. Help your daughter recognize the important lessons from this experience so the two of you can avoid a repeat experience.

Sometimes leaving private school is a mutual decision between parents and the school, and other times it is your decision not to return. Some parents find a private education more limiting for their daughters with ADHD, because private schools are not required to make as many accommodations as public schools and may have fewer resources. Although many private schools do make accommodations, it can vary widely by school. Do you feel like your daughter is a square peg being made to fit into a round opening? It's time for a change if the match between your daughter and her private school or public school is not correct.

In a public school, your daughter's ADHD may be tolerated more than in private school because of the student diversity found in most public schools. Exactly how much your daughter's ADHD behaviors are tolerated depends on her individual teacher. Some teachers have better classroom management skills and can handle your daughter's daydreaming, calling out answers, squirming while seated, or constantly picking away at her eraser. Having a teacher who understands your daughter makes life better for everyone.

However, some teachers may not understand children with ADHD. Try to help educate the teacher about your daughter and about girls with ADHD in general. Many teachers are willing to learn more about ADHD and techniques that they can use to help children, which in turn makes their classrooms run more smoothly. When we diagnose a girl with ADHD, we give her parents information about ADHD that they can read and share with their daughter's teacher such as the "Information for Your Teammates: Your Daughter's Teachers" box included on pages 132–136 of this book. Other fact sheets are available on websites such as http://www.CHADD.org or other parent support websites.

Sometimes things do not go well, despite your best efforts. If you've failed in numerous attempts to work with your daughter's teacher and engaged the principal, school psychologist, or guidance counselor to explore all options, and you still sense a growing despair in your daughter, then you may find it in her best interest to learn what other school choices might be open to her.

Ask yourself these questions:

◊ Am I receiving daily (or almost daily) phone calls about my daughter's school behavior or lack of academic progress?

◊ Is the majority of feedback I receive from my daughter's teacher or school negative?

◊ Has my daughter been suspended from school?

◊ Have I been asked to come pick my daughter up early from school on multiple occasions because of her behavior?

◊ Does my daughter say she hates school or does she feel sick each morning when it's time for school?

◊ Does my daughter's self-esteem seem low? Does she make statements such as, "I'm dumb," "I'm going to drop out of school," "My teacher doesn't like me," or "No one likes me"?

◊ Does my gut feeling or intuition tell me it's time for a change?

If you answered yes to the majority of these questions, it could be time for a change. If so, the next question is, "Where?" There are positives and negatives to any educational setting. Can you afford to send her to a private school? Does she need a special type of school? Should you homeschool or consider a virtual school? Often the answer is not obvious or easy.

If your daughter remains in the public school system, we recommend you talk to her principal to gain his or her support for making next year's teacher a good match with your daughter. Emphasize your daughter's strengths, needs, and the type of teaching style you believe works best for her. Although most principals cannot honor every parent request, many will listen carefully to what you have to say, especially about a child with a disability. Make an appointment and take notes to share. It may be helpful to have another person with you when meeting with the principal or school staff. Bring along your spouse, a friend, or a tutor.

Home and Community Issues

You know by now that your daughter doesn't leave her ADHD at school. She faces challenges at home, around the neighborhood, and in any activity she pursues, because ADHD permeates all areas of a girl's life. It is very common for girls with ADHD to have difficulties when interacting with their siblings and peers.

Siblings

If your daughter with ADHD has brothers and sisters, you understand there are times they fight like cats and dogs and other times they laugh like best friends. The sibling relationship is important for children with ADHD because it helps them learn to form appropriate interpersonal relationships. Home is usually where children with ADHD feel safest because of the unconditional love within a family. Therefore home is a great place to start teaching your daughter with ADHD how to appropriately interact with her siblings and others.

Many girls with ADHD require your specific advice and instruction to learn how to get along with their siblings. Forming solid, civil relationships may not come easily to many girls with ADHD, and siblings often find their sisters with ADHD annoying, interfering, and difficult. You must make it a priority to teach your daughter courteous and friendly behavior and provide her with opportunities to apply what she's learned with her siblings. The give and take required for siblings to get along well probably may not come naturally to her.

We recommend that you establish this primary family rule: "Treat others with respect." This directive must come from parents; after all, you are the head of the family. Your message must be, "We are a family. We treat each other nicely and we support each other." Teaching mutual respect starts with you. Model it and live it—and that means treating your children with respect and requiring that they treat you and one another with respect as well. Establish it as a theme in every family talk, especially when that discussion involves conflict. If this message isn't firmly established during the elementary years, adolescence can be very difficult. If you expect your daughter with ADHD to respect you and the other family members, then you must first show that same respect to her. She has to know what it looks like.

We understand that this can be so hard to do. Girls with ADHD sure know how to push your buttons, don't they? Young girls with ADHD often react with emotions rather than words because they feel emotions much faster than they can label and speak them as words. We've known girls who, when reprimanded for behavior, will roll their eyes, say "la la la la la," or sing song lyrics to block out the parent. If your daughter does this to you, try to remember how primal her first reaction can be. Help her to see how disrespectful this is and that she would not want you to respond to her in that way. If it continues to happen, just ignore it.

Name-Calling

When you establish the family rule of "treat others with respect," you take an important step toward creating family peace. Name-calling falls in the category of disrespectful behavior you're likely to have to address with all of your children, but your daughter with ADHD may need extra patience in learning that ugly names are absolutely not part of your family's vocabulary. This means you don't ever call your daughter an unkind name, and she never calls you or any of her siblings a mean or profane name. Agree on consequences and enforce them. This is one of Jim's most important family rules. In addition to the standard consequence, he and his wife also make each child pay $1 any time there is name-calling. It simply won't be tolerated, and this extra consequence really made the "treat each other with respect" rule hit home.

Counseling

Occasionally, sibling disagreements become so intense that the situation requires the help of a mental health counselor, family therapist, or psychologist. Family discord often makes everyone feel miserable, and this feeling spills over into your daughter's life at school, at her friends' homes, and everywhere she goes. Often within a half-dozen or so sessions, a well-trained counselor can help turn around family problems. In our experience, the time and money you spend working with a professional is time and money invested in family harmony.

Friendships

Some girls with ADHD are gifted communicators. If your daughter has this talent, continue to develop it, because it will carry her far in life. However, many girls with ADHD have communication and social difficulties because they speak before they think—which tends to get them in hot water. Some girls with ADHD seem to have difficulty processing language, which impacts their social skills. Many girls with ADHD don't think of others or about the way others perceive them. Sometimes kids with ADHD will act as if they have no filters, not thinking about how their questions or remarks will make the other person feel. One time a client said to Jim, "I like your head. How'd you get it so shiny?" Another one asked Mary Anne, "How did you get so old?" Often, whatever's on their mind just comes out. This is part of what gets them into trouble. Professionals call this "lack of inhibition," because girls with ADHD often don't have the little voice in their minds that says, "Don't do that, because it could get you in trouble," or "Don't say that, because it could hurt someone's feelings," or they don't pause long enough to listen if they do have that little voice. They don't hold back their automatic thoughts. The words or actions just happen. So the next time she gets into trouble and you ask, "Why did you do that?" and hear her reply, "I don't know," she's probably telling you the truth. It just happened.

This brings us to another point: Asking your daughter the question, "*Why* did you do that?" after she has caused a social problem is rarely helpful. We like the advice from Pete Wright (2009), an attorney and parent of two successful boys with ADHD and learning disabilities. He wrote,

> When my children misbehaved or messed up, I never asked them, "Why did you . . ." When the parent asks a child "why," the child learns to create good excuses, shifts blame onto others, views himself or herself as a "victim of circumstances"—and does not learn to take responsibility for his or her behavior.
>
> When you ask "why," it's easy to slip in some guilt—"Why did you do this? You upset Sally so much. You made her feel terrible." Ask these four questions instead:
>
> ◊ What did you do?
> ◊ What are you going to do about it?
> ◊ To ensure that this does not happen again, what should we do to you now?
> ◊ If this does happen again, despite your good intentions now, how much more severe shall the punishment be next time? (para. 7)

If your daughter's ADHD is on the severe side, you may find that she's excluded from birthday parties and other social events. Some girls with ADHD have such delayed social skills or can be so bossy and demanding that other kids shun them.

Many girls with ADHD benefit from structured play dates where a specific activity, like bowling or skating, is the focus. Depending on the level of your daughter's social skills, it might be helpful to role play some of the situations that might occur. Some children benefit from reading books and stories about how other children interact. As she gains more skills, allow her to help plan social activities with others her age. If you can help her improve her social competency, you will have helped her develop a gift of immeasurable value.

Whenever conflicts with other children arise, you need to listen to your daughter with ADHD. She is often telling you the truth. Over time, you can learn to recognize when she is being honest. Jim's wife has some type of "truth radar" and can always accurately identify when their son is not telling the truth, because he becomes very emotional and insistent. Perhaps you recognize these types of signals from your daughter. Does she have certain behaviors that signal when she's being sincere? As a parent, watch your daughter for nonverbal cues and pay attention to her actions as well as her words.

Some elementary girls have their own cell phones. Monitoring cell phone use, text messages, or any form of social media for inappropriate contacts or conversations will be important. Make sure your daughter understands your rules for cell phone and social media use and review them frequently.

Faith

If worship is a part of your life, you know the comfort your spiritual beliefs offer. You may also be seeking a way to integrate those beliefs and practices more fully into your daughter's life—and possibly finding that going to your religious services presents some of the same challenges she finds at school. See if any of these scenarios sound familiar:

◊ Getting ready is a struggle. For younger children, it's the everyday challenge to find shoes, get dressed, eat breakfast, and get out the door.

◊ It's hard for either of you to fully appreciate the service. Your daughter may find the service boring, or she may be totally overwhelmed by all the stimulation from the people, the lights, and the music. You're so preoccupied with her behavior, either trying to keep her engaged or trying to reign in her inappropriate outbursts, that you can't focus on the message.

◊ You feel you must explain your daughter's behavior to those around you, and often you can't help feeling judged by those around you for what they perceive as bad parenting.

◊ Your daughter's religious teachers or youth leaders are unequipped to work compassionately with a child who has ADHD.

Or there's this: By the time the weekend rolls around, all of you are simply exhausted. You can't muster the energy to add anything else to your lives.

We understand. And yet if you're inclined to find a way to pursue your spiritual beliefs with your daughter, know that it can be done. Like other areas of your lives with ADHD, there are strategies you can use (some of those we suggest sharing with teachers might be helpful for religious teachers too, for example). It's true that children with ADHD tend to struggle in religious settings (Hathaway & Barkley, 2005), both with socialization and with spiritual growth. Here are a few suggestions that may help your child:

◊ **Prayer or meditation:** Sitting meditation has been shown to reduce ADHD symptoms in students (Travis, Grosswald, & Stixrud, 2011). To us, it stands to reason that prayer could do the same. Because her ADHD may make it difficult for her to focus, help her start a prayer journal to help guide her quiet times. And because routines are so helpful for children with ADHD, you might also initiate a family prayer or meditation time.

◊ **Small groups:** If your daughter is uncomfortable in a religious service, she may thrive in a small-group setting where she can make a handful of intimate friends. Similarly, you may find you're able to form strong and supportive relationships in the small-group setting, where you can share the challenges of parenting a daughter with ADHD. Many religions incorporate small groups to help their members learn and grow together while they form strong bonds of friendship and fellowship.

◊ **Daily Devotional:** You can continue to develop your child's faith at home by reading a daily devotional with your child each night before bed. One program with short (5–10 minute) passages for kids and teens is *The One Year Josh McDowell's Youth Devotions*, which has monthly themes including self-control, respect, honesty, generosity, etc.

◊ **Helping Others:** One way to help yourself is to start helping others. If your daughter appears overly concerned about her own problems, set up opportunities for her to volunteer to help others who are less fortunate. This experience can help children learn to feel good about giving back and often helps them reframe their own situation.

Just as helping your daughter grow in her own faith can be an important component in managing her ADHD, some parents find comfort, guidance, and hope in pursuing their spiritual beliefs. Dez, the mother of Hannah, an 11-year-old girl with ADHD, reminded us of the ways the world tends to label children: "good," for those who are well-behaved and academically successful, and "bad" for those like children who struggle with ADHD, who are so often viewed as lazy, unmotivated, and a nuisance. She wrote to us that, "ADHD certainly has its challenges for Hannah, myself and our entire family, but oddly enough, it's been a blessing, too. Through my faith I am a better person, parent and teacher, because I am able to clearly see the struggles of children with ADHD." Another mother noted that praying helped her change the way she felt about her son's condition, as she was able to move from asking that he be changed to asking that his gifts be used in a positive way.

Sports

Some girls with ADHD are naturally athletic and excel in physical activities, like dancing and sports. It becomes a natural outlet where they can showcase their talents. Competing in activities may help your daughter with ADHD build a sense of accomplishment that could be missing from the academic areas of her life. These activities provide your daughter with focus, structure, and discipline. One of Jim's young clients struggled academically throughout elementary and middle school but always excelled in sports. During high school, she was so accomplished that she was the top player on her softball team and landed a college scholarship playing softball. This young woman's motivation to play softball was instrumental in helping her maintain her grade point average for athletic eligibility.

One of Mary Anne's clients had amazing agility and loved climbing on playground equipment. Gymnastics was a natural outlet for excess energy, provided a vehicle for making friends, and kept her interested in school. She knew she didn't like sitting at a desk in class, but her love for recess and physical education made the school day worthwhile in her eyes.

It is becoming increasingly clear that daily physical activity pays big dividends for everyone, but it can be especially important for your daughter's well-being. Even if she is inclined to be a "couch potato" or is not very coordinated, expose her to different sports opportunities from a young age. As soon as she is eligible, enroll her in organized youth sports. Try dance, T-ball, basketball, golf, tennis, roller or ice hockey, swimming, running, or martial arts. Once you find an activity where she has an interest and natural talent, build upon it. It does not matter whether it is a group or individual sport. Many girls we have worked with have been helped tremendously by karate and dance, which stress listening, discipline, respect, and following directions. Compliment your daughter's athletic ability in front of others. Remember to tell her you are proud of her, and encourage her to stick with it and practice.

An elementary school Mary Anne serves in her job as a school district psychologist has a running club modeled after a national program called Girls on the Run. Girls meet with several faculty members after school and run several miles. Several girls with ADHD benefit tremendously from this burst of activity after school. They are better able to focus later on homework and establish camaraderie with other children in the running club.

The tendency for many girls with ADHD is to jump from sport to sport because having a short attention span is part of their disorder. They find a sport and become passionate about it but lose the passion just as quickly. You can be the one to help your daughter persevere, at least until the season is over. Although quitting is often the easy way out, it does not build her character. Even if your daughter believes she is the worst player on the team, don't let her bail on her team. Let your daughter earn the feeling of accomplishment and satisfaction that comes from sticking it out until the end. Teach her to push through when things get tough. Pushing through tough times goes against everything she naturally wants to do, but she needs to develop this ability for success in school and sports. Mary Anne's son enrolled in competitive swimming because of how much he enjoyed recreational swimming. However, he hated the rigor of the swim practices, even though he was a natural at backstroke. As a young child, he would cry about going to practice, but was encouraged to stick it out until the session was over. He learned that once you commit to something, you have to see it through.

Not every girl with ADHD is going to find a sport she is willing to play. If your daughter has tried group and individual sports but still does not have the knack for any of them, then you know more about her gifts and personality and can nurture her other talents. Even though physical activity may not be a preference, it is still important for her to have some physical outlet in her daily routine, such as walking, swimming, jumping rope, skating, or doing yoga.

Camps

Attending a day or sleep-away camp can build your daughter's confidence. Camps that offer outdoor or hands-on activities during the summer can be a welcome change from the rigor of academics during the school year. Recreational, Scout, and church camps can all provide good lessons in being organized and keeping up with her belongings. Some girls may not be emotionally ready to sleep away from home or be as independent as sleep-away camps require, so local day camps might be a better idea. Check your local community for opportunities.

When carefully chosen, camps can boost self-esteem by providing opportunities for making new friendships and developing new skills. You know your daughter best and understand the type of camp she'd enjoy most. However, it takes due diligence on your part to locate just the right type of camp for your daughter. Sure, any parent can sign their daughter up for a camp and send her off, but it's different for girls with ADHD. You know her camp must be just the right fit, have the right type of activities, number of children, the best staff, and structure—or it could be a disaster. She'll come home early, say she hates camp, won't want to return, and give you a hard time. You know that if she feels miserable, some of it is going to rub off on you too.

In addition to more typical summer camps, some locations offer therapeutic camps for children whose ADHD requires more assistance than the average camp might offer. Dr. Bob Field operates the California-based, multisite Quest Therapeutic Camps for children with ADHD and other associated disorders. If you choose a therapeutic camp for your daughter, you want to make sure it offers a process similar to what Dr. Field describes below.

In a personal correspondence, Dr. Field explained that his Quest camps are fun for kids. He relies on parental input and an individual screening assessment to develop an individualized treatment plan that helps address a camper's most consequential problematic behaviors. The campers identify and understand specific behavioral goals. Using camp activities, therapy staff is able to observe difficulties as they occur and provide interventions right then and there. Counselors are advanced college or graduate students trained to help campers gain awareness as behaviors occur. In addition, during each hour of the day, campers receive specific staff feedback about the positive and negative aspects of their behavior. Campers are awarded points each hour based on their effort. As a camper progresses, higher points require increased effort, developing greater success. Combining a cognitive behavioral therapy approach and specially developed neurocognitive strategies, Quest's small-group therapy sessions facilitate the individualized goals of each camper. This model has been proven to successfully address problematic behaviors and help campers develop appropriate social skills.

Before you send your daughter to either a day or sleep-away camp, you need to think about a few important considerations:

1. Can I handle the stress of sending her off on her own?
2. Is she mentally prepared for camp?
3. What is the camper-to-counselor ratio?
4. What experience do the counselors have working with girls with ADHD?
5. How are discipline and interpersonal conflict between campers handled?
6. If my daughter has difficulty making friends, what steps are in place to help her?

If your daughter is attending a sleep-away camp, ask the camp staff these questions:

1. How do you handle bullying?
2. What happens if my daughter wets the bed?
3. Who keeps and administers her medication?
4. What happens if there is a medical emergency?
5. Are electronics allowed and monitored?
6. How can I communicate with my daughter?
7. What efforts are made to help children make friends?
8. What if she wants to come home early?

In addition to thoroughly researching and selecting the best choice for your daughter, mentally and emotionally prepare her for the experience. As mentioned previously, girls with ADHD do not tend to like unexpected change. Explain what a typical day at camp is like. If the facility is located close to your home, stop by and introduce her to the director. Try to anticipate her feelings on the first day of camp and give her words of encouragement that she can replay in her mind through the day. If your daughter is nervous about new situations and does not know any other campers, you might say something like, "On the first day of camp, a lot of kids won't know anyone. They may not look nervous on the outside, but I'll bet they feel nervous inside. Remember that and talk to lots of kids, because they are hoping they meet a good friend like you." These types of simple steps set your daughter up for a successful camp experience.

Video/Computer/Online Games

Video and noneducational computer games are generally not as big an issue for girls as for boys, but girls are very interested in using smartphones to connect with others through social media or games. Many young girls like virtual online games like Club Penguin or Webkinz, both of which have strong parental controls.

Games, like Minecraft with virtual LEGO-type figures, offer the opportunity to connect with other users via the Internet in a multiplayer mode or in chat rooms. Games often give children feelings of control and success. The fast pace and stimulation they produce feel great to a child with ADHD. Quite frequently we are asked our opinion on whether children with ADHD should be allowed to play video or online games at all.

Research is mixed on children with video games. Jim's rule of thumb is to allow children with ADHD some time to play video or online games because they can be a great reinforcement for good behavior. There are countless times when Jim has said to his son, "If you want to play your game, then I need your help doing so and so," or, "If you finish your homework without arguing, then you can play your game for 30 minutes." As we outline in Figure 8, video games have pros and cons. Jim suggests limiting video game time to a maximum of 2 hours on the weekend and 30 minutes on weekdays, if at all. We do not endorse allowing children to play without limits.

Clearly defining the amount of game time, rules for stopping, and consequences for arguing are important. Children with ADHD don't like new rules or things sprung on them, so with video games, and in everything you do, try to establish guidelines and procedures beforehand.

Children are becoming increasingly savvy about technology. As daunting as it may seem, it is your parental responsibility to stay abreast of the latest trends in social media and how to utilize parental controls to monitor how your elementary child is connecting with others. Many handheld devices, such as the Kindle Fire, have the ability to limit or time children as they play. It is important to know the passwords your daughter uses on social media or online accounts and make sure they are clear about how to recognize intimidation, bullies, and predators over the Internet.

Pros	Cons
Can be used as a reinforcement tool	May hyperfocus on the game
Some games promote physical or mental exercise	Some games are violent
Can develop hand-eye coordination	May become emotional or defiant when it's time to stop
May become a hobby that leads to employment	Video games can be expensive
May build focus and concentration	May spend too much time gaming
May build feelings of success	May engage in less physical activity and have fewer opportunities for socialization

Figure 8. Pros and cons of video games. *Note.* From *Raising Boys With ADHD* (p. 137) by J. W. Forgan and M. A. Richey, 2012, Waco, TX: Prufrock Press. Copyright 2012 by Prufrock Press. Reprinted with permission.

Self-Esteem

Think about your daughter's self-esteem. Does she appear to feel good about herself, or is she down in the dumps? When we complete an evaluation with clients, we believe it is important to assess a girl's self-esteem as part of the total process. Some psychologists see self-esteem as inconsequential, but we believe that if a girl has low self-esteem, then it permeates all areas of her life. If you work with a psychologist, our recommendation is to choose one who will assess your daughter's self-esteem. In our practices, we use a self-esteem measure that each girl completes independently.

If your daughter's self-esteem appears solid, you are fortunate. Her self-esteem will help provide her with the confidence she needs to navigate life. Continue to nurture her self-esteem, because it can give her a sense of resiliency, which she'll need to bounce back when she has a setback or challenge. Girls who do not develop a strong sense of self in elementary school may become overly sensitive and retiring as teens, making them more of a target for being ostracized or bullied. Good self-esteem will allow her to stand up, brush herself off, and try again—a key to success. This is an invaluable quality to develop. If you want to learn more about instilling this sense of resiliency in your daughter, we recommend *Raising Resilient Children: Fostering Strength, Hope, and Optimism in Your Child* by Drs. Robert Brooks and Sam Goldstein, because it is full of ideas for developing resiliency and self-esteem. *The Girl Guide* by Christine Fonseca is also a valuable resource, written for girls ages 10–14.

The self-esteem of many girls with ADHD is low. It can become low because of repeated failures, constant reprimands from adults, teasing from peers, or just because of the way she is wired. What we call "global self-esteem" comprises your daughter's behavior, anxiety, popularity, self-image, and general satisfaction in life. You may find your daughter's self-esteem is high in one area and lower in other areas. We find that many girls with ADHD feel nervous about school-related tasks such as taking a test or being called on by the teacher. Sometimes they act up in school and become the class clown to try to build confidence by making people laugh.

Your daughter's low self-esteem stifles her decision-making ability. Some girls with ADHD can't make even the simplest decisions. If your daughter thinks poorly of herself, then over time she may become anxious, frustrated, or depressed. These depressed thoughts create depressed actions, which lead to poor performance. Unchecked, it can become a difficult cycle to end.

If your daughter has low self-esteem, her automatic reaction to a new task that appears challenging is probably, "I can't." For many girls with ADHD, this "I can't" attitude turns into what professionals call "learned helplessness." Your daughter learns that it benefits her to become helpless. This develops over a period of time, because when your daughter automatically says, "I can't," many parents and teachers spring to complete the task for her. What you must do is determine if your daughter's problem is an "I can't" or an "I won't" type of problem. This allows you to decide how quickly you should step in to help. If it is an "I won't" problem, then you need to wait and let her try to work through it on her own. If the problem is "I can't," then you should step in, provide instruction, and step away to let her try. You want to do this to teach your daughter an "I can and I will" attitude.

You can help strengthen your daughter's self-esteem by affirming her in front of others. So often we reprimand and correct our daughters around other people, but we affirm them much less. Regardless of her age, your daughter needs to hear your encouragement and positive reinforcement, and she needs others to hear you giving it to her. She needs to hear you say statements like, "I'm proud of you. Your performance was awesome. You have a great heart. I love you." If parents don't affirm their daughter in this way, then she may find another way to get that affirmation, usually from peers or by engaging in dangerous behaviors. Build your child up by telling family or friends a positive story about her, send them an e-mail with a photo or a great story about her, or simply send her a note in her lunch box that she can read.

These are additional suggestions you can use to help develop your daughter's self-esteem:

◊ When age appropriate, explain her ADHD and help her understand it.

◊ Read age-appropriate books about self-esteem with your daughter. Search online booksellers with keywords such as "self-esteem children."

◊ Engage her in extracurricular activities (e.g., music, art, drama, sports, computers) where she can find success.

◊ Be aware of your positive-to-negative comment ratio, and increase your genuine praise.

◊ Comment on her positive qualities rather than her negative ones.

◇ Try to reduce family conflict by establishing routine, consistency, and structure.

◇ Help her identify and build at least one good friendship.

◇ Try to help her establish a positive relationship with her teacher.

◇ Identify a mentor (e.g., at school, within a club or other organization) who takes a special interest in your daughter and helps build her up.

◇ Work with a counselor.

Points to Consider

1. You can expect the elementary years to be challenging for you and your daughter. The demands of school shine a new spotlight on her deficits in executive functioning skills and her difficulties with behavior, attention, and social skills. Do you recognize these weaknesses?

2. Are you keeping a problem-solving perspective? Seek professional help when necessary and never give up.

3. How involved are you? Your daughter needs you to be involved at school to advocate for her and to work with her teachers to create interventions that will help her succeed at this critical time in her life.

4. Because your daughter is different than every other girl with ADHD, she requires interventions tailored to her needs. What do you have in place for her?

5. Is your daughter in a school and classroom where her needs are being met?

6. Your daughter's challenges spill over into family and community life. Are you helping her be her best self?

7. How is your daughter's self-esteem? What steps are you taking to develop her confidence? Are you providing supports to help her grow in her ability to self-regulate her behavior?

8. Review your self-assessment responses to decide if there are any areas where you still need to learn more.

Action Steps to Take Now

1. If you have not already done so, establish daily (or at least weekly) communication with your daughter's teacher.

2. Monitor your daughter's academic progress. Supplement where necessary.

3. Make sure you have a workable homework plan in place.

4. Try some of the techniques in this chapter to create a healthy home and community environment for your daughter.

5. Complete Step 3 in the Dynamic Action Plan.

Chapter 5

The Teenage Years

SELF-ASSESSMENT: Where Am I Now?

Each self-assessment helps you reflect on your daughter and your parenting practices and is a preview of the chapter's content.

1. When I think about my teenage daughter, I believe . . .

   a. She acts older than her chronological age.

   b. She acts younger than her chronological age.

   c. She acts her age.

   d. Her actions vary from day to day.

2. My daughter's organizational skills are . . .

   a. In need of a lot of work.

   b. Good enough to get by but could use some strengthening.

    c.   One of her strong points.

    d.   I don't know.

3.   When I think about my daughter's school . . .

    a.   We have her schedule optimized for the way ADHD affects her and accommodations in place.

    b.   She has an OK schedule, but we need to review her accommodations.

    c.   We need to have a school meeting ASAP to review everything.

    d.   My daughter does not want me involved in her school life.

4.   My daughter's study skills . . .

    a.   Are one of her strengths.

    b.   Are OK but could be improved.

    c.   Are nonexistent.

    d.   Are something we are working on now.

5.   My daughter's mood is . . .

    a.   Consistent.

    b.   Typical for a teenage girl.

    c.   Ever changing.

    d.   Out of control.

You're beginning to get more and more frequent glimpses of the young woman your daughter is becoming. She's growing out of her little-girl body, and that's as beautiful as it is unsettling—maybe to both of you. She wants independence, possibly more than you think she can handle. You worry for her well-being, both physically and emotionally, as her world gets bigger.

Your daughter's teenage years will test your limits and fortitude. Remember the Terrible Twos? With a scowl and a stamp of her little foot, she'd defy you with a pouty, "NO!" You can expect the teen years to be a bit like that. Her snippy attitude (maybe you've noticed it) is her way of saying, "I'm not a child. I can think for myself, and I want the freedom to make my own choices." At the same time, though, she's still unsteady and uncertain. She needs you to be consistent, fair, and compassionate, even if she's inconsistent, reactive, and insensitive. You're going to need to help her learn to navigate everything—school, nice girls, mean girls, hormones, sexuality, dating, driving, jobs—within the context of her ADHD.

You can expect that this will be a time of tremendous growth, but not just for your daughter. As she learns to become an independent young woman, your role transitions as well. You'll continue to be her biggest fan, her advisor, and her sounding board. But now, it's also your job to look for ways to start letting go.

If Your Daughter Was Recently Diagnosed

For many girls, ADHD isn't formally diagnosed until their tweens or teens. As you've already learned, boys with ADHD are simply easier to spot in elementary school classrooms, as hyperactive behavior draws more attention and more intervention (Nussbaum, 2012). Girls, however, tend to be quieter and better able to mask the kinds of difficulties ADHD causes. Also, ADHD in girls tends to be of the inattentive variety, which tends to be overlooked— sometimes until middle school, high school, or even adulthood.

If your daughter is one of these young women, ADHD is a new world for you. Neither of you have had years to implement the strategies, learning systems, or routines that will help her in a complex world. She may be scared or angry at the new label she's now asked to wear. She may also feel relief in knowing she has ADHD. At the debriefing meeting where she got her ADHD diagnosis, ninth-grader Ellen said, "I always knew there was something. I'm just glad I'm not dumb." The results seemed to validate her inner inkling that she needed more support.

ADHD and Executive Function

You can drive a car without understanding a thing about pistons and connecting rods. Likewise, you can help your daughter with ADHD without much of a grasp on the science behind it. But it will help you immensely if you can take a few minutes to review the concept of executive function and the role it plays in your daughter's diagnosis. You'll come to understand the brain of a girl with ADHD, and you'll be able to see a bit more clearly why your daughter struggles in some areas.

Consider this notion: The act of paying attention is actually the result of an intricate and complicated interaction between many regions of the brain and the emotions. Among other things, the prefrontal region of your daughter's brain governs what we call executive functioning. Here's a breakdown:

◊ *Defining and setting goals, and then breaking them down into a plan with manageable steps.* You already know your daughter may have a hard time getting started with . . . well, you fill in the blank. Completing a science project or her English homework. Emptying the dishwasher. Packing for a sleepover. She may know what she needs to do, and she may really want or intend to get it done. But she has an especially difficult time figuring out which part of the task to do first, and how to proceed once she's gotten started. Organization skills are a key part of this process, and she may find it overwhelming to try to organize her thoughts, her possessions, and her surroundings.

◊ *Paying attention and shifting focus as necessary.* It's likely your daughter may be especially easily distracted and unable to screen out the sounds, sights, smells, and other stimuli that are competing for her attention. Likewise, she may become so focused on one aspect of a project or activity that she can't move on to the next; she gets mired in the details.

◊ *Managing frustrations, and showing emotional flexibility.* In general, people with ADHD have a low tolerance for frustration and may show deeper sensitivity to emotional events. As Dr. Thomas Brown wrote in a 2008 edition of *Attention* magazine, "Many with ADD syndrome describe the following aspect of emotional experience: a feeling that emotion floods one's mind, taking up all available space" (p. 16). Once her emotions are triggered, your daughter may have an extraordinarily difficult time moving past the incident. Others may be able to adapt to disappointment, criticism, or frustration. Instead, she reacts.

◊ *Staying alert and focused.* Has your daughter ever mentioned that she feels sleepy when she has to sit still and be quiet, as she might when in class or reading a book? It's not unusual. People with ADHD show a chronic inability to stay alert in those kinds of environments. Your daughter isn't necessarily tired; her brain just tells her she is. Also, individuals with ADHD have been shown to display much slower processing speed than the general population, particularly when it comes to writing (Levine, 2003). Not only is it hard for your daughter to stay focused and on task for what seems like a simple assignment (e.g., write a paragraph describing the plot of this book), but it takes her a long, long time. It can be frustrating, bordering on excruciating, for a parent to watch. Again, remember that her brain is the traffic cop here, and there's a good chance it's slowing her down.

◊ *Working memory relates to the ability to process, store, and recall information in order to complete a task.* This is a complex brain function that we rely on nearly every moment of every day; our working memory is like the search engine of the brain. When you're dialing a telephone, you need to remember the name of the person you're calling and the reason for the call, and you need to have that information at your fingertips when they answer. If you get the person's voicemail, you need to remember all that information, plus you need to remember how to leave a polite, complete message. It's not hard for a person with fully functioning working memory to do this, or to solve a math problem, summarize a magazine article, or make a cake. But many people with ADHD struggle with working memory and simply aren't able to access information they need to do a job or complete a task, even if they knew that information 3 minutes ago.

◊ *Self-monitoring allows an individual to control her own behavior in socially acceptable ways.* It's a function that requires an individual not only to monitor herself, but to notice the impact she is having on the people around her. Some girls with ADHD may struggle in social settings because they can't hold back inappropriate outbursts. They talk nonstop and don't realize how annoyed others are becoming. On the other extreme, they may be so self-conscious that they withdraw from social interactions entirely for fear of making a mistake. Her brain restricts her impulses too much, or not enough.

Back to the science. Because the prefrontal area of the brain is one of the last to mature, it's not unusual for many teenagers to take a while to fully develop the kind of executive functioning abilities that will allow them to operate in the real world. Neuropathologists have determined that individuals with ADHD demonstrate reduced activity in the frontal and striatal regions of the brain, even into their adult years (Nussbaum, 2012). Additionally, girls with ADHD have been shown to have smaller volume in several regions of the brain than other girls. Those size differences have been found to have a direct correlation to the severity of ADHD symptoms (Castellanos et al., 2001).

In other words, the regions of your daughter's brain that have been affected by delayed or otherwise atypical development are the very same ones that govern impulse control, attention, alertness, focus, recall, and emotional balance. It's the medical, physiological reason she struggles.

Gender plays a role, too. It's not surprising that boys' brains and girls' brains develop differently, and that major changes occur in the brain during adolescence. Those differences may account for the increase in the number of teenage girls diagnosed with ADHD for the first time, and the fact that girls are far less likely to demonstrate hyperactive/impulsive symptoms than boys (Nussbaum, 2012). For many decades, most of what we knew about ADHD came from research into the "boy variety." Your daughter's brain is different, and her ADHD will be different, too. For the rest of this chapter, we'll look at how ADHD may show up in your daughter's life. We want you to be informed parents, even as she starts to manage her ADHD on her own. Here's what's ahead:

◊ Section 1: School (the challenges, the changes, and the ways you can help your daughter succeed).
◊ Section 2: Community Issues (her relationships with family and friends, dating, driving, money, jobs).
◊ Section 3: Your Daughter's Physical and Emotional Health.

We hope you'll find all three sections valuable, but we're hoping you pay special attention to the final section. She's undergoing profound physical changes as her body matures. Often burdened by acceptance issues and impulse-control problems, girls with ADHD often engage in risky sexual behavior that you'll want to help your daughter avoid. Your daughter's ADHD also carries with it a greater likelihood that she may also experience depression, anxiety, eating disorders, self-injury, and/or low self-esteem. As a community, we're just starting to understand the complex nature of ADHD in young women. New research has shown that over the long term, ADHD in adolescent girls is a persistent disorder with symptoms that can carry into adulthood (Biederman, Petty, O'Connor, Hyder, & Faraone, 2011). Some of what you read in this final section may come as a shock to you, and we want you to be prepared without being scared.

School

Your daughter has many strengths that she'll take into her middle school and high school experience. Remind her of this, and take the time to explore areas you may not have considered before. Is she an especially sharp observer? Does she have an exceptional memory for intricate details? Is she gifted in music or art or math? More and more, she'll have opportunities to use and develop her special talents and abilities. Everyone's different, but certain strengths have been identified in many individuals with ADHD. Maybe your daughter falls among them, if she's:

◊ a creative thinker,
◊ a good negotiator,
◊ highly intelligent,
◊ willing to take a risk to achieve a positive outcome,
◊ intuitive and perceptive, and
◊ able to focus intently on a subject or topic of extreme interest.

As a student with ADHD enters the upper grades, teachers and parents often dwell on the struggles she's likely to encounter. It's important that you regularly remind your daughter of how she's unique. Encourage her to find ways to use and develop her natural gifts in the more adult world she's about to enter.

And it *is* a more adult world. In elementary school, the focus is often on the child. In middle school, the focus moves away from the student and onto the curriculum. With her ADHD, your daughter may have trouble remembering things, paying attention, organizing her time, and balancing her emotions. Success in higher education requires memory, attention, organization, and self-control—the very things that can be so difficult when you have ADHD.

As schoolwork gets more challenging and demands grow greater, the performance gap between students with ADHD and their friends without ADHD tends to widen. That can begin to happen in middle school. Sometimes, it doesn't manifest itself until high school, where there's even more to juggle, a quicker pace, and often, a less-friendly schedule. So, just as you've worked hard to make your daughter's elementary years unique, you and she need to form a team to tailor her middle school and high school educational experience.

Middle School

Middle school will offer a chance for your daughter to grow, to make different friends, and to try interesting things. As she leaves the more nurturing environment of elementary school, you naturally hope her past successes will carry over into this new learning environment. She'll hopefully be surrounded by people who are going to be eager to give her a chance to shine. If she's experienced frustrations or problems before, it's a chance for her to start fresh.

Your daughter probably takes a lot of cues from you. It's a big step, but if your first response is fear, it's very likely you'll convey that to her, and she'll become worried and nervous, too. It's true that there will be challenges—there will *always* be challenges for a girl with ADHD and for her parents. But do your best to reassure her that you're prepared, and that she will be too.

Multiple teachers. This may be the first time your daughter is changing classes and having more than one primary teacher.

Suddenly, keeping in close communication with your daughter's school just got six or seven times harder. How will you manage it?

Many parents begin planning the transition to middle school many months in advance. You may request to meet with school administrators and guidance counselors to discuss the curriculum and teacher selection and to let your daughter introduce herself. More and more, your daughter needs to be involved in school meetings and speak on her own behalf. This will be easier for some students than others. Still, encourage your daughter to contribute. It's a skill she'll need to practice.

You may find you have less input on teacher selection as your daughter moves into the upper grades. Instead of making specific requests, you may wish to express your preference that your daughter be assigned to a specific "type" of teacher, like a highly organized or an energetic teacher. This won't only benefit your daughter but in the long run, the teacher and the class as well.

Generally, girls with ADHD do better with teachers who are willing to go the extra mile to help a student succeed. Some characteristics you might look for in a teacher include being:

◇ *Flexible.* This teacher grants extensions when your daughter misunderstands a homework assignment, leaves her work at home, or simply forgets to do it.

◇ *Open to modifying assignments.* This teacher understands that the goal is to have the student grasp ideas and concepts. If a student struggles with a long essay but can demonstrate command of the material another way, like making a video or an art project, this teacher is willing to let her do so.

◇ *Knowledgeable about ADHD.* Some teachers have far greater understanding of the disability and what to expect of a student with ADHD.

◇ *Attentive.* This teacher takes note when students seem to be falling behind and alerts their parents. This is especially important when a student has ADHD and may not remember to keep her parents updated when she's having trouble.

◊ *Cooperative.* Some teachers are very willing to work with parents. Keeping lines of communication open remains important in middle school. Your daughter with ADHD probably hasn't learned all of the skills she needs to be her own advocate. You'll need to stay in close touch with all of her teachers as much as possible.

Maintaining communication with multiple teachers doesn't have to be the overwhelming task it sounds. You will, however, have to do a little homework. We suggest taking the time to learn how each of your daughter's teachers prefers to communicate and honoring that. One may have office hours on Fridays between 10 a.m. and noon. Another may wish to receive only e-mails or text messages. One may give you his cell phone number and invite you to call any time.

Be sure to establish a courteous, respectful relationship with your daughter's teachers and with the school's administration and guidance staff. Get to know them, and show your appreciation for the jobs they do. Together, you can form a powerful partnership on your daughter's behalf.

More classes, more work. In the confusion of changing from one classroom to the next, having to find books and notebooks and reports in her locker, and getting the right books in her backpack to take to the right classes, how's a girl with ADHD supposed to manage during the day? And what about Thursday night at 9:30, when she mentions the blockbuster science project that's due the next day? Here are a few coping skills:

◊ *Establish a routine.* Before school starts, get permission to walk the halls with your daughter. Map out a route for her daily schedule. Together, determine when it makes sense for her stop at her locker to drop off and pick up books.

Color-coding books and notebooks can help her know at a glance what she needs for each class.

◊ *Enlist a "coach."* Someone at school may be willing to serve as your daughter's coach or mentor. This could be a favorite teacher, her homeroom teacher, a guidance counselor, or a teacher's aide. This person's role would be to help your daughter stay organized while at school and stay ahead of assignments and coursework. Your daughter and her coach may need to meet in the morning and again before the end of the day, once a day, or weekly. You'll know your daughter will have a little extra help staying on track. You'll also feel more confident that any small problems will be flagged before they become big problems.

◊ *Find out about big projects early.* Your daughter may be studying a half-dozen subjects with a half-dozen different teachers. There's a good chance you won't be kept personally informed on every single homework assignment. Keeping track of those needs to be her job. But you may wish to ask about any larger or more complex projects your daughter will be expected to complete during the semester or year. Girls with ADHD have a more difficult time with long-term planning and organizing multiple components. Larger school projects are going to require you and your daughter to establish a game plan. For the sake of your family harmony, you want to avoid unpleasant surprises— like learning about a 10-page paper with accompanying 3-D maps and video—the night before they're due.

Setting reasonable expectations. You have a right to have expectations of your daughter. She has a right to expect certain things of you, too. Your daughter isn't perfect. You can't demand more than she's equipped to give. At the same time, don't ever expect complete failure. Most of all, don't assume that the things your daughter does are deliberately designed to drive you crazy. They're not.

What's reasonable to ask of your daughter? As she goes through middle school, you can make it clear that she is required to:

◊ Complete her homework on time, without a struggle.
◊ Get acceptable grades. You need to define, together, what acceptable looks like. If she's extremely gifted in one subject, she might be expected to maintain an A average in that class. In other areas, a solid C might represent success.

What's reasonable for your daughter to ask of you?

◊ Begin to release control. Allow her to make some mistakes, understanding that children with ADHD tend to take quite a bit longer to learn from their mistakes. Be patient. She will learn.
◊ Trust her. When she demonstrates that she can handle a little responsibility, allow her a little more.

Dealing with cyberbullying. Just when you thought you had more than you could handle, a new danger pops up requiring your attention and vigilance—cyberbullying. It is defined as sending or posting mean, embarrassing, or threatening texts or images over the Internet via computer, cell phone, or iPads/tablets. It can happen on social networking sites, in chat rooms, on message boards, via text message or Twitter, or on Snap Chat, the most difficult of all to monitor.

In her 2009 testimony before the U.S. House of Representatives, Nancy Willard, Director of the Center for Safe and Responsible Internet Use, said, "The young people who are at the greatest risk online are the ones who are already at greater risk in the real world." Risk factors include vulnerable, socially naïve, or unpopular teens; youth who have impaired relations with parents and/or peers; and those who suffer from depression, anxiety, or are fearful (Feinberg & Robey, 2009). The emotional impact of cyberbullying can be significant. Many girls are reluctant to report the incident out of fear, embarrassment, or guilt that they may have brought it on themselves or out of concern that their phones or online activities will be curtailed. If it happens to your daughter, your support and understanding will be important.

Steps your daughter should take with your support if she is the victim of cyberbullying:

◊ Discuss the incident immediately with a trusted adult so the next step can be formulated. It may be important for the adult to contact the parents of the cyberbully, depending on the circumstances.

◊ Make a hard copy of the material posted, whether it is a screen shot, photo, e-mail, or text message. Record the dates, times, and circumstances.

◊ Don't respond to the message and don't forward it.

◊ Remove the offensive material if possible and block the cyberbully.

◊ Do not try to bully those who have bullied her.

◊ File a complaint with the website, Internet service provider, or cell phone company so they can take action against the person abusing terms of service.

◊ Contact the police if the cyberbullying includes threats of bodily harm or hate-motivated violence.

What you can do to manage the threat of cyberbullying:

◊ Encourage use of computers and devices in family areas when possible.

◊ Keep lines of communication open with your daughter about her online activities.

◊ Make sure your daughter understands what cyberbullying is and what the serious ramifications can be.

◊ Encourage your daughter to tell you or a trusted adult immediately when she becomes aware of cyberbullying.

◊ Be actively involved in your daughter's online activity. Have access to her online communication and review it if there is reason for concern.

◊ Visit social media safety centers to learn how to block users and change settings to control who can contact your daughter.

◊ Install parental control filtering software and/or tracking programs.

◊ Be aware of signs your daughter may be bullied, such as withdrawing from activities, becoming moody and sullen, or being reluctant to use the computer or refusing to go to school.

Keep abreast of trends and new developments by visiting social media safety centers, such as Stop Bullying, a governmental website (http://www.stopbullying.gov).

High School

Much of what we've written about middle school holds true for high school as well. The academic and social challenges continue to increase year by year, and by this point, your daughter's ADHD symptoms may become increasingly more well-defined. But these are the years when a young person moves into independence and self-reliance. It's no different for a teen with ADHD, just more challenging in many ways. In fact, it may be even *more* crucial that your daughter learn to advocate for herself. This will be a major step for both of you, one of many during the teen years. But remember, your primary job as a parent isn't just to get your daughter with ADHD through school. It's to prepare your girl to be a strong, self-assured young woman.

Self-advocacy. From the time they enter high school, we believe students should be present at all meetings that concern their disability. There may be obvious exceptions—conferences when other students' privacy is at issue. But your daughter is now old enough to be part of the discussion, and you need to let her answer the questions that pertain to her. Resist the urge to answer for her. As she becomes more comfortable in this role, it's possible she may attend such meetings without you.

It is appropriate for your daughter to initiate discussions with her teachers about her ADHD. Many teachers respond well when a student approaches them directly about a disability. She should be prepared to describe what ADHD means for her—what it might look like in the classroom, the kinds of assignments that have been hard for her in the past, and what's helped her succeed. It might go something like this:

> Mrs. Nelson? Can I talk to you for a couple minutes? I don't know if you know this, but I have ADHD. For me that means I have trouble paying attention and remembering things. Sometimes in class you might see me daydreaming, and it's sometimes really hard for me to remember what we've already learned. It's not because I'm not interested or because I don't want to learn. It's because I have a really hard time focusing and holding onto information. I have a 504 plan and last year in history, Mrs. Williams gave me a copy of her notes before every class. That really helped me pay attention better. I have other accommodations on my plan like extra time on tests and assignments. These things really help me and I know they will help me in your class too. I don't mind talking about my ADHD, so do you have any questions for me?

Much of this, of course, depends on the severity of your daughter's ADHD and whether she has any additional learning disabilities that may require your more active involvement. And please don't misunderstand. We're not suggesting you abandon your daughter and let her figure out everything on her own. Nationwide, educators report that lack of parental involvement is a major frustration and causes setbacks for children with ADHD. By reading this book, you've already proven yourself to be a concerned and caring parent. We're simply advising you to step back when it's appropriate to do so and see how your daughter does when she gets the chance to take the reins. This will build skills for college and the workplace. Jennifer explained how she helped her teenage daughter, Kali. "At the beginning of the year we explained her IEP accommodations. We reminded her during the school year to use these accommodations. Kali also sat in on a recent IEP meeting to talk about what she believes she needs to succeed."

Sleep and the high school student. Most current research shows that a typical teenager's body is designed to stay up late into the night and sleep well into the morning. Our school systems, on the other hand, still run on up-with-the-chickens time. In many parts of the country, high school students are in class by 7 a.m. Studies suggest that half of all teens with ADHD have additional sleep challenges. They report finding it hard to quiet their brains and go to sleep. Their sleep can be restless, or they may wake frequently in the night. They often feel tired in the morning.

Your daughter can't learn well if she can't get proper rest. In addition to trying common-sense procedures at bedtime (e.g., no caffeine, no cell phones or texting, no video games), you might explore the following:

◊ *Establish a reasonable bedtime.* Talk this through. For instance, your daughter may observe that she usually feels tired at about 10 but gets a "second wind" after 11. Together, you'll probably see that it would be wise for her to get to bed by 10:30 or 10:45.

◊ *Don't start projects after a certain time.* Whether they're school-related or just for fun, big projects can make a person with ADHD lose track of time. If she becomes absorbed, she might look up to see that it's 3 a.m.

◊ *Get plenty of exercise.* There's a lot to be said for taking a bike ride, a swim, or a run after school. A tired body sleeps better.

◊ *Arrange the school schedule to avoid your daughter's typical groggy times.* It may be possible to set up her school day so she has nonacademic classes (e.g., P.E., art, music) early in the morning, while she's waking up. Or schedule them for the end of the day if she tends to run out of steam.

Clubs and sports. Extracurricular activities are a valuable part of the middle school and high school experience. Surrounded by girls and boys with similar interests, your daughter will have the chance to make new friends. This is especially important for those teenagers with ADHD who struggle in social situations. She'll gain a sense of belonging. Her life will become more balanced as she gets to turn her focus temporarily from the challenges of school and homework.

We encourage parents to let their daughters explore a wide range of activities, though not all at once. Try new things one or two at a time, and see what works for your daughter and your family. If a particular activity, group, or sport isn't a good fit, require that your daughter fulfill her commitment and then move on to something else. We've put together some guidelines for you and your daughter to consider:

◊ We find that many girls with ADHD love to draw, paint, sing, or act. These are wonderful activities that encourage self-expression and help her keep emotions from getting bottled up inside her. You can be her biggest fan in creative pursuits, displaying her work or taking her to galleries, plays, and concerts. Sharing a common love of the arts can be a powerful relationship builder.

◊ Remember that every added activity is one more thing for your daughter's daily planner, and one more thing for her to remember. You probably already know that overloading a child with ADHD is a bad idea. Remember this when you're thumbing through her school's activity booklet or reading your city's online recreation flyer.

◊ Every child is different, and your daughter may be an exceptional athlete. But hand-eye coordination often tends to be less developed in girls with ADHD. This can make some team sports—like softball or volleyball—a challenge because they require agility in catching, throwing, and hitting. Your daughter may have more success in sports that emphasize gross motor skills—swimming or running, for instance.

Homework. Think for a minute of the executive functioning skills required for efficient homework management:

◊ Organizing large projects into smaller steps.

◊ Retaining focus on work your daughter may find both uninteresting and difficult.

◊ Storing, recalling, and processing information she's already learned.

These are the very same functions that are compromised in an individual with ADHD. You want to help your daughter recognize that homework isn't something to be feared or avoided, but a necessary part of her education. Homework isn't an option, but it doesn't need to be an ordeal.

If you've already spent years sitting beside your daughter at homework time, you're ready to turn the responsibility over to her. You're eager to help her develop a study routine that works. If you have a middle schooler, this may be a gradual transition, but the goal is to have your daughter be as self-directed as possible.

Getting her off to a good start. Helping your daughter get organized is the first step. Far more than their friends without ADHD, teens with ADHD need a way to keep track of every assignment, every report, every project, every swim meet, and every band rehearsal. Help your daughter set up a homework area so all of the supplies she'll need will be within reach of a quiet, comfortable place she chooses.

We also suggest that you and your daughter spend some time brainstorming about an age-appropriate planner system she finds workable and interesting. Go shopping together and see what makes sense to both of you, based on her needs. *What* you get is far less important than *how* she uses it and *how faithfully* she uses it.

Girls with ADHD tend to procrastinate. But to her, it won't seem like procrastination at all. She'll be very busy trying to create some sense of order in the mass of papers in her backpack and on her desk, or even just clearing a space to work. She calls a friend to get a homework assignment and they talk for a half-hour. She does an online search for a definition, which leads her to a cool website on the subject, which eventually leads her to YouTube. An hour has passed, and she's no closer to finishing her work. You and she need to collaborate on creating a system so she won't have to spend a lot of time thinking about how to get started on homework—she'll just do it. Here are some guidelines:

◊ Let her set the time she's going to do her homework every day. Help her find a way to stick to it, whether it's by using an alarm on her watch, a computer alert, or some other reminder.

◊ Encourage your daughter to tackle her more difficult (or least favorite) homework assignments first.

◊ It's important that she be able to take short breaks. It may be effective for your daughter to set small goals for herself (e.g., read one section, do 10 problems) and then assess whether she's fresh enough to continue. If she is, she sets another small goal. If not, she takes a short timed break. If your daughter is prone to forgetting the books she needs, investigate whether you can borrow or buy an extra set of textbooks for your home. Perhaps the textbook can be found in a digital version online.

Studying. Often, girls with ADHD will confuse preparing with studying. An example: Your daughter may be very proud of the flashcards she painstakingly prepared for her geometry class. But if she doesn't then study the flashcards and learn the material, those cards really haven't served their purpose. The older your daughter, the more she needs to be involved in working with her teachers so she'll understand what she needs to study and in what depth. Here are some suggestions we've found helpful:

◊ *Ask the teacher for a study guide.* This can include a reading schedule and which content is to be covered in every class, and it will help keep her from falling behind.

◊ *When possible, find out the format for upcoming tests and quizzes.* Your daughter will need to study differently for an essay test than she will for a multiple-choice test. Some girls are extremely hesitant to approach a teacher for this information, but remind her that it's an important part of self-advocacy. She's not asking for the answers. She's asking for information about testing procedures.

◊ *Working in groups can be effective for many girls with ADHD.* See if your daughter can organize a study group of friends. They can help remind her of work requirements, and participating in discussions of the material will help her learn.

The following suggestions can help your daughter develop good study habits:

◊ Studying in smaller time blocks is better than studying for an extended period of time.

◊ Take breaks when you feel fatigued.

◊ Try to study at the same time each day.

◊ Try to set realistic goals for studying, such as, "I'll memorize these 15 vocabulary words and then take a break."

◊ Avoid procrastination and begin studying at the time you planned to start.

◊ Work on your most difficult assignment first.

◊ Study in sequence. Only study one subject at a time or you will confuse yourself.

◊ Review notes before beginning an assignment.

◊ Avoid the temptation to study with social media sites open on your computer. You'll accomplish less if you are distracted by these websites.

Extra help. Organization and routine still may not be enough. If your daughter continues to have trouble grasping course content or needs hours and hours to finish her homework, it may be time to bring in reinforcements. You want to be her loving parent, not a sentry who keeps her locked in her room at night slaving over her desk. Some solutions include:

◊ *A tutor.* If you can afford it, this is often a wonderful option for a student with ADHD. The one-on-one attention helps her maintain focus, and talking through the material is an effective learning method when a student has ADHD. Teachers and education professionals are obvious choices, but sometimes a special neighbor or college student can make a great tutor. A gifted tutor can build a strong relationship with your daughter, will see her value, and help her realize her abilities. No less important, if there are struggles over homework, then they're on someone else's watch. You're not the bad guy anymore.

◊ *An accommodation plan.* If your daughter is laboring over the sheer amount of homework she is given, then ask her teachers about reducing her workload. With the appropriate paperwork (discussed in Chapter 6), she may be eligible for an accommodation plan. It may be acceptable for her to complete only the even-numbered math problems, for example, as long as she can demonstrate mastery of the concepts.

◊ *A deadline extension:* Occasionally, your daughter may need to ask for extra time to complete an assignment. If this is part of her accommodation plan, then it's already available for her to use. We stress that this should be the exception, rather than the rule. Many students with ADHD tend to put things off, and being given extra time simply means their work piles up even more.

Planning for college and career. Your daughter's high school years are the time for both of you to shift your focus from what's immediately before you to the future—college, career, life plans. It's a time for the boundaries to expand again.

In high school, your daughter will be given the opportunity to choose the classes and electives she wants to take. She'll start to consider where—and whether—to go to college. She'll think about what she wants to do for a living. She'll need your guidance, along with the input of other wise mentors.

Encourage your daughter to think about college early, even during her freshman year. She'll feel your support, and it will help keep her focused on her goals and the reasons she continues to work so hard in high school. One of our young clients offered this advice to other teens:

> Use college as a goal for motivation. You have one part of your brain that says give up, but the other half says you'll feel worse if you give up so you have to try your best. You have to identify where you are, identify what you want, and figure out how you are going to get there. Think of it as having a master plan.

There are two web-based tools you can use with your daughter if she is uncertain about her interests and future career possibilities. One is the Self Directed Search by PAR Industries (http://www.self-directed-search.com). This search is a tool to help your daughter discover the majors, fields of study, and potential jobs that match her interests. After completing the survey, you'll instantly receive a written report that matches her personality type to potential occupations. Each occupation is linked to the *Occupational Information Network* database, which lists specific details about education, job requirements, employment outlook, and salary. This information is useful for researching a career in greater detail.

If your daughter needs help identifying her natural strengths and talents, a second web-based tool is the Kolbe Y Index for Youth (http://www.kolbe.com). This is an online survey that also produces a written report for the student and parent. Once completed, you daughter can learn how to use her natural talents to excel in school and life. Ideally, parents and teens would discuss the results together and then incorporate them into the Dynamic Action Plan.

Have her make a list of target and/or dream colleges. Not 20 schools. A half-dozen, maybe, and talk about why she's interested in them. Be objective and realistic. For instance, going to school near the beach is a legitimate draw for a young person, but it might not quite match what you're looking for in a curriculum. Make an appointment for the two of you to sit down with your daughter's high school guidance counselor and talk about what it's going to take to get into her target colleges.

Visit as many schools as possible. Just being on campus, sitting in on classes, and talking to students will help your daughter see that college isn't just an extension of high school. It's a different world. She'll need different, new skills.

Begin to coach her on the life skills she'll need. If she doesn't already know how, teach her to do her own laundry. Let her begin to navigate bureaucracy herself. She'll need to do those kinds of things, and many more, at college and when she's out on her own.

One great way to teach her life skills is by planning a trip together and teaching her the responsibility of taking care of details.

Help her stay on track with her classes. Teens with ADHD sometimes make impulsive choices. A student with ADHD might decide to take a class not because she's interested in it, but because her best friend is going to be in the class. In high school, the choices your daughter makes about her curriculum will start to affect her potential for admission to college in general, and to the colleges of her choice. She needs to understand what goes into wise, long-term decision making.

Her career options. We feel strongly about this point: There are no careers that a woman with ADHD can't do. Some of the best publications on ADHD, such as *ADDitude* magazine and *Attention* magazine, regularly publish profiles of highly successful women with ADHD across a range of industries, from medicine to law to business to entertainment and the arts. Your daughter needs to understand that fulfilling careers result from a combination of talent, dedication, passion, and a great deal of hard work.

Even in college, your daughter will benefit from your career guidance, as long as it's positive. Some thoughts:

◊ Help her find a job-shadowing program or volunteer opportunities in the field or fields she's interested in, so she can discover for herself whether it's work she does well. Don't discourage her because you think a particular career isn't a good fit for someone with ADHD.

◊ Suggest she visit her school's career center, where she might receive one-on-one career counseling.

◊ Make sure she's aware of the interest and career assessment tools discussed above. These kinds of assessments can help pinpoint your daughter's personality traits, talents, and interests, and match them to careers that will build on her natural strengths and abilities.

Home and Community Issues

Of course you love your daughter. But living with her? (Believe us, living with *you* drives *her* crazy, too.)

In their excellent book, *Understanding Girls With AD/HD*, Drs. Kathleen G. Nadeau, Ellen B. Littman, and Patricia O. Quinn write, "The internal experience of a girl with ADHD is frequently one of chaotic disorganization, a whirling barrage of thoughts and feelings from within, as well as a relentless stream of unfiltered external stimuli" (p. 67). It's exhausting to be her, but it's also exhausting to be you. Her chaos spills over into your home and into your relationship. How do you manage?

ADHD at Home

Research has shown us that families of children with ADHD have more negative, stressful, intense interactions. Not surprisingly, it's the relationship with Mom that is affected most drastically. Mothers reported nearly twice as many conflicts with their ADHD teens as fathers did and seem to be much more directly affected by the stress those conflicts cause (Laursen, Coy, & Collins, 1998). Fathers tend to argue with teens about clothes, loud music, and fighting with their brothers and sisters. As one father told us, "Susan doesn't know when to shut her mouth!" Mothers report those same arguments, but also tend to take over an "enforcer" role when it comes to grades, bedtime, homework, and their teen's choice of friend. If that teenager is a girl, the mother-daughter relationship is particularly fragile (Laursen et al., 1998).

Part of that is a practical matter—Mom is typically the one who manages the day-to-day events in a child's life. Mothers have more contact, and from that results the potential for more conflict. Sometimes it's the daughter who initiates the dispute, but it can also be a frustrated, exhausted, or insensitive mother. Jim once tested a

14-year-old girl with ADHD who showed very strong visual and spatial abilities for remembering pictures, as well as understanding how puzzle pieces fit together. He tried to build this up as one of her natural areas of strength by telling her she might be naturally good at design, graphics, or photography. Her eyes lit up. "I love taking pictures!" she exclaimed. "I asked for a camera for my birthday, but I didn't get it." At the end of the evaluation, the girl's mother came in to pick her up. The young lady reported her natural ability for seeing things spatially, and mentioned again that she'd hoped for a camera. Her mother answered, "For the amount I had to pay for this testing, I could have bought one."

Those words hurt. The girl's mood immediately changed, and she became sullen and withdrawn. It's just one example of the tumultuous relationship between mother and daughter, and it shows how one sentence can make a big difference in how you relate to one another. What if, instead, the mother were to congratulate her daughter for possessing such a special gift, and agree to help her pursue her dream?

Parents, for the next few days, take note of how you speak to your daughter. Because the majority of girls with ADHD have the inattentive variety, they'll often seem daydreamy, mentally checking out in the middle of a conversation. That's how she's wired. If you constantly voice your frustration in negative terms, your daughter will start to view her entire being in negative terms as well. Remember, her tendency is to internalize behaviors and interactions. As much as you're able, try to keep your communication respectful. Research has shown that girls with ADHD respond poorly to authoritarian parenting (Hinshaw, 2002). If your daughter doesn't think you're in her corner, it's not a big leap for her to assume the rest of the world will be mean to her, too.

If your daughter has siblings, keep an eye on how they relate to each other as well. A young person with ADHD can be entertaining, talkative, and engaging, but endless chatter can easily become annoying to her brothers and sisters. Help your children get a break from one another, so that annoyance doesn't escalate. Also—and it's not new advice—try to give your non-ADHD children the individual attention they deserve. That goes a long way toward alleviating any resentments they feel toward their ADHD sister. Try to level the playing field as much as possible, so you treat all of your children equally. Make sure house rules—sharing, showing courtesy and respect, doing chores—are enforced uniformly.

Remember, life in your family is going to be more conflicted simply because you have a child with ADHD. As the adults, your goal is to maintain and restore balance at home.

Discipline That Works

Even though she's a teenager, your daughter still may be experiencing delays in impulse control, attention to detail, decision-making ability, problem solving, and social skills. In fact, she may be months or years behind her peers without ADHD but desire independence just as much as any other teenager. She's almost a grownup—but not yet. Just as many of your other parenting strategies have evolved, you also need to find discipline techniques that are appropriate and effective. Your new approach needs to respect your daughter's increasing maturity and preserve your relationship with her.

We can't possibly foresee every situation you might encounter. Instead, we'd like to outline a handful of discipline strategies we've observed. We'll tell you what tends to work and what doesn't, and you can "rent to own" them for yourself.

Natural consequences. Many mainstream child psychologists suggest that a teenager be allowed to face the consequences of her own choices, without any intervention from her parents. If she neglects her homework, she'll fail her classes. If she annoys all of her classmates, she'll struggle to make friends. If she can't remember to go to work, she'll get fired from her job. This may be effective in the general population, but girls with ADHD are much more easily discouraged. If she fails at any one of these things, she may convince herself that she'll never succeed at anything. Or, because her memory may be poor, she may not remember the consequences long enough for them to have the desired effect. She needs more encouragement and support than this form of discipline typically provides, particularly in more important matters like school performance.

Consistent, mild consequences. This tactic, we find, can be a more effective solution to chronic discipline problems for a young person with ADHD. Instead of seeking a harsh punishment, start with the least restrictive, most lenient punishment possible. Teenagers with ADHD remember one thing: That they were punished. They don't tend to remember how long they were punished. Lengthy punishments often end up hurting the entire family, without any additional benefit. Teens with ADHD often repeat the unacceptable behavior, even when they've been punished. You may have to take away your daughter's iPod or cell phone for 20 two-day periods over the course of a year, but eventually she'll get the point. We recommend you never threaten consequences you aren't prepared to impose. When you do that, your daughter will quickly learn that you don't mean what you say and therefore will continue to argue and test your limits.

Grounding. It's rare for any teenager to escape getting grounded. But you need to proceed with caution if you're going to go down this road. Grounding your daughter will take her out of activities for a week, 2 weeks, a month—whatever sentence you've pronounced. That's a long time for a kid whose social network is already probably very fragile and whose social skills need daily practice. If you isolate her, the effects could range from rebellion to depression. If you must use this as a method of discipline, we recommend it only for short periods of time (a day or two). We also suggest that you warn your daughter ahead of time that this is the consequence she'll face for particular rule violations.

Losing car or electronic privileges. Neither of these are given rights, although your teenager might be surprised to learn this. It's perfectly reasonable to refuse her the right to talk on the phone for a while if she runs up a monumental cell phone bill. If she's old enough to drive, you can also take the car keys for a week if she's chronically late getting home and it's become a major inconvenience. But don't take away car privileges for 2 months if her room is messy. That's an overreaction.

Negotiate. There should be room in your relationship for both of you to express your opinions about whatever you feel she did wrong. You both need to speak respectfully and calmly. For a girl with ADHD, this can be an empowering way to build conflict-resolution skills in a nonthreatening environment.

Second chances. Far more than other kids, teens with ADHD need plenty of second (and third and fourth) chances to regain your trust and prove they have learned whatever lesson you've meant to teach. If your daughter messes up, by all means, discipline her. But after a while, give her another chance along with a hearty dose of forgiveness and encouragement.

Admit you don't know it all. By now, your daughter has you pretty well figured out. She knows you're not perfect. Why not admit it every once in a while? When she makes a mistake, let her off the hook. Instead of punishing her, tell her about one of the dopey things you did when you were growing up, maybe something you never told your parents. You don't always have to be the enforcer.

The last word on the last word. Your daughter may argue every point. Some teens with ADHD do. It can be next to impossible for her to resist. But it's a no-win situation for you. Try not to let yourself get drawn into pointless arguments with your daughter. If you do, either let her have the last word or simply refuse to discuss the matter until she stops arguing.

You've spent a lifetime—your daughter's lifetime—helping her in countless ways, large and small. Now you're in the strange and uneasy position of needing to pull back a little here, a lot there. How will you know when to stop helping? Well, one mom put it this way: "She's my daughter and I'll always be there for her."

Teaching Her to Fail Forward

At one point or another, everyone fails. It's especially important for high school girls with ADHD to know how to develop resiliency and understand how to learn from their failures. You want your daughter to understand that failure is an opportunity to learn, adjust, and try again. Equally important, you'll be helping her resist the urge to internalize her failure and beat herself up over it.

To help you and your daughter grasp these concepts, we recommend the book *Failing Forward: Turning Mistakes Into Stepping Stones for Success* (2000) by Dr. John C. Maxwell. We encourage parents, family members, and important adult friends to read the book ahead of time or together with the teen. This allows for important common ground. In other words, everyone has the same information. That opens the way for discussion and shared experiences or ideas.

Failing Forward presents real-world examples of people who fail at one undertaking, but go on to succeed at something much bigger as a direct result of what they learned. Dr. Maxwell lists several abilities that an individual can work on to help this process along:

◊ *Reject rejection.* In other words, don't base self-worth on performance. It's important for your teenage daughter to truly understand that even if she fails, *she* is not a failure.

◊ *See failure as temporary.* Your daughter must believe in herself and in her potential. She needs to believe that she can overcome her present situation, and that success is within her reach.

◊ *See failures as isolated incidents.* Your daughter may have conditioned herself to expect poor results. Help her identify her failures as short-term setbacks, not as a permanent condition. When things go wrong, help her move past it smoothly and with as little drama as possible.

◊ *Keep expectations realistic.* You can work with your daughter on helping her define reasonable, achievable goals for herself. She will gain a great deal from a series of small successes, which is especially important for a young person with ADHD. Teens with ADHD have likely experienced more than their fair share of failures, so imagine the boost your daughter will get when she learns she doesn't have to expect the world of herself.

In Chapter 10 of *Failing Forward*, Dr. Maxwell writes about the benefits of adversity, and how it can develop resilience, maturity, and innovation. If your daughter can reframe her ADHD in this light, she'll be better able to see it as a gift, rather than a burden.

We think your entire family will be encouraged by the stories of people who refuse to give up. How might your family work this valuable book into your routine? Here are two ways you might do so:

◊ *Have a weekly family discussion.* Each week for 4 months, read one of the 16 chapters and discuss it with your daughter and family. You, or another family member, can read portions of the chapter to illustrate key points and how they apply to your daughter's situation.

◊ *Provide incentive to read and summarize.* You can offer this book as "extra credit" for your daughter. She may read the book and receive extra credit in the form of payment or earning an incentive. She could read a chapter and then write a short summary or create discussion points that she shares with you. Consider doing the first chapter with her to provide a model for how this works, and then allow her to take over. This opportunity allows your daughter to experience feelings of accomplishment.

As Dr. Maxwell states, "I know of only one factor that separates those who consistently shine from those who don't. The difference between average people and achieving people is their perception of and response to failure" (p. 2).

Her First Job

Much like an extracurricular activity, finding a part-time or summer job can give your daughter a place where she can excel. There are many valuable skills and lessons she can learn in the workplace:

◊ employer, coworker, and customer relations;
◊ the importance of being on time;
◊ remembering and following directions;
◊ a sense of independence;
◊ money management; and
◊ building a resume for future positions.

If you and your daughter decide the time is right for her to find a job, talk through the kind of commitment it takes to be a dedicated employee. There are any number of entry-level jobs that are well-suited to a creative, enthusiastic teen with ADHD, so take the time to help her find a job she can really get excited about.

If she's had difficulties maintaining relationships, your daughter may be concerned about having a boss. If you can't meet the person in charge, make every effort to have your daughter meet the supervisor she'll work with before she accepts a job. She needs to feel comfortable that this person will be flexible and understanding. Depending on the severity of her ADHD, it's up to you and your daughter whether or not the employer is informed of your daughter's disability. Whether or not you inform the employer, your daughter needs to feel that her supervisor will support her as she learns the job.

Because working, even part-time, will be a new challenge, be prepared to help your daughter succeed. She'll need to establish a new routine and may need to practice some new skills before she feels comfortable tackling this big step on her own. For instance, you can help her:

◊ Learn how to fill out a job application.

◊ Understand the interview process. If conducting a two-way conversation is difficult for your daughter, practice this at home. She needs to be comfortable answering questions about herself, but also needs to know when to stop talking and listen. Together, you could role-play through a typical interview scenario: Why are you interested in this job? Can you tell me about your strengths? What experiences have you had working on a team? Your daughter should also be ready to ask some basic questions about the job. This indicates her interest level to a potential supervisor.

◊ Learn to be on time. You may need to wake her up, or remind her it's time to leave for work, until it becomes habit. You don't want her to lose the job as a consequence of being late. Having a job is a confidence-builder and an important step toward independence. Also, arriving at the job 5–10 minutes early should become part of her routine. Especially at the beginning, do whatever you need to do to help her with this. That might mean setting two alarm clocks, leaving reminder notes on her mirror, or having someone call or text her when it's time to get ready for work.

◊ Manage her clothing and work-related items. She may have a uniform or other gear she always needs to have. Develop a routine to make sure her work clothes get laundered and the other items are ready to go when she is. A teen with ADHD is just as likely to misplace her plastic nametag as her homework.

◊ Work on her manners. No matter where she goes, your daughter will need to have adult, appropriate interactions with the people she encounters. It's likely they won't know her. They won't know the background of her ADHD. If she blurts out inappropriate remarks, interrupts people, or chatters to her coworkers, she'll jeopardize her job. Employers need to see the same kinds of self-control she's been working to develop in other areas of life. Help her by talking through situations that didn't go well on the job.

◊ Show her how to be a team player. It's unlikely your daughter will be working alone. Having a job will be a wonderful experience for her to bring her unique perspective to a group effort, but she also has to be willing to consider other ideas and figure out how to work with people she might not like.

◊ Explain the value of extra effort. By nature, your daughter may be a people-pleaser, so this might come naturally to her. But when she is being paid to do a job, she should try to do it in an exceptional way that wins notice and praise and can result in an increased sense of self-worth. It may be eye-opening to her that this part of her nature comes with such positive affirmation

Having a "work-for-it" attitude. Some kids believe that showing up to a job is really all that should be required of them. Young people get into trouble when they feel certain work is "beneath them." An attitude of entitlement is dangerous and unrealistic, and you need to make sure your daughter doesn't buy into that kind of thinking.

Any job is worth doing well. But developing that kind of determination can be tricky for kids with ADHD, who not only have trouble thinking in the long term, but are easily bored with the kinds of mundane tasks that require ongoing, sustained effort. The exception? Something she's highly interested in.

It will be great if your daughter can find a summer job that sparks her interest 100% of the time. But she needs to practice her ability to work steadily no matter what the circumstances. You can help her develop this patience by assigning her chores that she does not do for pay, but for the gratification of a job well done. It's a great way to give her a sense of success and mastery, and she'll get used to doing what's required of her.

Money Management

Once your daughter has an income (or if you give her an allowance), she'll need your guidance in learning to manage her money. Together, you can begin to explore basic financial principles such as:

◇ how a checking account works and how to balance it,
◇ how compound interest works, and
◇ how to pay bills and expenses on time. This is a little like homework. But in this case, if she fails to do it (or forgets), the penalty isn't failing the course. The consequences will be additional fees and eventually, a poor credit score. A thousand reminders from you may not be as effective as the first $35 late fee that comes out of her own pocket.

People with ADHD are especially vulnerable to spending their money impulsively. Saving is a very difficult concept for them to grasp because it's so abstract. Saving her money to buy something later is not nearly as stimulating as your daughter buying something—almost anything—right now. As she matures, she needs to understand that the concepts of self-control and delayed gratification apply to her finances as well. Depending on the severity of your daughter's ADHD, she might be months or years behind her peers in her ability to handle money soundly.

It's a fairly simple coping strategy, but if your daughter is saving for a big purchase, she should not take a wallet full of cash every time she goes with her friends to the movies or the mall. Restricted-access accounts, like long-term CDs, are a great place to park money meant for a car or another big purchase. Credit cards can be very difficult for a teen with ADHD to manage. They simply provide temptation to spend more than she has. If you feel your daughter needs to carry a card for emergencies, we recommend a card with a prepaid balance or a debit card you monitor carefully. Show your daughter that you trust her with a small amount. You can increase her access as she shows that she can handle it.

Driving

Another major milestone for your daughter will be when she slides behind the wheel of a car. It represents freedom, independence, and being on the brink of adulthood. For you, it represents a major loss of control. Unlike many of the other obstacles you've navigated, this one truly is a matter of life and death.

We know that distractibility and difficulty paying attention are traits of girls with ADHD. It's dangerous if you can't focus when you drive. You may have a sense that your daughter may not be able to handle the responsibility of driving when her friends without ADHD begin getting their licenses. This is common. A study of teenage girls with ADHD showed a direct association between inattention and moving vehicle citations (Cardoos, Loya, & Hinshaw, 2013). Many teens with ADHD wait 6 months, a year, or more before pursuing their drivers' licenses. This allows them a bit of additional time to mature and develop the necessary skills to operate a vehicle safely.

Some parents tell us, "I dread teaching my daughter to drive. She's so sensitive to correction." That's a valid point. Think back to the time when you were learning to drive. How many times did your own Mom or Dad stomp on the floor of the passenger side of the car, hoping to find that a brake had miraculously appeared? It's tough for both of you. She'll be nervous and unsure. You'll be worried and tense. Remember, preserving your relationship is essential. This is a great time to enlist backup. If your school has a driver's education program, make sure your daughter signs up. Or if it's in your budget, sign her up with a professional driving school. If that's not possible, maybe there's another trusted adult who'd be willing to teach her. Some communities and schools are even beginning to introduce high-tech driver simulation programs. Much like flight simulators, these machines expose inexperienced drivers to dangerous and unfamiliar situations to give them practice in safe driving techniques. They're expensive and not readily available, but they offer a wonderful way for learners to practice until they get it right, without risking anyone or anything in the process.

When you think your daughter may be ready to begin driving, here are some of the elements that need to be part of your family discussion:

◊ Do you believe your daughter is mature enough to drive? Does she?

◊ Does she feel ready to pass all of the parts of the driver's test? Does she need extra help with the written portion?

◊ Will she be expected to pay for the expenses associated with driving? Can she afford it?

◊ When she gets her license, how often will she be allowed to use the car? Will she be able to drive at night? In bad weather? With friends in the car?

◊ What happens if she breaks one of your rules?

This last point is an important one. You must have immediate, preestablished consequences for violating rules associated with her use of the car, and they need to be reasonable and proportionate. It's not reasonable to remove her car privileges altogether if she's a half-hour late getting home one day or if she forgets to fill the gas tank. That kind of offense might warrant loss of driving privileges for a week. But if you find she's been drinking and driving or driving recklessly, the penalty needs to be strict and severe. She needs to know this.

The day your daughter earns her license is a day she'll never forget. Celebrate this moment together. But also emphasize that driving is a privilege, not a right. She needs to earn and continue to earn the privilege of driving a car.

It's also recommended that a reminder of your family's driving rules be posted prominently in the car your daughter drives (Katz, 2007). Especially in the case of a young driver with ADHD, it's important to see that reminder every time she gets behind the wheel. We recommend that your list include the following:

◊ Absolutely NO alcohol or drugs.

◊ Keep music low.

◊ No wearing headphones.

◊ No texting. There are, in fact, mobile phone apps you can download to your daughter's phone that will disable it when she is behind the wheel.

◊ No talking on your cell phone, unless it's a parent calling. You may advise your daughter to pull off the road safely before she takes or returns your call.

◊ No other teens in the car. This is a smart rule for the first few months. But we believe that after your daughter has earned your trust, you should allow her to drive one of her friends. Talk with her about whether she's able to stay focused on the road with her friends in the car, though.

Beyond these basic rules, there are a number of additional precautionary measures we recommend for teen drivers with ADHD:

◊ Make sure she gets plenty of practice behind the wheel, with you or another responsible adult in the car. Don't give her permission to take her driver's test until you are convinced she meets the criteria for being a safe driver.

◊ Make sure she understands the long-term consequences of reckless driving. This includes death to herself or others, injury, property damage, and loss of her driver's license.

◊ Make sure your daughter knows what to do in case of emergency. Does she know how to handle an accident? A flat tire or other mechanical breakdown? How should she respond to a stranger who has pulled over to offer help? Does your family have a roadside assistance program? Go over the scenarios with her not to frighten her, but to help her be prepared.

◊ Sign a safe driver contract with your daughter. There are plenty of examples of these kinds of documents online, or you can draft your own. In a typical contract, the teen agrees that she and all passengers will wear seatbelts, that she will obey all traffic laws, and that she will not drive under the influence of drugs or alcohol. You promise to give her calm and respectful feedback on her driving, and you agree not to punish her if she calls you for a ride home because she's under the influence of drugs or alcohol. Often, such an agreement also outlines who is responsible for various car-related expenses. Posting your contract in a prominent place will help a teen with ADHD remember what she agreed to do.

◊ Set a good example for her. If you want her to drive safely, make sure she sees you driving safely. Your behavior, in this or any situation, will always have a powerful impact on your daughter.

Your Daughter's Physical and Emotional Health

When a boy with ADHD reaches adolescence, he may be seeing a decrease in symptoms. But it's just the opposite for girls. Clearly, teen girls with an ADHD diagnosis are going to need extra help and guidance in several areas—understanding their own bodies, dating, moods and emotions, and maintaining a healthy, positive self-image.

Her Hormones

It's not news that girls begin to develop earlier than boys. Because of her ADHD, your daughter already may feel awkward and out of place among her peers, and puberty can make those feelings more pronounced. So make sure that your daughter understands what's happening to her body.

The hormones that regulate her menstrual cycle affect her mood and functioning. During the first 2 weeks of the menstrual cycle (starting with the first day of the period), levels of estrogen are on the rise. This elevates the levels of serotonin and dopamine, the feel-good neurotransmitters in the brain. During weeks 3 and 4, progesterone levels rise and diminish those feel-good effects. Fluctuating hormone levels can affect your daughter with ADHD both emotionally and in relation to practical areas like memory and medication. She may struggle more to stay focused in school or might be especially irritable or withdrawn. If you notice your daughter's ADHD symptoms are worse at certain times of the month, try to identify a pattern and work with her doctor to adjust her medication or treat any depression or anxiety that may result.

During adolescence, you daughter will probably start to feel the sexual flutterings that are normal for any teenager. For teens with ADHD, the line between dating and sexuality is a fine one. Dr. Russell Barkley (2000b) has conducted exhaustive studies of children, adolescents, and teens with ADHD. His research is often shocking and showed that:

◊ Thirty-eight percent of teens with ADHD are involved in a pregnancy.

◊ Teens with ADHD begin having sexual intercourse earlier than their average peers.

◊ Teens with ADHD have more sexual partners and are less likely to use contraception.

Parents, sit up and take notice. You already know that girls with ADHD have little self-control. They can be impulsive. They find it difficult to delay gratification. So from a physical perspective, the temptation to have sex is powerful. Girls with ADHD often feel socially rejected and may seek affirmation through sexual relationships. Because the teen with ADHD is delayed emotionally, she may seek out behaviors that may make her seem more mature—including sex—in order to fit in. Because she has trouble projecting long-term consequences of her actions, your daughter may not be affected by fear of getting pregnant or the threat of contracting a sexually transmitted disease.

We urge you not to turn a blind eye to the possibility that your daughter is acting on her strong sexual urges. Here are some tools and guidelines to help her:

◊ Talk to her about the rest of her life. If she becomes pregnant, it will forever change her, no matter the outcome. She may not understand that millions of teens contract STDs every year and that for many of them, like HIV and herpes, there is no cure. She will take them into every relationship she has and into her marriage.

◊ Don't rely on school sex-education classes alone. Anticipate the physical changes she's experiencing and discuss them openly. If this is impossible or difficult for you or her, make sure she has access to good resources she can read or watch. Just because your daughter has ADHD and has had difficulty with reading material, don't presume she won't read a book about sex. One of Jim's clients had success with Dr. James Dobson's book and CD series, *Preparing for Adolescence: How to Survive the Coming Years of Change.*

The family was able to listen to the CDs together, discuss them, and talk through dating, peer pressure, and other physical and emotional issues.

◊ Make sure she knows your family's moral code. Reinforce that she is precious and loved, and that she does not need to go outside of your home to experience love and affection.

◊ Many parents presume their daughters know how to say "no" to a boy. That can be a dangerous and false assumption. Make sure she understands that she has the right to say no to sexual activity, and the right to be respected.

◊ Decide how you are going to handle the issue of birth control. This is highly personal and can be overlooked because some parents find birth control uncomfortable to discuss; however, it's a conversation you'll want to have with your daughter so that she's not left wondering. Let her know your stance on birth control, and make sure she understands carefully how it is used correctly, if that is a decision you make.

Mostly importantly, be available to discuss—calmly and thoughtfully—any issues of sexuality that come up. Remember, you *want* her to come to you.

Dating

Whatever your daughter's chronological age, you need to discuss your family's dating rules before she starts to have romantic relationships. This will help her know what to expect when the time comes. These include:

◊ When she can go on dates and how often. You may have different rules for the school year and for school holidays and the summertime.

◊ Who can she date? What if you don't know the boy? Typically, your daughter will date a friend from school, church, or the community. But she might wish to date someone you don't know. Meet him.

◊ Where they're going, what they'll be doing, and whom they'll be with. If you would not permit your daughter to attend unsupervised parties alone, she shouldn't be allowed to go to one on a date.

◊ Guidelines for when her boyfriend comes to your house. Her boyfriend should be welcome in your home. Whether you approve of him or not, make him feel comfortable. If he's not the guy for her, she'll figure it out eventually. But she's never to have him over when she's home alone, and you'll want to limit the time they're alone together in a room with closed doors.

◊ What if she breaks a rule? Your daughter needs to know in advance that she will face consequences for breaking one of your rules about dating. Dating is a privilege that shows you trust her. If she loses that trust, take away that privilege for a week or two, and then return it for a trial period. For girls with ADHD, a short removal of a privilege is as effective as a long one.

Coexisting Mood Disorders

One of the most upsetting characteristics of ADHD in girls is this—there is a far higher rate of major depressive disorders and anxiety disorders among young women with ADHD than among young men (Hinshaw, Owens et al., 2012), and the rate of mood disorders continues to climb into adulthood. Women with ADHD suffer disproportionately from bipolar disorder (Biederman et al., 2010). Hinshaw, Owens et al.,'s 2012 research arrived at this striking conclusion: "The sheer range of negative outcomes is noteworthy; the most striking include the high occurrences of suicide attempts and self-injury in the ADHD sample, confined to the childhood-diagnosed combined type" (p. 1049).

Indeed, Dr. Hinshaw's research presents some staggering statistics. In a 10-year follow-up study of young women aged 17–24, 93 had been diagnosed with combined-type ADHD in childhood, and the remainder with inattentive type. Of those girls with combined-type ADHD, half had engaged in some type of self-injury (e.g., cutting or scratching their skin, burning themselves, hitting themselves, or pulling out their hair). Almost 20% had attempted suicide.

It's important to note that those figures don't represent the general population of girls with ADHD; Dr. Hinshaw's 2012 study had more girls with combined-type ADHD, while the majority of young women with ADHD have the inattentive variety. Keep in mind that the research is consistent in concluding that by young adulthood, females with ADHD are at risk for coexisting psychological conditions, including addictive, mood, anxiety, and eating disorders (Biederman et al., 2010; Hinshaw, Owens et al., 2012).

We'd like to present a brief discussion of some of those disorders to begin to build your awareness. Clearly if your daughter experiences any of these you should seek professional help

Cutting and self-harm. These behaviors provide a means to express deep emotional distress. Those who injure themselves feel as though they have no choice, and injuring themselves actually makes them feel better—but only temporarily. Self-harm is accompanied by feelings of shame, guilt, and loneliness, because it's rare that the sufferer feels able to share their actions with family or friends. They aren't trying to get attention. In fact, they will usually do everything they can to keep the act a secret.

Because young women with ADHD tend to internalize their pain, some turn to self-harm as a way to cope with the vastness of their emotions. Red flags include unexplained wounds, usually on the wrists, arms, thighs, or chest; bloodstains on clothing or linens; withdrawal; irritability; and an unwillingness to reveal her arms or legs even in hot weather.

The father of one of our clients shared with us his perspective about his daughter's cutting.

> The day I found out that she had cut, I was heart-broken. I quickly scanned the Internet for articles about cutting, why girls did it, and fear took over me. Although I saw one cause that seemed to fit (stuffing feelings and a rocky relationship with Mom), I also saw a few that scared me (abuse and other harms of that nature). Not wanting to put words in her mouth, I approached her room with love and understanding and confronted her about it. I told her that I knew and asked if she wanted to talk about it. She was open and scared that I knew but seemed to be truthful in her answers. I left there feeling confident that the reasons were an inability to express her emotions and an inability to please Mom. I let my daughter know that she could talk to me about anything. I would never judge her. I wanted to be available to teach her to express her emotions in a healthy way.
>
> I also worked with her Mom to communicate in a more positive way. We began to restrict time away from home with friends that we felt were a negative influence, opting for time at our house with these friends. At the time, we felt absolute restriction from friends would be more destructive as this was one of her issues and would leave her with no friends. This also gave us an opportunity to invest in the friend's life as well. We also arranged a counselor but our daughter didn't seem to take to this. So, while searching for a new one, the counseling was left to us. Increased Daddy-daughter time seemed to help. Over time, it seems she is

getting better and better at expressing herself, and honestly, we are getting better at accepting who she is rather than what we might want her to be. The cutting stopped, although the emotional outbursts have not. It is a constant teaching and learning process to battle the lies that so abundantly exist in our culture. She is an incredibly gifted and wonderful child! I just have to never miss an opportunity to tell her that because the world around her tells her differently.

Eating disorders. These disorders include anorexia (the inability to consume enough calories to maintain a healthy body weight); bulimia (cycling between eating and purging by the use of vomiting, laxatives, or excessive exercise); binge eating; and compulsive overeating. Puberty is a common time for the onset of eating disorders, which can be fatal or cause long-term physical injury. Girls with ADHD are susceptible to begin self-medicating with food, especially sugar, chocolate, and carbohydrates. That behavior can become addictive, and coupled with our society's preoccupation with weight and physical beauty, can lead a girl to follow those comforting binges with purges in an attempt to achieve "perfection." But it's important to note that while symptoms of eating disorders begin earlier for girls with ADHD, by young adulthood there is little difference in the rate of diagnosed eating disorders between girls with ADHD and the general population of women (Hinshaw et al., 2012).

Mood disorders. We've already mentioned that a young woman with ADHD is at greater risk of being diagnosed with depression, anxiety, and/or Obsessive-Compulsive Disorder. Bipolar disorder is also overrepresented. It's crucial to note that the rate of mood disorders in women with ADHD continued to climb between the ages of 25 and 30, and that many do not develop until after age 25 (Biederman et al., 2010).

Addictive behaviors. Girls with ADHD are often plagued with the feeling that they don't fit in. Girls in general have a far greater need than boys for relationships and emotional connection. Girls with ADHD may be willing to risk substance abuse so they can achieve a kind of peer acceptance they may never have had. They want to belong, and if they have to smoke, drink, or do drugs to make that happen, they may be willing.

We want to make clear that it's not our intention to scare you. Although the research suggests an increased rate of these disorders in girls diagnosed with ADHD, it does not mean it will automatically happen to your daughter. We want only to stress how important it will be for you to observe her, listen to her, and support her. If she is faced with any of these issues, there is a great chance that she's feeling shame and guilt. Please do your very best not to judge, lecture, or criticize. Instead, understand that these are deeply rooted psychopathologies that require serious, compassionate, and often immediate treatment.

If you have the sense that something is wrong, seek professional help for your daughter. Don't be afraid to seek a second opinion, and keep digging until you can get at the root of the problem. Often a team approach is the best means of identifying and treating coexisting conditions, and that could include input from a psychiatrist, clinical psychologist, physician, or university-affiliated hospital. The most important thing is to get her the help she needs.

Self-Esteem

If your daughter has been struggling with ADHD since she was a little girl, there's a chance her self-esteem may already have taken a hard hit. Many labels may have been attached to her over the years, and she may still carry the hurt from them. Is it any wonder that by the time they're in their early teens, some girls find it impossible to list even one of their strengths? And if her diagnosis is relatively recent, she may look at it as a crushing blow, something to set her apart from her peers.

Indeed, when you ask your daughter about how she feels, a lot of the time her answer will be, "different." Adolescence is a time when fitting in becomes as important to a young person as almost anything, and we find that particularly true for girls. More relational by nature than boys, girls are also more likely to define themselves by how other people feel about them—whether they have ADHD or not. By the time she reaches middle or high school, your daughter may have been feeling left out or misunderstood for a very long time.

See if you could apply any of these traits to your daughter (Teach, 2012):

◊ She is anxious, eager to please.
◊ She is a perfectionist.
◊ She is easily wounded in social situations.
◊ She feels isolated.
◊ She is verbally impulsive (e.g., interrupting, talking too loudly, speaking before thinking).
◊ She is bullied, either physically or emotionally.
◊ She struggles to be what society calls "a good girl."

Every one of these characteristics depends in some part on the quality of your daughter's relationships, and the quality of your daughter's relationships can have a direct impact on her self-esteem. Whereas boys with ADHD tend to be more active and physically aggressive, girls with ADHD tend to turn that energy inward—and it can create havoc with their self-esteem. Girls' friendships are more complex. They are held to a more strict code socially, from the way they look, to the way they dress, to the way they act. Because girls with ADHD have so much difficulty keying in to social clues and navigating relationships, they suffer. But they often suffer in silence.

As a caring parent, you can take measures to restore or protect your daughter's self-confidence. In fact, it's essential that you do so. Her self-esteem is closely linked to her likelihood for success now and into adulthood.

Components of self-esteem. An individual builds self-esteem bit by bit, by succeeding in life, at school, with friends, and in relationships. True positive self-worth, particularly in the case of a young woman with ADHD, needs to include a number of elements:

◊ She believes she is lovable and valuable.

◊ She tries. Many teens with ADHD have become the unwitting victims of "learned helplessness." It's often quicker and easier for adults to do something for a child with ADHD than it is to teach that child to do it for herself. Sadly, when that child grows up, she comes to believe there are many things she's incapable of doing on her own. That can result in an extremely low sense of self-worth. On the other hand, a young woman who's willing to take a risk and attempt to figure things out—even if she's not successful all of the time—is likely to have higher self-esteem. She will believe that trying may result in success, at least sometimes.

◊ She views her ADHD not as a problem but as something that makes her different and special. Believing that you're unique is a key component to healthy self-esteem. As she grows older, your daughter may begin to see her ADHD as a sort of gift that sets her apart. Encourage this sort of thinking, and she'll feel good about who she is and how she's wired.

◊ She believes she can identify and fix things when they go wrong. Your daughter already knows that life with ADHD is extra challenging. If her self-esteem is healthy, she has begun to develop the ability to identify when there's a problem and to have confidence that she can, with effort, work toward a solution. If her grades have slipped, she's aware of the steps she needs to take. If she's had an argument with a friend, she doesn't give up on the friendship. She figures out what went wrong and works it out. The key to this aspect of self-esteem is her *belief* that her efforts will be productive.

◊ She develops and maintains self-control. A person with high self-esteem is in command of herself, her feelings, and her reactions. Although this ability may be naturally delayed in a young woman with ADHD, it's a crucial part of self-confidence to know that you can trust yourself to stay in control.

◊ She acknowledges her own efforts and rewards herself. If your daughter feels valued and confident, then she'll understand it's OK to give herself a pat on the back when she really tries hard at something. She might even buy herself a gift or do something fun to celebrate. If she's feeling good about herself, then she'll realize that it's the effort that earns the reward, not the outcome. She's not after perfection, which is unhealthy. She's rewarding persistence.

◊ She has a parent or parents who support her, praise her, and love her for who she is. Time and again, adults with ADHD report that their parents were their most consistent encouragers. As children and teens, they knew home was a safe place. They never doubted their self-worth, because they always felt loved by the people who mattered most in their lives. If you remember only one sentence from this book, remember this one: *The best predictor of success for a child with ADHD is having someone believe in her while she is growing up.* This finding comes from more than 15 years of research conducted by Dr. Gabrielle Weiss, coauthor of the 1993 book *Hyperactive Children Grown Up*.

So what does healthy self-esteem look like? In this case, that may be better answered by discussing what it doesn't look like. Your daughter shouldn't be walking around feeling inferior every day of her life. She should know that she has strengths and weaknesses; that she's wonderfully flawed just like the rest of us. Like everything in your walk with ADHD, the pursuit of healthy self-esteem is about balance.

Self-esteem strategies for teen girls. As your daughter matures, she becomes more capable of understanding how her own actions and thought patterns contribute to her self-esteem. Encourage her to boost her own self-esteem with strategies like the following:

◊ *Teach her how to make and keep friends.* Friendships are an important defense against the tumult of adolescent life. The good news? She doesn't have to have dozens of friends in order to get a boost. One study found that the presence of just one friend reduced the likelihood that a girl with ADHD would be mistreated by other girls (Cardoos & Hinshaw, 2011).

◊ *Make sure she can develop "islands of competence."* This concept comes from Dr. Robert Brooks, educator and faculty member at Harvard Medical School. Everyone has some special gift, and some people have many. Your daughter needs to have at least one special area in which she can shine.

◊ *Inventory the life skills that will serve her well as an adult.* Ironically, the same qualities that are considered a drawback in a child with ADHD can be really beneficial to an adult in the workplace. It can be an eye-opening exercise to look at your daughter's individual characteristics and define which ones might be extremely valuable to her later in life. ADHD-related magazines are full of stories about successful surgeons, educators, artists, and entrepreneurs— women often diagnosed in adolescence or as young adults.

◊ *Set small goals.* It can be self-defeating to look at an overwhelming challenge, particularly for a teenager with ADHD. It's far gentler on the self-confidence to set smaller goals and feel the confidence boost that comes from achieving each one. Imagine your daughter thinking about saving enough money to buy a car. Now help her break that down into small, manageable pieces: $25 a month, for instance. Maybe you'll even match all (or a portion) of it if she's faithful to her goal. By overcoming the challenge bit by bit, her confidence will build and she'll see she *can* do it.

◊ *Have hope.* Things tend to happen just a little later for people with ADHD. Encourage her not to lose sight of the fact that good things will still happen for her, even if she feels like ADHD has really messed up her life. She might try keeping a "gratitude journal" so she can remember the times things went right for her. It's easy to forget.

Your daughter may relate to and find the following books helpful.

◊ *You Grow Girl!: A Self-Empowering Workbook for Tweens and Teens*

◊ *The Self-Esteem Workbook for Teens: Activities to Help You Build Confidence and Achieve Your Goals*

◊ *Don't Let Your Emotions Run Your Life for Teens: Dialectical Behavior Therapy Skills for Helping You Manage Mood Swings, Control Angry Outbursts, and Get Along with Others*

◊ *The Anxiety Workbook for Teens: Activities to Help You Deal With Anxiety and Worry*

◊ *Stopping the Pain: A Workbook for Teens Who Cut and Self Injure*

◊ *The Girl Guide: Finding Your Place in a Mixed-Up World*

Strategies for parents. Your teenaged daughter comes into contact with a lot of people, directly or indirectly—friends, teachers, neighbors, coaches, and TV and movie characters. However, don't for a minute forget the influence *you* continue to have in building and nurturing her feelings of self-worth.

◊ Love her unconditionally. Love your daughter exactly as she is—her gifts, her talents, her quirks, her faults. When a girl is accepted and cherished in her own family, what other kids think of her tends to matter a whole lot less. Your love goes a long way to offset the actions and words of mean-spirited peers.

◊ Make a list of her strengths. Begin to list all of your daughter's gifts and talents. Once you get going, it's hard to stop. Find a quiet time to share your list with her, and make sure she has a copy of it. It may become one of her most cherished possessions. And after you've made the list . . .

◊ Help her build on those strengths. As a parent of a young woman with ADHD, you need to keep her engaged and growing. Once her eyes have been opened to her many gifts, explore together how she can build upon them. Find seminars she can attend, books she can read, or volunteer opportunities she can pursue.

◊ Have fun with her. Make sure to laugh together. Enjoy each other. Create memories.

◊ Stay engaged. As your daughter matures, continue teaching her the skills she needs to feel confident in life.

◊ Teach by example. You cannot simply bestow self-esteem upon someone. You need to demonstrate how your choices and actions produce your own feelings of self-worth. Show your daughter where your self-esteem comes from.

◊ Praise her. But do so genuinely. Like all kids, your daughter has a finely tuned "fake praise" meter. She'll know when she deserves praise and when she doesn't. If you gush with praise over trivial things, your true admiration will become meaningless. (And remember to praise effort, not outcome.)

◊ Don't let your fears become her fears. Many parents of children with ADHD develop a "worst-case" mindset. They end up envisioning the darkest possible future for their kids. Most children are very perceptive. Watch the words you use, your tone of voice, the looks you give. You can tell her a lot without ever saying a word.

◊ Read the book *200 Ways to Raise a Girl's Self-Esteem: An Indispensable Guide for Parents, Teachers & Other Concerned Caregivers.*

Remember, the most effective support she'll ever get comes from you, when you say and believe with your whole heart, "I know you can do it."

Points to Consider

1. Remember to nurture the relationship you have with your daughter. Nearly everything else is secondary.

2. There are no careers a person with ADHD can't pursue, and no jobs a person with ADHD can't do. Remind your child she has what it takes to succeed in any area she's passionate about, gifted in, and dedicated to.

3. Be very, very cautious how you speak to and about your daughter, and what your expressions and body language say to her. She needs to know you see her value. Children who do best in overcoming the challenges of ADHD are the ones who can say, "Somebody believes in me." Are you that person for your daughter?

4. Review your self-assessment responses to decide if there are any areas where you still need to learn more.

Action Steps to Take Now

1. Complete Step 4 in the Dynamic Action Plan.

2. Set reasonable expectations for your daughter's performance at school, at home, and in the community, and require her to live up to her end of the bargain. She is not a child.

3. Together with your daughter, explore clubs, activities, sports, volunteer work, and part-time job opportunities that are interesting and appealing to her.

4. Buy or borrow a copy of *Failing Forward* by Dr. John C. Maxwell. Involve the whole family in reading and reviewing its principles.

5. Be sure you understand the significance of your daughter's ADHD as it relates to issues of sexuality and impulse control. Have open and honest discussions with her about dating, sex, and pregnancy.

6. Stay actively involved in your daughter's life, and watch carefully for signs of depression, anxiety, self-injury, eating disorders, or addictive behavior.

7. Praise your daughter when she tries, listen when she speaks, and love her all of the time.

Chapter 6

When More Support Is Needed

SELF-ASSESSMENT: Where Am I Now?

Each self-assessment helps you reflect on your daughter and your parenting practices and is a preview of the chapter's content.

1. When I think about my daughter's struggles in elementary school, I . . .

    a. realize I need to learn more about the types of eligibilities that might be available to help her.

    b. had no idea additional help could be available.

    c. am totally opposed to my daughter being labeled as having a disability.

    d. am going to talk to her teacher to determine what is currently being done and what else might be available to her in her current school.

2. When thinking about eligibilities for my daughter, I . . .
    a. have never heard of a 504 plan or IEP eligibility.
    b. have talked to some parents who have encouraged me to look into eligibility because they felt it was helpful for their child.
    c. need to find out more about a 504 and an IEP eligibility.
    d. feel like I have a good understanding of both plans, their benefits and limitations.

3. When looking into the future for high school and college, I . . .
    a. am afraid to think about it.
    b. feel she is on a good path to acquire the skills she will need.
    c. think I need to get serious about identifying potential problems and then getting her remediation or assistance in those areas.
    d. feel completely incapable of figuring that out for myself and need to find someone who can guide me and assist in locating supports.

4. When thinking about virtual or homeschool options, I . . .
    a. would never consider either.
    b. need to learn more about them—both their benefits and limitations.
    c. know people who have had good experiences with them.
    d. am seriously considering it as a good educational option for my daughter.

5. I think my child will qualify for a 504 plan or an IEP, and I . . .

    a. have no idea what kinds of accommodations or services are allowed or provided.

    b. have to research the school district's website or the Internet to find out more about which accommodations would be most helpful.

    c. need to talk to other parents to gain knowledge about their experience.

    d. am confident I can count on her school to determine the most appropriate services and accommodations.

Sometimes even your most effective parenting tools and your daughter's best efforts are not enough to enable her to succeed in the classroom without interventions. Could your daughter use additional time on tests, frequent cueing to stay focused, or a behavior plan? If so, how do you go about advocating for your daughter? We tell our clients that learning information about accommodations and services the school can provide is critical. If your daughter's ADHD significantly impacts her life at school, the following federal laws could enable her to receive assistance if she meets the qualifications:

◊ **Section 504** of the Rehabilitation Act of 1973 (referred to as Section 504) and its companion federal laws—Americans with Disabilities Act (ADA) and Americans with Disabilities Act Amendments Act of 2008 (ADAAA); and

◊ Individuals with Disabilities Educational Improvement Act of 2004 (called IDEA), which began as Public Law 94–142, the Education of All Handicapped Children's Act in 1975, and has been amended multiple times.

Sometimes the school will initiate the process for services and accommodations. Often, however, parents need to take the leadership role. In cases where you have to initiate and drive the process, it will be important for you to understand the parameters of both Section 504 and IDEA to help you determine which best fits your daughter's needs. The following sections give you the information you will need to have a basic understanding of both 504 and IDEA.

What Is Section 504?

Section 504 is a federal civil rights law that protects a child from ages 3–21 with a record of impairment or who is regarded as having an impairment against discrimination in public and nonreligious schools, including colleges and technical schools receiving federal funds. A student is eligible for accommodations under Section 504 if the student is determined to have a physical or mental impairment that substantially limits one or more major life activities, which in a child's case would be school functioning. However, Section 504 does not provide funding; it simply mandates accommodations and some services. The intent is to provide a level playing field so the student's disability will not interfere with her access to education. Section 504 states:

> No qualified individual with a disability shall, on the basis of disability, be excluded from participation in or be denied the benefits of the services, programs or activities of a public entity, or be subjected to discrimination by any public entity. (35.130, Subpart B, p. 549)

According to the Americans with Disabilities Act of 1990 (ADA),

> The term "disability" means, with respect to an individual—

A. a physical or mental impairment that substantially limits one or more major life activities
B. a record of such impairment
C. being regarded as having such impairment. (HR 3195 RH)

Your daughter could meet items B or C above and be guaranteed freedom from discrimination, but she may *not* be eligible for services and accommodations under a 504 plan *unless* she has met the first requirement—"a physical or mental impairment that *substantially limits* one or more major life activities." In essence, your child can be diagnosed with ADHD by an outside source or can be suspected of having ADHD and receive the protection against discrimination but still not be determined eligible for services and/or accommodations through a 504 plan because she does not demonstrate a substantial impairment in the school setting. A team of personnel from the school, which isn't tightly defined by 504 and doesn't always include parents, must determine if the ADHD *substantially limits* your child's access to an education on a case-by-case basis.

The impact of American with Disabilities Act Amendments Act of 2008 (ADAAA) included the following changes:

◇ the definition of "disability" under Section 504 was broadened to include "learning, reading, concentrating, thinking, communicating, and working" (Section 2A);

◇ it clarified that an impairment could limit one major activity but not others and could be episodic but should not be transitory, meaning it should have been present and last for at least 6 months or more;

◇ it stated that effects of medication and other forms of assistance should not be considered when determining if impairment substantially limits a major activity (that means that if your daughter is receiving medication, the team should consider what her performance would be like without the medication. Why? If those supports were withdrawn, your daughter's performance might decline significantly); and

◊ broad interpretation is given to the term "substantially limits."

What Does the 504 Process Look Like?

Most schools will follow similar steps to these to determine if you daughter is eligible under Section 504:

1. The school will gather information about your daughter's classroom performance, which might include teacher observations, grades, results of standardized assessments, and any outside medical or psychological information you might provide.

2. The school team may or may not require additional evaluation. As a parent, you have the right to request an evaluation of your child through the school district. Once permission is signed for the evaluation, it must be completed within 60 school days.

3. An eligibility determination will be made by the 504 team. If the team determines that your daughter's ADHD substantially limits her academic performance, functioning, or behavior at school, it would determine her eligible for a formal 504 plan.

4. A written 504 plan will be developed to delineate services and accommodations. It is reviewed annually but can be revisited at any time and is kept in place as long as needed. Even though a 504 plan includes strategies and assistance that an effective teacher would normally implement, it is always important to have it in writing. Without it, one year you may have a teacher who makes accommodations, and the next year you may have one who does not, or you could move to a different school and have no written record of accommodations. Going forward, you want to ensure your

daughter has the accommodations she needs and that they are provided consistently from classroom to classroom.

Jim's son has a 504 plan for his ADHD that was established at the end of his kindergarten year. Jim and his wife had their son privately evaluated by a psychologist and brought the paperwork to school. After reviewing the report, the school met with the Forgans and determined he was eligible for a 504 plan. Because he was struggling, there was no resistance from the school toward writing the 504 plan, and Jim and his wife were pleased with the accommodations. Some of the accommodations written on his first-grade 504 plan included not taking away all of his recess, allowing reduced homework, providing spelling words on Friday instead of Monday, and allowing frequent breaks.

What Is IDEA?

IDEA is the federal law that states that a free and appropriate education must be provided to all students who have a disability, meet their state's eligibility criteria, and have an *educational need* for special education services. IDEA provides funding for instruction addressing your child's unique needs, usually from a special education teacher, and can provide related services like occupational therapy or counseling when needed. The federal law specifies 13 disability categories. Other Health Impairment (OHI) is the eligibility category most often considered for children with ADHD. Other disability categories could be considered, depending on your daughter's specific difficulties. If she has academic problems, she may qualify under Specific Learning Disabilities. If your daughter has serious behavioral or emotional problems, she may qualify under Emotional Behavioral Disorder, although the number of girls labeled with this eligibility is far less than boys because boys' disruptive and externalizing behaviors come to the attention of school personnel far more readily than girls, who generally have more internalizing behaviors. If you are considering this option, make sure that the programming provided would meet your daughter's needs.

If a child is considered for services under the Other Health Impairment eligibility, she must have a disability (such as ADHD) that significantly impacts her ability to learn and perform in the classroom to the extent that she would require special education services. Factors other than her test scores should be considered. Those factors might include "grades, homework completion, independent work habits, alertness, sleeping in class, class participation and attendance, ability to complete schoolwork and tests within specified time frames, relationships with peers, and compliance with rules" (Durheim & Zeigler Dendy, 2006, p. 128).

How Is the Disability Category OHI Defined Under IDEA?

Federal law defines OHI as

having limited strength, vitality or alertness, including a heightened alertness to environmental stimuli, that results in limited alertness with respect to the educational environment, that:

A. Is due to chronic or acute health problems such as asthma, attention deficit disorder, or attention deficit hyperactivity disorder, diabetes, epilepsy, a heart condition, hemophilia, lead poisoning, leukemia, nephritis, rheumatic fever, and sickle cell anemia; and

B. Adversely affects a child's educational performance. (IDEA, 2004, Section 300.8©(9))

If your daughter qualifies as having a disability under IDEA, then the school staff meets with you to write an Individualized Education Program (IEP). IDEA requires that your child must be educated in the least restrictive environment (LRE) that will enable her to progress in the general curriculum to the maximum extent possible, meaning that she must be educated in a general education classroom setting as much as possible. Schools have different options for delivering educational services. Many have inclusion classrooms where a special education teacher comes into the classroom for part of the day or the general education teacher is trained in techniques for instructing children with disabilities. Elsewhere, the child leaves the general education classroom for a portion of the day to receive instruction in areas where she needs extra help.

What Would the IDEA Process Look Like?

The school may follow steps similar to these in determining if your child qualifies under IDEA:

1. The school would gather information about your daughter's classroom performance, which might include teacher observations, grades, results of standardized assessments, and any outside medical or psychological information you might provide.

2. A formal evaluation is required, either done through the school district or provided by you from an acceptable outside source or a combination of the above. As a parent, you have the right to request an evaluation of your child. Once permission is signed for the evaluation, it must be completed within 60 school days in which the child is in attendance.

3. An eligibility determination will be made by the IEP team, which includes you, the parent, as a member. If the team determines that your daughter's ADHD is a disability that

requires special education services, then it would determine her eligible for a disability category.

4. A written IEP would be developed to delineate services and accommodations. It is reviewed annually, and a reevaluation is considered every 3 years.

How Are 504 and IDEA Different?

Generally, children who qualify for IDEA are more impaired and require more services than those best served by a 504 plan. IDEA provides actual funding to schools for special education instruction specified in an IEP, while a 504 plan provides no additional funding to schools but affords your daughter accommodations and some services such as a quiet place to work, use of educational aids such as computers, or small-group instruction. As you would expect, the qualification procedure is less stringent for Section 504.

IDEA requires the development of an IEP that specifies the student's current levels of performance, specific goals written for a year in all areas where she is below her grade level peers (with specification about how these goals will be monitored), and details about where and for how long during the school day special education services will be provided. A 504 plan requires only written documentation of accommodations.

Members of the IEP team under IDEA are specified by law and must include the parents; a teacher knowledgeable about the child; a special education teacher; an administrator (usually called a Local Education Authority or LEA), who is knowledgeable about the laws, disabilities, and general curriculum; and someone who can interpret test results such as a school psychologist or speech-language pathologist. Members of the 504 team are not as clearly defined.

IDEA requires a formalized evaluation that might include a psychoeducational evaluation of the child's intelligence, academic levels, and processing abilities and possibly behavior rating scales. It could require a medical diagnosis of ADHD. Eligibility criteria can vary by school districts. Section 504 requires some documentation of the child's difficulties, but it could include results of rating scales, teacher and parent information, and/or medical information.

IDEA requires consideration of reevaluation needs every 3 years. Many times those reevaluations might be results of assessments and written observations provided by the classroom teacher. If your daughter has a 504 plan, it does not have a specific 3-year reevaluation component.

More specific parental rights come into play with IDEA, such as clearly defined due process rights when there is a serious disagreement between the school district and the parents over the need for an evaluation or services. Section 504 provides for parent rights, usually left up to the discretion of local school districts, which are not as extensive but still allow parents to contest a 504 determination.

Paperwork required in IDEA is more stringent and requires specific written notice of eligibility or ineligibility. Under IDEA, an official IEP meeting is required before any change in placement can occur. The 504 requires no such meeting, but parents of a student with a Section 504 plan must be notified of any proposed changes to the plan and given the opportunity to provide input. Table 5 further outlines the differences between the two laws.

How Are 504 and IDEA Alike?

Both are based on federal laws requiring that a child with a disability receive a free and appropriate public education (FAPE). As we've said earlier, the laws attempt to level the playing field so

Table 5
How IDEA and Section 504 Differ

IDEA	504
Office of Special Education of the U.S. Department of Education responsible for enforcement	Office for Civil Rights of the U.S. Department of Education responsible for enforcement
Students generally more impaired and require more service	Students generally don't require special instruction
Funding provided based on disability category	No funding provided to schools, but schools receiving IDEA funds must meet 504 requirements
More stringent qualification procedure	Less stringent qualification procedure
Individualized Education Plan (IEP) developed	504 plan written
Members of IEP team specified by law	504 team may vary by school district
Formal evaluation necessary	Some documentation of difficulties necessary
Reevaluation to be considered every 3 years	No reevaluation specified
More specific parental rights	Parent rights provided but not as stringent as IDEA
Official IEP meeting and parent permission required before change in placement can occur	No meeting required, but parent should be informed

Note. From *Raising Boys With ADHD* (p. 198) by J. W. Forgan and M. A. Richey, 2012, Waco, TX: Prufrock Press. Copyright 2012 by Prufrock Press. Reprinted with permission.

your daughter will have the same access to education as her non-disabled peers. For example, if she processes information slowly or loses her focus so frequently that she can't finish her work in a specified amount of time, she may be given extended time to complete her work.

Both can provide accommodations such as extended time to complete work, lessons broken down into smaller segments or "chunked," and copies of notes provided for the student's use.

Both require a formal eligibility process with paperwork that must be kept confidential. This allows the teacher and those working with the child to have knowledge of her disability and the required accommodations. Each plan requires an annual review, although parents can request a review at any time.

Both laws require that the child be educated in the least restrictive environment (LRE) with nondisabled peers as much as possible. Both eligibilities transfer if your child moves to a different school, but they may have to be rewritten.

Due process rights are provided by both laws when a parent disagrees with a school district over a child being eligible or services provided. The due process in IDEA is specified by federal law, whereas the due process in Section 504 is left up to the local school district. The similarities between IDEA and Section 504 are further summarized in Figure 9.

What Determines Which Is Most Appropriate for My Daughter?

The decision will be based on the needs of your daughter and the extent of her impairment. If she needs individualized instruction from a special education teacher, eligibility under IDEA should be considered. Remember that if your daughter is eligible for special education, the goal will be to have her remain in a general classroom as much as possible. With an eligibility under IDEA, she could also access other services as needed, such as occupational or language therapy.

Girls with ADHD often may be eligible for IDEA services under multiple categories. For example, a comprehensive evaluation may determine that she has a Specific Learning Disability (SLD), an Other Health Impairment (OHI) or an Emotional/Behavioral Disorder (EBD). If so, her IEP would address those issues.

How are IDEA and Section 504 alike?

- Both are federal laws requiring FAPE.
- Both have accommodations and some services available.
- A formal eligibility process is required for both.
- Paperwork for both laws must be kept confidential.
- Under both laws, the child is to be educated in the least restrictive environment with her nondisabled peers as much as possible.
- Eligibilities under both laws transfer from school to school but may have to be rewritten.
- Under both laws, due process rights are provided when a parent disagrees with the school district.

Figure 9. Similarities between IDEA and Section 504. *Note.* From *Raising Boys With ADHD* (p. 199) by J. W. Forgan and M. A. Richey, 2012, Waco, TX: Prufrock Press. Copyright 2012 by Prufrock Press. Reprinted with permission.

On the other hand, if your daughter is doing relatively well, she may only need accommodations in the classroom, such as being reminded to pay attention, permissible movement, or extended time, so her needs could be met through a 504 plan.

What Can Parents Do?

◊ Try to maintain good communication with your daughter's teacher(s).

◊ Advocate for your daughter and make sure the 504 or IEP (IDEA) team has a clear picture of your daughter and her struggles.

◊ Provide any outside documentation that might help the team.

◊ Request an evaluation if more information is needed. Put your request in writing and keep a copy.

◊ Try to understand the eligibility process and parental rights for your school district, often addressed on its website, and make yourself an integral part of the team by doing what you can do to help your daughter. Some school districts have parent advocates who can attend the meetings with parents to help them understand the process. Check with your school district to determine if parent advocates are available to assist with problem solving and support. Some parents bring attorneys to the table, but Mary Anne's experience as a school psychologist has been that this is usually unnecessary. As a parent, you have the option to request mediation or a due process hearing if you and the school cannot agree on what your daughter needs.

What if I Don't Want to Label My Child?

Some parents are reluctant to create a "paper trail" and formalize their child's disability in the school's records, but it is better for your daughter's chronic problems to be understood for what they are—deficits in neurocognitive processes that affect her day-to-day functioning. It's not laziness, lack of ability, or obstinacy. At times, early intervention provided through accommodations on a 504 plan could prevent the need for special education services later. The goal of a 504 plan or IDEA eligibility is not to provide a crutch or an easy out for your daughter, but to enable her to receive the support she needs to be as successful as possible when she's at school.

Jenny was having significantly more difficulty in her third-grade classroom than in any of her previous grades. When her parents attempted to help her with homework, they felt as if she had not heard one thing taught in the classroom that day. A conference with her teacher was an eye-opener for the parents. Her teacher observed that Jenny was often daydreaming, especially when reading long passages or completing difficult, multistep math problems. She frequently failed to turn in homework her parents had spent hours helping her complete. Her teacher questioned Jenny's organizational skills, observing she seemed to have great difficulty getting out the correct materials for each subject. Her parents felt they could not possibly help Jenny any more than they were currently doing and asked for Jenny to be discussed at the school based team meeting to come up with additional ideas. The school implemented a Response to Intervention (RtI) plan targeting specific reading skills, one of the first steps in most states to look at whether a child has a learning disability. Her RtI plan involved additional time spent during the school day on reading comprehension. Jenny was taught additional strategies for comprehension in a small-group setting. Her teacher noted she was much more able to concentrate on what she was reading in a small setting where there were fewer distractions. Her progress was monitored weekly over a 6–8 week period. With the additional assistance on reading, she showed improvement and seemed more engaged in the reading process as her skill level increased.

Because Jenny seemed to be making progress, the school did not pursue formalized testing to determine if she had a learning disability. However, she was still having difficulty staying focused on the teacher, doing her best work, and finishing assignments in the large classroom setting. Her parents brought Jenny to us for an evaluation. She was not found to have a learning disability, but tests of neurocognitive functioning suggested deficits in attention and working memory, commonly seen in children with ADHD. Rating scales completed by her parents and teachers showed significantly more inattentive and disorganized behaviors than would be expected given her age. The school initiated a meeting to discuss her eligibility for a 504 plan. Her parents brought in documentation of her ADHD diagnosis (not required but helpful), and the team developed a 504 plan. It included an individualized task-monitoring plan, which her teacher used to help Jenny keep track of her responsibilities. She received a star for each item completed and turned in, for checking her work, and for self-monitoring her reading. She was able to earn special privileges, such as additional time on the computer, with the stars she received. In addition, she received frequent cueing on tasks by her teacher and opportunities to move about the classroom to different stations when her work was completed. She showed progress and benefited from the provisions of her 504 plan. If her difficulties had been ignored, she may have fallen further and further behind in her academics.

The Importance of Establishing Eligibility Before College

Many students benefit from the structure provided at home and the efforts of elementary and secondary school faculties. When they get to college, they sometimes fall apart without those supports. If you suspect your daughter's ADHD might cause her significant difficulty in college, then it is important to establish eligibility for 504 or IDEA before she leaves secondary school, so her needs and accommodations will already be documented. The eligibilities don't transfer to the college setting, but the paper trail can be helpful.

Requirements for receiving accommodations on the SAT and ACT for students with ADHD have become more stringent in recent years. In addition to a diagnosis, the student must provide a comprehensive psychoeducational evaluation that was completed by a licensed professional. Postsecondary institutions do provide accommodations and services but generally require more information such as updated testing.

Classroom Accommodations and Supports

As your daughter's advocate, you should be familiar with the universe of options that could be available to her. Listed on the following pages are examples of some of the accommodations that can be made with either a 504 plan or an IEP (take note that it is not an all-inclusive list). It is important to be realistic about what a teacher can be expected to do for your child and still manage an entire classroom. The best advice is to focus on the accommodations that you feel would be most beneficial to your daughter. The quality will likely be more effective than the quantity of interventions.

Classroom Structure

◊ Warnings should be provided before transitions. For example, the teacher gives your daughter a 5-minute warning before she must put away her work and begin a new task. It is helpful for some children to be allowed to begin cleaning up a few minutes before the rest of the class, allowing extra time to improve organizational skills.

◊ Placement of your child's desk in an area that is as free of distraction as possible. For example, you wouldn't want your child's desk in an area where other students are constantly walking past it.

◊ A clean and clutter-free workspace to avoid distractions.

◊ Provision of a quiet workspace, such as a study carrel or quiet corner of the room, where your daughter could take her work.

◊ Placement near a positive role model.

◊ Scheduling accommodations. If there is an option, schedule more demanding classes earlier in the day and try to include some activity, such as physical education or recess, during the middle of the day.

◊ A specified place for turning in homework. Some students e-mail homework.

◊ Permissible movement, such as allowing your daughter to get out of her desk and go to another area of the classroom for a specific purpose—to get materials or a drink of water or to run an errand for the teacher. Gaining the self-discipline not to bother other children is important.

◊ Permission to stand beside her desk and work.
◊ Specific classroom routines and structure, such as a specific routine for turning in homework.
◊ Establishing eye contact with the student when providing important information.
◊ Ignoring slight movement behaviors, like twirling a pencil, that do not interfere with classroom instruction.

Assignments

◊ Reduction in the amount of work to be completed. For example, in math, your daughter could complete the even-numbered problems rather than doing all of the problems. This can have a downside, because your daughter may need the repetition of doing more problems in order to have the concept cemented in her mind.
◊ Assignments presented in manageable chunks. Your daughter could be given an assignment in several different parts so she isn't overwhelmed by the amount of work.
◊ Masking her papers. In this strategy, the student is encouraged to use a plain sheet of paper to cover up a portion of the page she is working on. This helps minimize distraction from so much information on a page.
◊ Assistance in breaking down large assignments into manageable chunks.
◊ A monitoring plan to check work for careless mistakes before submitting it for grading.
◊ Positive reinforcement when grading papers, such as marking correct responses rather than wrong answers, if that would be more motivating to your daughter.
◊ Use of highlighter for key words in reading or for mathematical signs.

◊ Frequent checks to ensure that the student has understood directions. Sometimes it may be helpful for your daughter to repeat directions to the teacher.

◊ Watching for signs that the student does not understand the assignment and providing additional instruction.

◊ An example of what the finished product should look like.

◊ Multimodal instructions—visual and auditory instructions paired with hands-on learning when possible.

◊ Use of technology such as computer programs—often an effective way for a girl with ADHD to practice skills.

◊ Study guides in writing when possible, as well as copies of notes or board work.

◊ Access to word processing programs on computers to produce written work.

Self-Regulatory Skills

◊ Training in turn-taking, waiting in line, remaining seated, and identifying cause and effect of behaviors, especially important in kindergarten and first grade.

◊ Opportunities to regain self-control by removing herself from overwhelming situations.

◊ Holding "stress" balls or fidget toys in her hands, especially if they enhance concentration.

◊ Assistance in organizational strategies such as writing items in an agenda and keeping papers in their proper place.

◊ Opportunities to self-manage behavior. For example, your daughter counts and records a specific behavior with teacher assistance and receives positive, corrective feedback and some reward such as verbal praise or a tangible item.

◊ Placement on an individualized behavior management plan where the teacher monitors behavior in specific areas and your daughter earns rewards such as additional computer time, lunch with the teacher or a special friend, or tokens.

These are most effective when the system carries over to the home and parents are reinforcing the same behaviors.

Memory

◊ Frequent repetition and review of previously learned material.
◊ Provision of cue cards that would outline steps, especially important in solving math problems requiring sequential steps like long division.
◊ Use of a calculator.
◊ Assistance in attaching new learning to previously learned material.
◊ Use of memory techniques such as mnemonics.
◊ Overlearning until it becomes firmly embedded in long-term memory. This may require intensive practice, repetition, and review.
◊ Assistance in organizing information into meaningful categories.
◊ Assistance in using verbal rehearsal (repeating information to herself) or using visual imagery to assist with recall.

During his school-age years, Mary Anne's son never required a 504 plan or special education eligibility. There were times he could have benefited from some accommodations, such as being allowed to make up tests he had missed in a quiet environment or receiving extended time on complex testing, but his strong self-regulation skills helped him do well. His organization skills improved over time, and even though it was often a scramble at the end, he was always able to produce projects on time. Mary Anne made sure he had a quiet place to work and tools that he needed, and encouraged him to break large assignments into manageable components well ahead of the due date. However, he seemed to work more effectively under the pressure of time. The summer prior to his senior year in high school, Mary Anne was conducting a college preparatory camp where he had ample time to write his college essays. However, true to form, he generally completed each one the night before he mailed the application. Once attending college, he found the academic demands were much greater than in high school, and he needed the accommodation of extended time on classroom tests, which was allowed after an updated psychological evaluation documented the need.

When the Current School Setting Isn't Working

In some cases, girls with ADHD cannot function in a public school with special education eligibility or 504 accommodations or in a private school providing some support. Other alternatives can include a special day or private school specializing in ADHD, learning disabilities, behavioral difficulties, or all three; specialized boarding schools; homeschooling; or virtual school. All of these options will require extensive research.

Homeschooling

Homeschooling is legal in all 50 states, so if you are interested in your state's specific requirements, contact your state's Department of Education or check with your local school district. Homeschooling may be an option if a parent can commit the time, patience, and knowledge. It would require registering with your local school district; if it is large enough, then it may have a separate office to handle homeschooling. There, you would be informed about state requirements, which usually entail annual evaluations to assess progress and written documentation of educational activities and curriculum used. Some states require portfolios of student work.

We believe that homeschooling is a viable choice for girls with ADHD and have recommended this option to some of our families. There are many considerations you must establish, including a structured and comprehensive curriculum, adequate supervision, and social opportunities with peers. Although we recognize that homeschooling is not for everyone, it works for many. Homeschooling provides parents the ability to give their daughter an individualized curriculum, no homework, opportunities for hands-on learning, and the possibility for her to be more active. In Jim's personal experience, homeschooling can allow your child to gain academic confidence and build self-esteem. Some of our families homeschool their daughters because it presents flexibility and does not require participation in high-stakes testing.

It is a myth that homeschooling is isolating and does not allow your daughter to have social interactions. Many communities have homeschool cooperatives (or co-ops) that you can join. There are also national, state, local, and online homeschool groups for you to investigate. Homeschooling affords your daughter the flexibility to interact with others as little or as much as you wish. Our advice is to ignore the naysayer who makes statements like, "She won't have any friends," "You'll feel alone," or "Homeschooling doesn't work for girls with ADHD." Jim knows firsthand that homeschooling can and does work for many children with ADHD.

Our belief is that the homeschool movement will continue to expand and more resources will become available to support homeschooled girls with ADHD. These supports will include stronger curriculums, improved approaches to teaching executive functioning skills, and educational options. In many states, registered home education students can take a partial or full schedule of classes through a virtual school.

In some cases, parents choose to provide the instruction for their daughter rather than use a homeschooling center or virtual school. Although it is beyond the scope of this book to discuss specific curriculum choices, parents can choose between traditional, online, or virtual school homeschool experiences. When you're deciding, look for key features that include the quality of instructor resources for you, the types of hands-on activities offered for your daughter, the availability of computer-aided instruction, and the quality of the tracking system for recording your daughter's progress.

Of course, a prime secret for a successful homeschooling experience is having a good working relationship between the homeschooling parent and daughter. We use the term working relationship to emphasize that your daughter must be able and willing to complete schoolwork for you, the homeschool parent. You should have good organizational skills and the time to plan your instruction. We understand it is a full-time job to adequately homeschool your daughter and that parents benefit from the support of networking with other parents who are also homeschooling their children with ADHD. Figure 10 includes our pros and cons of homeschooling a girl with ADHD.

You can weigh the pros and cons of homeschooling your daughter by creating your own chart. Check resources in your community and determine if there are homeschool centers or co-ops nearby. We have seen homeschooling work and understand it can be a viable option for children with ADHD.

Virtual School

Many school districts offer virtual schools, where students access courses online. Some students enroll in virtual school full-time and take all of their coursework online. In many states, a student who is a full-time student attending a traditional public school can enroll in virtual school to take a remedial course, an extra course, or an advanced course with permission from her school counselor and principal. Students have some interaction with a teacher but do the majority of their work on the computer. Some students with ADHD are successful with computerized instruction because it can

Pros	Cons
Customized curriculum	Parent as teacher (typically)
Online curriculum options	No paycheck for teaching your daughter
Flexibility	Patience required
Shortened school day	High structure necessary
Can work at a slower or faster pace	Difficult to stay disciplined and make progress
Increased opportunity for hands-on projects	Fewer social opportunities
Opportunity for movement	Dealing with her academic frustrations
No high-stakes state testing	Slower work speed means learning takes longer
Teach to her learning style	Reduced freedom for the teaching parent
No homework	High burnout rate
Freedom to teach your religious beliefs	Requires teaching multiple subjects
Opportunity to teach more real-life skills	Record keeping required to monitor progress
Support of other homeschool parents	Can't take advantage of benefits of public school (e.g., intensive tutoring, teacher expertise)

Figure 10. Pros and cons of homeschooling. *Note.* From *Raising Boys With ADHD* (p. 213) by J. W. Forgan and M. A. Richey, 2012, Waco, TX: Prufrock Press. Copyright 2012 by Prufrock Press. Reprinted with permission.

be faster paced than traditional classroom instruction, can allow for more review of the material, and much of the monotonous repetition can be eliminated. It is usually more effective with children in the upper elementary grades, middle school, and high school students. Attending a virtual school requires consistent parental supervision and access to a computer with Internet access. Contact your local school district for more information.

Specialized Day Schools

For some families, there comes a point when their daughter's academic and/or behavioral difficulties approach the disaster level. Your daughter's ADHD may be so severe that she needs more than you or her current school can offer. Her behavior and emotionality may have escalated to the point that you don't know what to do for her, and you may be concerned for her safety and that of your family. She may be taking up the majority of your time and energy. Other family members may feel resentment or jealousy because of all of the time you spend on your daughter. This includes your time thinking and worrying about your daughter, talking to school staff, going to therapy, making and attending doctor's appointments, and doing online research. You likely feel exhausted and worn down. At times you may feel hopeless and worry that you might lose your temper and hurt her. When this happens, it is time to consider either a special day school or a boarding school.

We recognize that you should do what is best for your child and your family. If your daughter attends a special day school or boarding school, try not to worry about what her grandma, cousin, or aunt so-and-so is going to say about your decision. They don't walk in your shoes or truly understand how stressful your daily life has become. Some parents cope with the stress their daughter creates by keeping her in so many activities that she is constantly away from them and the family. This may provide a temporary escape, but in the long run, it does not help her or you.

We recommend that when our clients choose a specialized day school for their daughter, they should look for one that offers these qualities:

◇ small classrooms with no more than 14 students (less is better);

◇ a student-to-teacher ratio of no more than 7 to 1;

◇ an environment with minimal distractions and unnecessary interruptions;

◇ a school philosophy of building upon strengths rather than just remediating deficits;

◇ an administrator who understands ADHD and provides teachers with ongoing professional development;

◇ teachers with specialized training in teaching and understanding children with ADHD;

◇ teachers who know how to make accommodations and provide differentiated instruction;

◇ a daily schedule that places academics in the morning hours;

◇ a schedule that includes physical activity every day; and

◇ a curriculum that teaches study skills and organizational strategies and utilizes multisensory and hands-on learning techniques.

Boarding Schools

Despite your best efforts and the effort of the school staff, your daughter may require an overwhelming amount of support that is all-consuming. If she is out with friends and your phone rings, your heart skips a beat because you wonder if she is safe. Perhaps she continually and blatantly disobeys you and comes home way past her curfew. When this level of utter disobedience occurs, it may be time for her to attend a boarding school.

In fact, you may have threatened to send her to boarding school so many times you've lost count. In our experience, many parents issue that empty threat but few follow through. One mother said, "We constantly threaten to send my daughter to boarding school. We tell her that it's going to be her own choice because if she doesn't start making the right choices, she'll be going." This mom went on to say, "I don't know if I would ever have the nerve to do it, but it crosses my mind more than I'd like to think." Using boarding school as an empty threat is never helpful. Our advice to you is for you to rationally make the decision and then inform your daughter.

When you tell her about your decision, expect anger and shock. We find that often there will be tears from both of you. Frame the discussion with your daughter in humility rather than anger or victory. Explain to her this is the "real deal" and she really is going. Remember that most girls with ADHD feel things before they can express them verbally, so expect her to be angry, cuss, kick or punch something, and shed tears. As one mom put it, "She was mad and upset, but then once she calmed down, she began to listen to us and accept what was happening." Give your daughter alone time if she needs it, but tell her you love her and that this is going help her change for the better. She may scream at you and say, "You don't love me or you wouldn't be doing this! You must hate me and I hate you too!" Explain that you can't accept any more empty promises from her to change, because you know she needs more assistance than she can get at home. Tell her that attending boarding school is short-term until she can learn to abide by your rules.

After telling her of your decision, you may consider involving her in the process of researching and making a final school selection. Ask her what she thinks of two different schools, both of which are acceptable to you. Show her the schools' websites and literature to teach her about what they offer. This can create buy-in and help your daughter believe she has some input and that her opinions are valued. She should definitely attend the campus visit with you.

One concern we hear from parents is that the boarding school will not know their daughter as well as they do. Most parents ask endless "what if" questions. What if she gets into fights with other kids? What if her medications get mixed up? What if she doesn't go to the bathroom for weeks on end? What if she gets sick? What if she misses us so much that she cries herself to sleep? What if she feels abandoned? What if she hates us for doing this? To overcome this, you have to do your research, ask countless questions, make your choice, and then stay in contact with the administration and your daughter. Provide the emotional support that she needs.

We find it helpful to consider pros and cons when making any important decision. It's also important to teach your daughter how to make decisions using this structured approach. Although any decision is always more than a simple count of pros vs. cons, it provides a starting point to help make your decision. Always consider the extraneous factors in your life and focus on the most important issues to your particular circumstances. Figure 11 includes our chart of boarding school pros and cons.

Once you've made the decision that boarding school is the right place for your daughter, the main question is, "How do we make the right boarding school choice when there are many to choose from?" This is a potentially life-changing decision, and it can be hard to know where to start. We find parents benefit when working with an educational consultant who specializes in boarding schools for children with ADHD, if one is available in your area. This person can help provide support and guide you down the right path.

If your daughter requires a boarding school, then a good educational consultant can help point you in the right direction. If you decide to forgo working with an educational consultant or can't locate one, then these are some of the questions you should ask when speaking with boarding school admissions directors. Make a chart with these questions on the left side and columns to the right where you can place each school's answers.

◊ How many counselors, psychologists, and/or psychiatrists are on staff at one time?

◊ What is the teacher-to-student ratio?

◊ How long does the average teacher stay employed with the school? Are they certified or licensed?

Pros	Cons
Small class size	Expensive tuition
Increased individualized attention	May be isolating
Counseling services may be available	Emotionally difficult to separate from your daughter
Fresh start	Lack of appropriate role models
May increase her self-esteem	Cost of travel to and from home for holidays, weekends, etc.
Mentoring	Family separation
Highly structured, around-the-clock supervision	Requires adjustment to new environment

Figure 11. Boarding school pros and cons. *Note.* From *Raising Boys With ADHD* (p. 218) by J. W. Forgan and M. A. Richey, 2012, Waco, TX: Prufrock Press. Copyright 2012 by Prufrock Press. Reprinted with permission.

◇ How will my daughter be disciplined? What is the school's discipline plan?

◇ Is physical restraint used with students? If so, under what circumstances?

◇ Are parents encouraged to have their daughter take ADHD medication?

◇ What does a student's typical daily schedule look like?

◇ How frequently do parents get to talk and e-mail with their daughter?

◇ How long is your average student's stay?

◇ Is your school accredited, and will my daughter's coursework transfer to another school?

◇ What happens on weekends, long weekends, and holidays?

After you narrow your decision to the top two, visit each school's campus before making a final selection. The school may sound like the perfect fit when you talk with staff on the phone, read the catalogue, and study their website. Seeing the campus in person and talking to students and other parents will help finalize your decision.

Points to Consider

1. If your daughter's ADHD is impairing her school functioning significantly, she could meet the criteria for a 504 plan or Individualized Education Program (IEP).
2. Even though the disability perspective is difficult to accept, isn't it better for people to have an understanding of the neurobiological nature of her ADHD than to think she is just being difficult?
3. You are your daughter's most important advocate and always will be.
4. What specific struggles does your daughter have in her current classroom?
5. Are homeschooling or virtual school viable options for your daughter, and what resources exist in your community?
6. What benefits would there be in sending your daughter to a specialized day school or boarding school?
7. Review your self-assessment responses to decide if there are any areas where you still need to learn more.

Action Steps to Take Now

1. Continue to educate yourself about your child's legal rights within the school system.
2. Think about your daughter's learning style, strengths, and weaknesses. What does she need in the classroom in order to do her best?

3. If she is struggling behaviorally or academically in the classroom with no support, contact the school about the necessity of a 504 plan or IDEA eligibility. Make sure you educate yourself so you can be a good advocate for her.

4. Develop a good working relationship with her teacher(s) and with other staff members who could assist her.

5. Complete Step 5 in the Dynamic Action Plan.

Chapter 7

Pulling It All Together: The Dynamic Action Plan

Throughout this book we've given you action steps at the end of each chapter. Whether or not you've had the opportunity to apply them, our message to you is the same: Your daughter needs you, even if she says she doesn't. The Dynamic Action Plan you are creating is a reflective tool to help you prioritize your steps. As parents ourselves, we've found that although we may have unwritten goals for our child, they become much clearer if we write them. This allows you to see your daughter's growth.

At times, you may become overwhelmed by your daughter's needs. You worry about what lies ahead. Despite her challenges, she is a unique person with a special purpose in life. You know there is hope for her future. You can use the Dynamic Action Plan to help your daughter discover her purpose and grow in her journey.

Begin by identifying your daughter's strengths and needs to use as a reference point to guide your thinking. Consider all aspects of her life—school, family, friends, leisure time and extracurricular activities, health and fitness, religion, etc.—as you complete the plan.

Step 1. Strengths and Needs

I/we believe my daughter's strengths include:

1. _____

    _____

    _____

    _____

2. _____

    _____

    _____

    _____

3. _____

    _____

    _____

    _____

4. _____

    _____

    _____

    _____

5. _____

    _____

    _____

    _____

I/we need to communicate these strengths to her by doing or saying the following:

1. _____

_____

_____

_____

2. _____

_____

_____

_____

3. _____

_____

_____

_____

4. _____

_____

_____

_____

5. _____

_____

_____

_____

I/we believe the following need to be addressed for my daughter to maximize her strengths:

1. _____

_____

_____

_____

2. _____

_____

_____

_____

3. _____

_____

_____

_____

4. _____

_____

_____

_____

5. _____

_____

_____

_____

Step 2. Vision

The key here is to begin by reflecting upon where you see your daughter 5 years from now, and if she's mature enough, to ask her to consider her next 5 years as well. Together, think about her future in the following ways:

◊   How old will she be?

◊   What will she physically look like?

◊   What will her personality be like?

◊   What do you expect from her behavior?

◊   How will she feel about herself?

◊   What will her ethics and character be like?

◊   Will she be able to make good decisions?

◊   What type of school will she attend?

◊   What interests and hobbies will she pursue?

◊   Who will her friends be?

◊   Will she have a job?

◊   Will she be taking medication?

◊   What strategies will she be using to manage her ADHD?

◊   What kind of support will she need at school? From her family?

We find that thinking about and predicting what your daughter will be doing in 5 years is an interesting exercise. For you, it will stir various emotions, and you'll realize just how fast those years will pass. Again, consider all aspects of her life—school, family, friends, leisure time and extracurricular activities, health and fitness, religion, etc.—as you complete this section.

◊   In 5 years, I/we see my daughter doing/being . . .

_____

_____

_____

_____

_____

◊   In 3 years, I/we see my daughter doing/being . . .

_____

_____

_____

_____

◊   In one year, I/we see my daughter doing/being . . .

_____

_____

_____

_____

In some cases you and your daughter completed this section together. If not, then you should communicate the vision to her and motivate her to become an active participant.

Step 3. Action

In order for my daughter to achieve the vision I/we have for her at the 5-year mark, I/we need to do the following:

◊ Today—Make a to do list:

_____

_____

_____

_____

_____

◊ Tomorrow—Prioritize and begin following through:

_____

_____

_____

_____

_____

◊ Within one month:

_____

_____

_____

_____

_____

◊   Within 6 months:

_____

_____

_____

_____

_____

Your daughter's involvement and participation is crucial to the plan's success. In order for my daughter to achieve the vision I/we have for her at the 5-year mark, she needs to do the following:

◊   Tomorrow:

_____

_____

_____

_____

_____

◊   Within one month:

_____

_____

_____

_____

_____

◊　Within 6 months:

_____

_____

_____

_____

_____

◊　Within one year:

_____

_____

_____

_____

_____

Step 4. Support

In order for my daughter to achieve the vision I/we have for her at the 5-year mark, I/we need to obtain the support of the following individuals or professionals:

1. _____

2. _____

3. _____

4. _____

5. _____

Step 5. Roadblocks

When I/we become discouraged or frustrated with her behavior or performance, I/we need to remember these things:

1. _____
   _____
   _____
   _____

2. _____
   _____
   _____
   _____

3. _____
   _____
   _____
   _____

4. _____
   _____
   _____
   _____

5. _____
   _____
   _____

When I/we become discouraged or frustrated with her behavior or performance, I/we can count on these people for support:

1. _____

2. _____

3. _____

4. _____

5. _____

When my daughter becomes discouraged or frustrated with us or with her ADHD, she needs to remind herself of these things:

1. _____

_____

_____

_____

2. _____

_____

_____

_____

3. _____

_____

_____

_____

4. _____

_____

_____

_____

5. _____

_____

_____

_____

When my daughter becomes discouraged or frustrated with me or with her ADHD, she can turn to the following people for support (other than myself):

1. _____

2. _____

3. _____

4. _____

5. _____

Now that you've completed your daughter's Dynamic Action Plan, remember to review and refine it as necessary.

We'd like to close by thanking you for your effort and for the hard work you are doing on behalf of your daughter. In our experience as parents, we don't often hear many people say "Thank you" for how we are raising our kids with ADHD, but we know you deserve thanks. We understand your journey because we've traveled similar paths. Each day you work hard at raising your daughter, and one day she'll realize this. Helping your daughter make the most of her capabilities will be an accomplishment you can cherish all of your life. We can assure you that it will be worth every ounce of effort you put into it. Our compassion goes out to you.

References

Aronson-Ramos, J. (n.d.). A guide to nutritional supplements and dietary interventions in children. Retrieved from http://draronsonramos.com/wp-content/themes/drramos/articles/Supplements%20Nutrition/NutritionandSupplementGuide.pdf

Alderson, R. M., Rapport, M. D., Hudec, K. L., Sarver, D. E., & Kofler, M. J. (2010). Competing core processes in attention-deficit/hyperactivity disorder (ADHD): Do working memory deficiencies underlie behavioral inhibition deficits? *Journal of Abnormal Child Psychology, 38,* 497–507.

Alexander-Roberts, A. (2006). *AD/HD parenting handbook: Practical advice for parents from parents.* Lanham, MD: Rowman Littlefield.

American Academy of Pediatrics. (n.d.). *Connected kids: Safe, strong, secure.* Retrieved from http://www.aap.org/connectedkids/samples/tvviolence.htm

American Psychiatric Association. (2013). *Diagnostic and statistical manual of mental disorders* (5th ed.). Washington, DC: Author.

Americans with Disabilities Act, 42 U.S.C. §§ 12102 et seq. (1990).

Americans with Disabilities Act Amendments Act of 2008 €3(4)(E)(i), 42 U.S.C. € 12102(4)(E).

Armstrong, T. (1995). *The myth of the A.D.D. child.* New York, NY: Penguin.

Arns, M., de Ridder, S., Strehl, U., Breteler, M., & Coenen, A. (2009). Efficacy of neurofeedback treatment in ADHD: The effects on inattention, impulsivity and hyperactivity: A meta-analysis. *Clinical EEG and Neuroscience, 40,* 180–189.

Bailey, E. (2009). *ADHD in young children.* Retrieved from http://www.healthcentral.com/adhd/children-40947-5.html

Barkley, R. A. (2000a). *A new look at ADHD: Inhibition, time and self-control.* New York, NY: Guilford Press.

Barkley, R. A. (2000b). *Taking charge of ADHD. The complete, authoritative guide for parents.* New York, NY: Guilford Press.

Barkley, R. A. (2006). *Attention-Deficit Hyperactivity Disorder: A handbook for diagnosis and treatment* (3rd ed.). New York, NY: Guilford Press.

Barkley, R. A. (2007). School intervention for attention deficit hyperactivity disorder: Where to from here? *School Psychology Review, 36,* 279–286.

Barkley, R. A. (2012). Distinguishing sluggish cognitive tempo from attention-deficit/hyperactivity disorder in adults. *Journal of Abnormal Psychology, 121,* 978–990. doi:10.1037/a0023961

Biederman, J., Petty, C. R., Monuteaux, M., Freid, R., Byrne, D., Mirto, T., . . . Faraone, S. (2010). Adult psychiatric outcomes of girls with attention deficit hyperactivity disorder: 11-year follow-up in a longitudinal case-control study. *American Journal of Psychiatry, 167,* 409–417.

Biederman, J., Petty, C. R., O'Connor, K. B., Hyder, L. L., & Faraone, S. V. (2011). Predictors of persistence in girls with attention deficit hyperactivity disorder: results from an 11-year controlled follow-up study. *Acta Psychiatrica Scandinavia, 125,* 147–156.

Bower, B. (2006, October 28). Med-start kids: Pros, cons of Ritalin for preschool ADHD. *Science News, 170,* 12.

Breaden, M. (2007, September 12). Preschoolers with ADHD. *Education Week,* 5.

Brown, T. E. (2008, February). Executive: Describing six aspects of a complex syndrome. *Attention,* 12–17.

Cardoos, S. L., & Hinshaw, S. P. (2011). Friendship as protection from peer victimization for girls with and without ADHD. *Journal of Abnormal Child Psychology, 39,* 1035–1045.

Cardoos, S. L., Loya, F., & Hinshaw, S. P. (2013). Adolescent girls' ADHD symptoms and young adult driving: The role of perceived deviant peer affiliation. *Journal of Clinical Child & Adolescent Psychology, 0*(0), 1–11. Retrieved from: http://dx.doi.org/10.1080/15374416.2012.759117

Castellanos, F., Giedd, J. N., Berquin, P. C., Walter, J. M., Sharp, W., Thanhlan, T., . . . Rapoport, J. L. (2001). Quantitative brain magnetic resonance imaging in girls with attention-deficit/hyperactivity disorder. *Archives of General Psychiatry, 58,* 289–295. doi:10.1001/archpsyc.58.3.289.

Centers for Disease Control and Prevention. (2010, December). Summary health statistics for US children: National Health Interview Survey, 2009. *Vital and Health Statistics, 10*(247). Retrieved from http://www.cdc.gov/nchs/data/series/sr_10/sr10_247.pdf

Children and Adults With Attention Deficit/Hyperactivity Disorder. (2011). *Understanding ADHD: How is ADHD treated?* Retrieved from http://www.chadd.org/Content/CHADD/Understanding/Treatment/default.htm

Dahlin, K. I. E. (2011). Effects of working memory training on reading in children with special needs. *Reading and Writing, 24,* 479–491.

Dawson, M. M. (2007). The ideal versus the feasible when designing interventions for students with attention deficit hyperactivity disorder. *School Psychology Review, 36,* 274–278.

Dorsett, K. (2013, February). Embracing differences: Understanding and meeting the needs of women with ADHD. *Attention,* 24–27. Retrieved from http://www.chadd.org/Membership/Attention-Magazine/View-Articles/Embracing-Differences.aspx#.Uo4woRYp8gg

DuPaul, G. J. (2007). School-based interventions for students with attention deficit hyperactivity disorder: Current status and future directions. *School Psychology Review, 36,* 183–194.

Durheim, M., & Zeigler Dendy, C. A. (2006). Educational laws regarding students with AD/HD. In *CHADD educator's manual* (pp. 125–134). Landover, MD: CHADD.

Feinberg, T., & Robey, N. (2009). Cyberbullying: Intervention and preventions strategies. *Communique, 38,* 21–23.

Goldstein, S. (1999). Attention-deficit/hyperactivity disorder. In S. Goldstein & C. R. Reynolds (Eds.), *Handbook of neurodevelopmental and genetic disorders in children* (pp. 154–175). New York, NY: Guilford Press.

Goldstein, S. (2004). *What do we want from children with ADHD? Keeping a moving target in mind.* Retrieved from http://www.samgoldstein.com/cms/index.php/2004/09/what-do-we-want-from-children-with-adhd

Grady, M. M. (2010). The Multimodal Treatment Study of children with ADHD: Questions, answers, and controversies. *Psychopharmacology Educational Updates.* Retrieved from http://edb.pbclibrary.org:2077/ps/i.do?&id=GALE%7CA238349066&v=2.1&u=d0_mlpbcls&it=r&p=AONE&sw=w

Harvard Health Publications. (2007). *Preschool ADHD.* Retrieved from http://www.health.harvard.edu/press_releases/preschool-adhd

Hathaway, W. L., & Barkley, R. A. (2003). Self-regulation, ADHD, & child religiousness. *Journal of Psychology and Christianity, 22,* 101–114.

Hinshaw, S. P. (2002). Preadolescent girls with Attention-Deficit/ Hyperactivity Disorder: Background characteristics, comorbidity, cognitive and social functioning, and parenting practices. *Journal of Consulting and Clinical Psychology, 70,* 1086–1098.

Hinshaw, S., Owens, E., Zalecki, C., Montenegro-Nevado, A., Huggins, S., Schrodek, E., & Swanson, E. (2012). Prospective follow-up of girls with Attention-Deficit/Hyperactivity Disorder into early adulthood: Continuing impairment includes elevated risk for suicide attempt and self-injury. *Journal of Consulting and Clinical Psychology, 80,* 1041–1051.

Hinshaw, S., Barkley, R., & Hechtman, L. (2012, November). *I: Montreal study: Milwaukee study; Berkeley girls ADHD longitudinal study.* Presented at the Research Symposium at the 24th Annual International Conference on ADHD, San Francisco, CA.

Holmes, J. H., Gathercole, S. E., Place, M., Dunning, D. L., Hilton, K. A., & Elliott, J. G. (2009). Working memory deficits can be overcome: Impacts of training and medication on working memory in children with ADHD. *Applied Cognitive Psychology, 24,* 827–836.

Individuals with Disabilities Education Improvement Act, Pub. Law 108-446 (December 3, 2004).

Katz, M. (2007, December). AD/HD safe driving program: A graduated license plan. *Attention,* 6–7.

Kofler, M. J., Rapport, M. D., Bolden, J., Sarver, D. E., & Raiker, J. S. (2010). ADHD and working memory: The impact of central executive deficits and exceeding storage/rehearsal capacity on observed inattentive behavior. *Journal of Abnormal Child Psychology, 38,* 149–161.

Laursen, B., Coy, K. C., & Collins, W. A. (1998). Reconsidering changes in parent-child conflict across adolescence: A meta-analysis. *Child Development, 69,* 817–832.

Levine, M. (2003). *The myth of laziness.* New York, NY: Simon and Schuster.

Littman, E. (2012, December). The secret lives of girls with ADHD. *Attention, 19,* 18–20.

Lofthouse, N., Arnold, L. E., Hersch, S., Hurt, E., & DeBeus, R. (2011). A review of neurofeedback treatment for pediatric ADHD. *Journal of Attention Disorders, 16,* 351–372.

Maxwell, J. C. (2000). *Failing forward: Turning mistakes into stepping stones for success.* Nashville, TN: Thomas Nelson.

McConaughy, S., Volpe, R., Antshel, K., Gordon, M., & Eiraldi, R. (2011). Academic and social impairments of elementary school children with attention deficit hyperactivity disorder. *School Psychology Review, 40,* 200–225.

Melby-Lervåg, M., & Hulme, C. (2013). Is working memory training effective? A meta-analytic review. *Developmental Psychology, 49,* 270–291.

Mezzacappa, E., & Bucker, J. C. (2010). Working memory training for children with attention problems or hyperactivity: A school-based pilot study. *School Mental Health, 2,* 202–208.

Monastra, V. J. (2004). *Parenting children with ADHD: Lessons that medicine cannot teach.* Washington, DC: American Psychological Association.

Monastra, V. J., Lynn, S., Linden, M., Lubar, J. F., Gruzelier, J., & LaVaque, T. J. (2005). Electroencephalographic biofeedback in the treatment of attention-deficit/hyperactivity disorder. *Applied Psychophysiology and Biofeedback, 30,* 95–114.

Monastra, V. J., Monastra, D. M., & George, S. (2002). The effects of stimulant therapy, EEG biofeedback, and parenting style on the primary symptoms of attention-deficit/hyperactivity disorder. *Applied Psychophysiology and Biofeedback, 27,* 231–249.

Nadeau, K.G., Littman, E. B., & Quinn, P .O. (1999). *Understanding girls with AD/HD.* Silver Spring, MD: Advantage Books.

National Institute of Mental Health. (2009). *The Multimodal Treatment of Attention Deficit Hyperactivity Disorder study (MTA): Questions and answers.* Retrieved from http://www.nimh.nih.gov/trials/practial/mta

National Resource Center on ADHD. (2008). *Complementary and alternative treatments.* Retrieved from http://www.help4adhd.org/en/treatment/complementary/WWK6

NIH News. (2006). *Preschoolers with ADHD improve with low doses of medication.* Retrieved from http://www.nih.gov/news/pr/oct2006/nimh-16.htm

Nussbaum, N. L. (2012). ADHD and female specific concerns: A review of the literature and clinical implications. *Journal of Attention Disorders, 16,* 87–100.

Parker, H. C. (2005). *Accommodations help students with attention deficit disorders* (ADAPT). Retrieved from http://www.addconsults.com/articles/full.php3?id=1353

Pelham, W. E., & Fabiano, G. A. (2008). Evidence-based psychosocial treatments for attention-deficit/hyperactivity disorder. *Journal of Clinical Child & Adolescent Psychology, 37,* 184–214.

Pharmacological and behavioral treatments for ADHD in preschoolers. (2009, April). *The Brown University Child and Adolescent Behavior Letter, 25*(4), 1–8.

Pliszka, S., & AACAP Work Group on Quality Issues. (2007). Practice parameter for the assessment and treatment of children and adolescents with attention-deficit/hyperactivity disorder. *Journal of American Academy of Child and Adolescent Psychiatry, 46,* 894–921.

Rapport, M. D., Bolden, J., Kofler, M. J., Sarver, D. E., Raiker, J. S., & Alderon, R. M. (2008). Hyperactivity in boys with attention-deficit/hyperactivity disorder (ADHD): A ubiquitous core symptom or manifestation of working memory deficits? *Journal of Abnormal Child Psychology, 37,* 521–534.

Ratey, N. A. (2008). *The disorganized mind.* New York, NY: St. Martin's Griffin.

Rief, S. F. (2008). *The ADD/ADHD checklist: A practical reference for parents and teachers* (2nd ed.). San Francisco, CA: Jossey-Bass.

Section 504 of the Rehabilitation Act, 29 U.S.C. Section 706 et. Seq. (1973).

Taylor, J. F. (2001). *Helping your ADD child.* Roseville, CA: Prima.

Teach, J. K. (2012, November 9). *Lost and unidentified: The plight of the ADHD inattentive female.* Presented at the 24th Annual International Conference on ADHD, San Francisco, CA.

Teeter, P. A. (1998). *Interventions for ADHD: Treatment in developmental context.* New York, NY: Guilford Press.

Travis, F., Grosswald, S., & Stixrud, W. (2011). ADHD, brain functioning, and transcendental meditation practice. *Mind & Brain, The Journal of Psychiatry, 2*(1), 73–80.

U.S. Department of Health and Human Services. (n.d.). *Stop bullying now.* Retrieved from http://www.stopbullying.gov/

Weiss, G., & Hechtman, L. T. (1993). *Hyperactive children grow up.* New York, NY: Guilford Press.

Wendling, P. (2008, December 1). Full exam guides ADHD diagnosis in preschoolers. *Family Practice News, 26.*

Willard, N., (2009, September 30). *Digital media safety and literacy education and youth risk online presentation and intervention.* Testimony presented before the Subcommittee on Crime, Terrorism, and Homeland Security, Committee on The Judiciary, House of Representatives.

Williams, N. I. (2010, September 30). Rare chromosomal deletions and duplications in attention-deficit hyperactivity disorder: A genome-wide analysis. *The Lancet, 376,* 1401–1408.

Wolraich, M. L. (2007, August). Preschoolers and AD/HD. *Attention,* 8–11.

Wright, P. (2009). *Four rules for raising children.* Retrieved from http://www.wrightslaw.com/nltr/09/nl.0106.htm#4

Wymbs, B. T., Pelham, W. T., Molina, B. S., Gnagy, E. M., Wilson, T. K., & Greenhouse, J. B. (2008). Rate and predictors of divorce among parents of youths with ADHD. *Journal of Consulting and Clinical Psychology, 76,* 735–744.

About the Authors

James W. Forgan and **Mary Anne Richey** have spent a combined 50 years working with children with ADHD in school settings, in private practice, and at home. The first thing you need to know about the authors is that each is the parent of a child with ADHD.

James W. Forgan, Ph.D., is an Associate Professor and Licensed School Psychologist. He teaches others how to teach and assess children with ADHD and other types of learning disabilities at Florida Atlantic University. In private practice, he works with families of children with ADHD and other learning differences. Jim consults with public and private schools doing workshops on ADHD, dyslexia, problem solving, and accommodations for learning disabilities.

Mary Anne Richey, M.Ed., also a Licensed School Psychologist, works for the school district of Palm Beach County and has a private practice. She also has experience as a middle school teacher, administrator, high school guidance counselor, and adjunct college instructor. Mary Anne has assisted many students with ADHD and their families over the years. In 2012, she was honored as School Psychologist of the Year by the Florida Association of School Psychologists and is a nominee for the 2013 National School Psychologist of the Year to be chosen by the National Association of School Psychologists.

Throughout this book, Jim and Mary Anne help parents manage the issues they face and incorporate strategies to help their daughters succeed in school and life. They have presented at national conventions and workshops for parents and professionals on strategies for helping those with ADHD maximize their potential. They are coauthors of *Raising Boys With ADHD: Secrets for Parenting Healthy, Happy Sons.* They share an integrated perspective on ADHD based on their experiences as parents and professionals, their academic research, and their interactions with so many other parents raising girls and boys with ADHD.